DESTINY TALKS

21 Brave Conversations With Sonia Hassey

SONIA HASSEY

© 2019 by Sonia Hassey

All rights are reserved.
ISBN: 9780578218342

First Printing: March 2019

DEDICATION

Why this book? I have been interviewing women for the past year, and have personally discovered such transformation in women that have struggled against all odds. They rose up in their courage and went after their dreams. I believe these stories of struggle and success need to be shared for the purpose of inspiring others to believe that they have a purpose on this planet, and to know that their circumstances do not define them.

This book is dedicated to all the women that have aspired to live their dream, and to believe that they can reach their greatest potential. Many women allow fear, doubt, or circumstance to stop them. Owning our story and loving ourselves in the process is the bravest thing we can do. The goal is to rise from our falls and overcome our mistakes that bring us more wisdom and ultimately lead us to our destiny.

Our life is made up of our story: we can run from it, or we can have the courage to face it. We can be willing to get vulnerable to allow us to process each challenge with authenticity and understanding. Being in our ultimate truth is key to our healing, clarity, and courage to bring transformation to our lives.

Facing your giants of fear can be the beginning of your transformation. Being in your truth about who you are and where you want to go is the beginning of rising up to your greatness.

Our pain eventually becomes a stepping stone to strength, character and fulfillment when we overcome what holds us back.

Remember when you were a child and you dreamed of being a star or a doctor? If you think about it, the ideas that came out of our heads were without limits, and we dreamed big! Unfortunately, those dreams sometimes dim over time through difficult circumstances, or by the negative messages that we hear from others or that we tell ourselves. When that happens, confidence is shattered and we can believe that all hope is lost. It's a belief that holds us back, and for some women it can feel permanent. I have been there and I fully understand what it's like to feel like you can't accomplish much because you don't feel worthy. It's like you're alive, but not really living. This book is about women that have faced failure and setbacks, but through it all they never quit! They never gave up on hope to reach their greatest potential. Their stories show that you can think creatively and discover the ability to lead with confidence. Now they are doing great things for themselves and their community, and ultimately leaving a lasting legacy!

Table of Contents

About Sonia Hassey 1

Chapter 1: I Know Who I Am and What I Can Be (Don Quijote, Chapter 5) 3

Chapter 2: The Truth Shall Make You Free 18

Chapter 3: You Got This! 42

Chapter 4: Do It or Die! 73

Chapter 5: Think Global Act Local 103

Chapter 6: Soul In Power: From Trauma To Triumph 125

Chapter 7: Grace – The Ultimate Gift 151

Chapter 8: Family, Community, and Faith 176

Chapter 9: Living My Best Life Fearlessly 196

Chapter 10: Who Am I? 222

Chapter 11: The Comfort Zone 244

Chapter 12: Near Death to Awakened Soul 270

Chapter 13: If You Can't Go Through It, Go Around It 305

Chapter 14: The Girl from El Paso and Her Dream 328

Chapter 15: Being Latina with a Vision 357

Chapter 16: Because You Are Worth It 377

Chapter 17: Because of My Sister Gina 392

Chapter 18: Rising Beyond My Limits 409

Chapter 19: Always Have a Plan B 417

Chapter 20: Ripple Effect 445

Chapter 21: Yes I Can! 467

About Sonia Hassey

Sonia Hassey is President and Founder of Women Inspired Network, Inc. and Destiny Women Global Leadership, a women's transformational leadership program empowering thousands of women globally to become heart-driven leaders. Sonia is an exciting speaker whose motivating messages, full of enthusiasm and heart, has been inspiring audiences for years.

After 32 years of her career as a hairstylist, Sonia realized her passion for coaching and mentoring women. She set her goal, saved up money, studied leadership nationwide, and then bravely launched her own business full time to reach more women as an author, speaker, and coach.

Her biggest "Why" is to see women transformed through renewed confidence in their ability to discover their purpose, believe in themselves and create the destiny they deserve.

Among Sonia's key programs are the Destiny Women Global Leadership Program, VIP Coaching, Accelerate Group Coaching Program, Millionaire Mindset Coaching, Mentoring Program, and Leadership Team Coaching Program. Sonia's programs have been attributed to driving significant transformation at the personal and organizational level, measurable by exponential increases in confidence, clarity of direction, clarity of goals, clarity of purpose, goal attainment, and the increase of revenue.

Sonia is a Certified Life Purpose Coach from Dream University, a Dale Carnegie graduate.

Author of the International best seller, Butt Naked Leadership, Compiler of the number #1 International Best Seller Destiny Talks, and Co-author of the book Catch Your Star.

www.destinywomenglobal.com

CHAPTER 1

I Know Who I Am and What I Can Be
(Don Quijote, Chapter 5)

Maica Gil

Sonia: Hello, I am here with Maica Gil. She is one incredible woman on a mission to empower other women. Maica, I would love for you to share your personal story and tell us about your global initiatives.

Maica: I'm a work in progress, for sure. I was born and raised in the Canary Islands, Spain. During that period, it was the end of the Franco dictatorship. I didn't come from a rich family or anything like that. It was a very hard-working family. I got my education through scholarships. I studied law, I have a law degree, and I also did my master's degree in international law and international business transactions.

One of the key moments in my life that made me the person I am today ... I was always looking out for the underdog. My mother always made me go to different nonprofits to work a couple of hours every Saturday so I could see what was going on out there. My mother always did a lot of nonprofit work to help others and she was well-known in the island for helping others, so I guess that's in the DNA code of our family. Another person who inspired me was my aunt Chona, my grandmother's sister. Aunt Chona used to cook for wealthy families in the island, and basically when she got home, she cooked for all the kids who lost their parents. I'm talking about a dark period in the islands, when lots of kids were getting orphaned and people were disappearing because we were in the middle of a conflict like the start of a civil war. It was really tough.

Another experience that helped me come out of my comfort zone is that when I was in my early years, I was bullied a lot. When I was six, seven, or eight years old, I was really tiny and older girls at school were taller and stronger than me. But I've always been very opinionated and that's when I got bullied and a little bit beaten up because the older and stronger ones were doing something, and I was complaining to them ... I was trying to defend other girls if I saw some kind of injustice. I couldn't be quiet. So they came after me. I wasn't strong enough to defend myself, so basically, I used my brains to defend myself.

Some of the bullies were in my class, and I knew they didn't have the homework done, so I would say to the teacher, "Oh, you know Pepita, she wants to share her homework." And the teacher would ask her, and no, she didn't have her homework, so she was grounded.

Sonia: Yes, you used strategy as your way of getting back to their bullying outside the classroom.

Maica: I had to be creative. I was also lucky because it was mostly a black eye or my knees. After those young years, I got taller and stronger, and then I was taller than the girls who bullied me, but I also had girls who were older than me backing me up or walking with me to certain areas. I remember one or two situations that were physically tough. One time I had to spend a whole month sitting on this inflatable cushion with a hole in the middle like a donut because they hit me on my tailbone, and I was in a lot of pain. I had to go to the hospital, and I couldn't do gymnastics or anything.

Years later, this is the cool thing about growing up, we all became friends and they apologized to me. Every time I go back home for Christmas, now that they are mothers, they say, "We were crazy back then." It's good to see that everyone grew up.

Sonia: How did it affect you emotionally?

Maica: I've always been surrounded by strong women in my family, so it was a challenge, but I figured out a way of getting out of it. I didn't like having scars. Right now, the women who used to beat me up back then are probably more traumatized than me.

Sonia: Would you say your strength and assertiveness came from the strong women in your family?

Maica: Yes, and I was an only child, so my father always educated me in a certain way, and my mother taught me to be independent. Our families are small, especially on my mother's side. My parents always wanted to give me the tools or resources so I could be on my own. My father, for his generation, was the biggest feminist that I've encountered. He used to cook. He used to work at the bank and do a lot of things, but was a different type of man. He was super happy to be with all the women in his family, and of course with his friends too.

Sonia: He was a great supporter of you.

Maica: Yes, and one thing I will never forget, he said, "Let's take you to Jiu-Jitsu." My uncle was really good at judo and won the national championship in Spain. It was actually quite funny, but my father said, "Just in case, it's good to learn how to protect yourself, so let me send you to Jiu-Jitsu as well." Also, he taught me how to drive when I was seventeen. He was always pushing me to try new things, and it was great to have him.

Sonia: It makes sense that you weren't emotionally set back. You were bullied, but you didn't think, "I'm not good enough," because you went home, and it was a whole different story. You were with strong women and your dad was a strong supporter.

Maica: I was bullied because I was trying to defend or protect someone else, even though I was the tiny one. I think it was more frustrating for them because they tried to beat me up and I'd have bloody knees. The next day, I was still telling them, "You shouldn't be doing that" when they were bothering someone else, so it was actually hilarious.

Sonia: You've always had a voice. You were an advocate for those girls who weren't strong enough to have a voice. What did your teenage years look like?

Maica: I was a typical teenager who had good relationships with the different groups in high school. I made good friends who are still my friends. We had a band called the Happy Hour. There were the different tribes, as we called them back in the day. A posh group of people, the people who were the gothics, the heavy metals, the British pop kind of look—the poppies. And I was more like the girls who loved to go to the beach, surf, and learn to sail. It was a cool exposure for me to go to the beach and create music.

I saw lots of people getting easy access to drugs. Our school had a sexologist coming in during our first year of high school. We had an hour or two with them to ask all kinds of questions privately. The girls were with a woman, and the guys were with a man. We could ask anything we wanted to know, and I think that's key. It's so sad that people don't talk about sex or puberty openly. I was in a Catholic school back then in Spain, but it was also liberal with certain things.

Sonia: Awareness of anything is good: the pros and the cons.

Maica: I remember once we went to a party and one of our friends was smoking weed, and I don't know what else he did, but he passed out, totally passed out. Nobody had the guts to call his parents and say, "Hey, we should take him to the hospital." But who called? I did. So my parents came and took him to the hospital. Everyone was like, "Oh my God, I'd be so grounded if my parents knew I was at this party." When I got home my father was not mad, and my mother said, "Okay, we can count on her." I was probably fifteen or sixteen.

We couldn't leave him without taking him to the hospital. To me, it was a no-brainer. We didn't have cell phones back in the day, so I had to use the home phone.

Sonia: What did you do after high school and college?

Maica: I became an attorney at twenty-two. Before that, unfortunately, my father passed away when I was seventeen, and it was my first year of law school. It was tough for all of us, but for my mother, it was really hard. I remember that her hair turned all gray. It was tough to see her like that because she was always a strong woman.

She still lives in the Canary Islands. She used to visit me here every other year but now I go there every Christmas.

Sonia: How did you end up in the United States?

Maica: I went to college where I could get a scholarship. I also did the exchange student program in college. I went to London to help a friend with a project. I ended up in New York and I started seeing that I wanted to get my master's degree in the international arena. I applied for different universities and got accepted at Golden Gate University, and that's how I ended up on the West Coast.

When I was ready to do my practical training, I talked with a big, famous university here, but they didn't have foreign attorneys and local attorneys in the same courses, and I thought, "How are we going to learn? What is the point of coming here?" I even had more experience than some of their training teachers. I wanted to learn from the good teachers who had experience. I met friends there who are attorneys and they're in other parts of the world, but we're still connected and see each other quite often. I got my LLM in International Law.

Later, I did an internship with a finance company, and I was an outside counsel for a big law firm here with privatizations in Latin America. One thing that shifted in me was that it was sad to see how dividing companies in foreign countries was affecting their communities in a big way. I didn't feel comfortable with that. Everyone was trying to get a tiny piece of those companies. It was affecting a sector of the population with kids and women. We always end up paying the biggest price. Again, my "helping others DNA" kicked in and I said that it wasn't for me. After that outside counsel role, I got a job in a startup that later got bought by Western Union, and it was an interesting process to see the corporate dynamics. I decided to go back to international trade and e-commerce. This is the job that allows me to pay the bills and do all the crazy things that I do for women now.

Sonia: That's so awesome. I would love for you to share about Heroikka and tell us about your mission and passion for it.

Maica: Five years ago, I started something called the San Francisco International Women Entrepreneurs Forum. I saw that there were many organizations in the Bay Area with programs, initiatives, and events for women entrepreneurs and professionals, but nobody was collaborating or sharing resources. Everyone was doing their own thing. I saw that different chambers of commerce or business associations and institutions were presenting the same topics and types of events. I thought, "This is a no-brainer. If you want to give more visibility to a broader community and do things in a different way, you should open up and collaborate with other organizations."

I started talking to executive directors from these institutions and organizations, and suggested we had one big event. I think we had the French Chamber, the British, the Australian, the German, the Italian, and others. We sold out the tickets and had a waiting list.

From there, we started connecting with other organizations, and then we decided to create a website. Now if you go to the website, you will see that we are the biggest alliance of organizations and institutions with programs, initiatives, and events for women entrepreneurs here in California, and one of the top three in the United States. Right now, the Forum includes more than thirty organizations.

At Heroikka, we connect global talent to female-led projects. And this is really important because what we're seeing is that women and girls are the biggest economic indicators in their communities. They're creating businesses and initiatives that are helping grow their communities. We also saw that these women need to have access to the talent and resources that will help their project grow, otherwise they're going to throw in the towel. At the same time as they run their businesses, they're mothers, they have their daily work, and they start side projects. They're the motor of the family, and it's hard to keep up with all of this.

We connect global talent to female-led projects, so women who don't have projects or businesses can still help others. They have amazing talents that they can share out there. All these women want to help their communities and support the right businesses, initiatives, institutions, or organizations.

We did a pilot in Mexico and had 548 women registered for our event. From those, three hundred registered in Heroikka, and they posted seventy projects.

Sonia: Whether coaching or free help, people could give back.

Maica: Yes, and even though we are a for-profit, we want to give back to the community. By being profitable in the future, we can reinvest in the community. Through Heroikka, we can share the projects with a global community to create more impact.

Sonia: It seems like it's for everyone, and you're building a global community and asking what people need and how you can help. All these people are willing to help.

Maica: Yes, it could be for a business plan, social media, or legal help or just promoting the projects on their own social media. They say, "I love your project so much, I'm going to post it on my Instagram or on my Facebook." We are facilitating a tool for women to be more proactive with what they are doing online. Many of them, for the first time, have all the information in different platforms, all in one place, regarding a project. A video on YouTube, or a description in another platform, a link to their website … It's all in one place. So you can send a link directly to the platform and others can see what you're working on without any problem. It's faster than writing all these templates and generating them to different people. Other women can then promote your project and send it to their contacts or collaborate with your project.

Once you create your project, there are four easy steps. We're not asking for personal information when you create a profile. We ask five or six questions, that's it. We are interested in what you're doing ... What we are really interested in is about what you want to do and how you can make things happen. We're creating a big global hub to help people discover what other women are doing around the world. This isn't something that even governments and institutions are doing, and for the first time, they're able to see what women in those communities are truly doing. We can go to governments and institutions and say, "Hey, you're not investing in the right places, because this is what women in your community are working on. This is what the girls in your community need." For the first time, we can have access to data that nobody else can get access to.

Sonia: Oh wow. This is very exciting, and now I can see it in detail. My mind is spinning and thinking that every woman needs this. We can give our talents and also receive talents from others. It's like reciprocity, and the site is the hub.

Maica: Yes, and of course, we work for profit, but we do not charge women to post in the platform, or to help other women —no way. We want to get our funding from governments and corporations, etc. Many communities are as wealthy as they are right now because of women. We say, "You should start paying attention to what really interests me. It's about time you start actually investing in us, in the same way that we are your clients and we trust in your companies."

Sonia: Absolutely wonderful. Where do you see yourself and Heroikka, this beautiful thing you've created, five years from now? What's your vision for it?

Maica: This is a feisty side of me that always comes with this quest.

Sonia: The out-of-the-box side; that's what we want.

Maica: I want to see as many women and girls as possible do what they really want to do. I don't want them to say, "I would love to do this, but I don't know the right people," or "It's hard for me to tap into the right networks to get access to capital or education or resources so I can do what matters to me." I don't want to see any girl or woman questioning that side. As women, we have to educate each other about what we are doing and how we can help each other. Heroikka fulfills that space of questioning.

The other thing that I envision is the Heroikka Innovation Lab, where we can invite women from all over the world to join us and create a tailored program, and they won't have to pay. We're trying to figure out how we can make it for free. So if you're a woman, maybe you're able to travel to one of our summits abroad.

The best ideas and things happen because we are in an ecosystem where everyone is so different, so diverse. But at the same time, they feel so inclusive in that ecosystem. They feel free to make their own decisions for wealth-building.

Sonia: Wow, that's empowering.

Maica: Yes but now I don't say that we need to empower women. No, I don't believe in that, we need to figure out that we were born empowered.

Sonia: Yes, I love it, not "we need" but "we are." We were created for greatness.

Maica: Some women grew up seeing certain role models around them and they think that's their role and they cannot get out of such a situation.

Sonia: Right, but in your case, you lived with your dad, your mom, and your grandmother's sister, and so you had mentors who were very strong. How important is mentorship for all women?

Maica: One thing we discovered when we interviewed so many women around the world is that they have a certain phobia to the word "mentorship." Why? Because the image they have is one person talking and the other listening, and basically what they want more is an exchange of ideas. I always give this example: What's the point of you inviting me to the table if I cannot order what I want from the menu? So yes, it's a big difference. Maybe a woman has expertise and is amazing in certain things, but she also has something to offer. Women sometimes forget that everyone has something to offer. They can still help someone else.

Throughout history, everything that women have accomplished, for instance, the right to an abortion, the right to vote, is because we got out there and created a social movement that translated into legislation. We always gather together as women. We gather with our friends, and to make the changes we need to make for our businesses and initiatives. That's why it's important to see more women in engineering, politics, and different industries with a focus on technology. We need to go out there and come out of the closet as women. And we need to show men that they can be excellent allies. It is up to us to help them understand that we're needed, and what we need.

I got into a conversation with a friend of mine; he's really funny. He said, "Wow if we had to breastfeed, I can imagine the rooms for this … they would have these amazing seats, non-alcoholic beer, the biggest TV to watch the game. If men could have babies, we would probably get a procreation bonus." I said, "Yeah, you're right, yes, for sure."

Sonia: Women and men need to say, "I don't know everything, you don't know everything, but we can help each other."

Maica: Yes, we need to stop competing. Let's collaborate and learn from each other and educate ourselves about each other.

Sonia: Yes, and many women we know lack confidence, and like you were saying, they don't know what they were born with. And they allow circumstances to define them. But that's your mission for women to rise up and say, "I can be whoever I was created to be and I'm going to go after it." Thank you so much for sharing this. You have a strong passion. I'm excited about your global mission for women to think big and aim high.

Maica: It's true, and women are coming from different backgrounds and they don't all have access to the same type of education or resources or networks. I believe in doers. It's not just about being someone; I believe we need to get back to "doing something."

Sonia: Yes, I would say both: Be who you were created to me, and also be a doer and take action.

Maica: For sure, and I believe our best legacy is going to be through our work and what we do for others in our communities … if they do something for others, it means they do something for themselves too. My mother always said to me, "If you want to do something for others, first you have to take care of yourself."

Sonia: Absolutely, I agree one hundred percent. How can you serve others while you're drowning?

Maica: So, take care of yourself, and then you're ready to bring the best of yourself.

Sonia: Thank you so much, Maica. Thousands of women are going to be very encouraged because they will see a resource and other women coming together to share gifts and information.

Maica: They can find me on LinkedIn at Maica Gil, and of course at Heroikka.com. Send us questions if you want to collaborate with us or if you want to start a project, initiative, or if you want to donate your talent to your community.

Sonia: Wonderful, thank you so much, Maica!

Sonia Hassey

ABOUT MAICA GIL

Founder at Heroikka and SF International Women Entrepreneurs Forum. Maica's extensive experience in entrepreneurship, government and non-profits, has helped her create a platform for diverse international organizations to collaborate, share resources and give visibility to various projects and initiatives, start-ups and businesses specific to women at the SF International Women Entrepreneurs Forum.

As Founder at Heroikka, Maica is passionate and committed to closing the gap by connecting women-led projects, funding and support systems around the world.

She is also on the Board of Directors for the "Association of American European Chambers of Commerce and Business Associations" and Co-Founder of the California – Spain Chamber of Commerce.

Heroikka.com

Twitter @be_heroikka

CHAPTER 2

The Truth Shall Make You Free

Brenda Rejamand

Sonia: Hello, I am here with Brenda Rejamand and she is the founder and CEO of BD Tax & Finance Group in Sacramento, California. Brenda is going to share her powerful story about how she came here to America, what made her become the woman that she is today, and what has given her the strength to persevere.

Brenda: My name is Brenda Rejamand and I was born and raised in San Salvador, El Salvador, in the year of 1974. My father had just graduated from medical school and my mother was a secretary and owner of a small business the year I was born. Because I was the first grandchild, my grandparents, Ricardo, Hilda, Justino, and Toyta, welcomed me with so much love and gifts. Justino and Toyta even gifted my dad a house so I could have a home.

My father was barely starting his career as a physician in general medicine and as a typical Salvadorean gentleman, he asked my mother to stay home and raise me. My mother drove me to my grandparents' house every afternoon. I was pretty much raised with my grandparents Ricardo and Hilda. Back then, my grandparents were very hard-working business owners; they were the perfect example of success and freedom. They loved to travel to beautiful beaches every weekend. I was always involved in their lives and I grew up not only being spoiled but pretty much having everything a girl could wish for. They taught me not only how to work hard but also to enjoy life as we go.

My father became one of the best and most reputable doctors, not only because he was good but also because he loved to help the community. I grew up watching him volunteering his time, collaborating with chambers and rotary clubs in El Salvador. One of my favorite places to go to with him was when my father visited foster homes. He would vaccinate all these beautiful, fragile children who didn't have parents due to the civil war in our country.

The children really needed medical assistance and because of my father's love and tender care, I enjoyed seeing him taking care of these kids with their glowing faces. It impacted my life because I had my parents' love, their education, and wealth. These kids didn't have any of the three. I also loved how they would hug my dad with so much gratitude. One of my favorite memories is the fact that because I was a doctor's daughter, they would take me on horses and entertain me while my dad was doing his job with the kids.

So I had a princess life! I had that advantage and I loved it. I loved it as a child. I had an incredible childhood. About two years later, my sister Amalia was born and she became my best buddy, but also my little competition for attention.

Amalia and I were raised together, and she also had the princess life. So pretty much it was the two of us for a while. My father continuously grew as a professional and that helped our family climb rapidly up the social ladder. We moved to an upscale neighborhood, and of course, with that came a more upscale school for us. I ended up going to one of the best bilingual schools in San Salvador. My father always planned for my future in the United States because my father's parents and siblings were residing in the United States. My grandmother, Toyta, became a citizen and she requested my father's family for permanent residency when I was in my childhood. I was continuously told to practice English on a daily basis because I was going to need it in the near future. I honestly HATED with a passion what it took to learn English ... English to me was like, "Okay no, I can't do this."

Sonia: Was that your father's dream to go to the United States because he wanted the best for you and his wife and the family? Was that his vision?

Brenda: Yes. He got so big in his career that he had a lot of jealousy from other doctors and by other people around him. When I turned nine, someone threatened his family's life and his life. By that time, I already had two more sisters, Margarita and Lucy, so it was four of us. And they told him, "If you don't pay us this amount of money, we know where your daughters are, and what school your daughters go to." My father felt so threatened that he immediately got us out of the country. So we ended up in Los Angeles with my aunt.

Sonia: How old were you at the time?

Brenda: I was probably ten and a half by then, almost eleven. It was a big change for me because not only was it a new country, but I was forced to start speaking English, the language I hated. Although we had already visited Miami and Orlando, Florida, back when I was seven years old, my parents took my sister Amalia and I to Disney World. We loved our family trip, but I felt lost in Florida, Everything looked so large to me.

L.A was all new to me. And I left all my friends behind. I come from a family where my mother used to have three maids for us because it was four girls, and we had a princess life that was very comfortable. So we had all the attention in El Salvador, and all of a sudden, we didn't have that attention here. My mom didn't know how to even handle us. She felt lost and so did we.

Sonia: Now you're a small fish in a big pond!

Brenda: Yes, my mom was not happy, and my dad ended up bringing one maid to assist her, but it was still not the same. Our life was different and starting from scratch. The culture was a mix in our new elementary school! I was in so much shock that I was struggling with the language. I was pretty much living in denial. My father was able to get a great job and he was only working three days a week in

Santa Barbara, California. On his time off, he was either having fun with us or traveling back and forth to El Salvador. He was also having a hard time adapting to his new life. The difference between him and me was that he was able to go back to his country and I was not. Every time he came back home, he was refreshed and ready to continue with the change of life, while I was still stuck in denial and in my past. But he was not whole. He missed practicing medicine and we felt that.

Sonia: You didn't feel at home?

Brenda: Absolutely! I remember back then, El Salvador went through a very destructive earthquake; my father's new boss in Santa Barbara asked him to take first aid and medicine to El Salvador. I saw my father on the L.A. news. His boss was promoting first aid respondents to the emergency in El Salvador. I was impressed to watch that neither the language nor a totally new country kept him away from his professional collaboration and success. The news reporters aired, "The Salvadorian doctor is taking medicine for the ones in need due to an earthquake," and that impacted my life forever. Every Sunday, we attended church and the church kids were expressing, "Wow! We saw your dad on TV and he's doing all this humanitarian work!" I felt so proud of him! I learned that it's not about how you feel or how uncomfortable you are, it's about who needs you, and how you will impact the one life in need under the circumstances.

Sonia: Your dad's impact stuck with you.

Brenda: Yes. I grew up as Catholic. Hispanic countries being Catholic means religious and judgmental, as a whole. It's either white or black, but no mediums. Before we left El Salvador, our family met

Jesus Christ as our Savior. That was an additional great change to our new lives ...

Sonia: How did it change for you? You mentioned that Catholicism is overly structured. But what gave your family that "wow" transformation?

Brenda: It changed as far as giving me faith. I was looking for a spiritual connection and I found it in Christ. Being far away from home made me more mature at a young age, and I felt empty. Jesus was my answer. Although my connection with God was stronger, the one thing that didn't change was my religious position. Jesus was starting to change my faith to another level, but it is up to us to let the religious position go. I can tell you, it's very hard to let go of something you are not aware of. I was too young for awareness, but I wasn't too young to fall into a judgmental religious position.

After two and a half years, my father decided to go back to El Salvador because our permanent residency was still not approved. It was going to take a few more years and we could not be living illegally in the United States. Our family was in danger to be deported and we could have lost our opportunity of having the Green Card.

We all went back to El Salvador. I was happy and excited to the point that I was giving away all my toys, gold rings, and other belongings to the church children that became my best friends at that time.

What I did not know is that when I went back to El Salvador, I was still going to feel very strange. I was already adopting the mixed culture of living in L.A, even though I did not accept it in my heart.

So when I go back, I'm already thirteen and a half years old and I don't know that my parents are going to get divorced. So not only did I feel like a foreigner, but I also lost my parents.

I had to worry about making new friends, new school rules, and a new way of living with my divorcing parents. Watching divorce fights were the ugliest scenes for me. I had never experienced watching my parents argue because they had always kept it private from us. It was unbelievably traumatic for me. I was no longer a princess, even though I was back living in my country. But what struck me was their divorce. Imagine my whole world collapsing in front of me. So my idols are not my idols anymore. I want to help but I don't know how.

Sonia: It's devastating.

Brenda: At my age, it was a tsunami. I was drowning and all I knew was that I was not going to make it. I started noticing my sisters were struggling too and I pretty much became their second mother. I saw myself that way. I thought, "If I don't take care of my sisters, nobody will." My parents were too involved in their divorce. I was obviously not ready to take that responsibility of being their second mother because of my young age, and I'd been spoiled all my life. I didn't know how to handle the situation. However, I managed in my own little way to protect them. My grandparents Ricardo and Hilda took over and protected us as much as they could, so we were not alone even though we felt alone.

I couldn't understand why my parents were going through a divorce. My childhood had been the most beautiful childhood anybody could have, so what happened? How did it happen? This was my question. My parents were not the same parents that would fight in front of us. All of a sudden, we have a broken family, a broken child that has to start a new life again. I was completely stuck in my sorrows ... When you have divorced parents in El Salvador, it's not okay. It's hard for society to accept you with divorced parents. Especially when you are trying to fit in again and make new friendships.

Sonia: It's a big deal.

Brenda: It's a big deal to everyone. They look at you differently. You become a black sheep, unfortunately. They see you like, "Oh, you don't have a mother," or "You don't have a father" and that means that you are not completely fitted for that friendship or you are not being raised to the society standards.

Sonia: It's almost like you lose your identity!

Brenda: That's exactly what happened to me, I lost my identity. I didn't know what I wanted. I lost my sense of direction, and my self-esteem was low. One thing I never forgot about was my faith. I cried to Jesus for help and I did feel His love and care. I remember my mother tried to cope with the situation, but she couldn't. She ended up leaving to the U.S. again and she started a new life. She started all over again without us.

Sonia: So did she come back?

Brenda: She came back to L.A. So now I'm left with my grandparents, who I love, and my father. Even though they've been there for me all my life, it's not the same because my mother is missing. Being a teenager is hard as it is; can you imagine not having your mother around? It's just horrifying! Now that my mother has left, I'm definitely the mom to my sisters.

Sonia: You didn't have a choice.

Brenda: I did not have a choice. I had to step up, and of course, my grades were not good at all. I couldn't concentrate or focus. I started getting migraines for not sleeping well. My dad started taking me to specialists in the subject matter, colleagues' visits, but I could not sleep nor could I ever be the same. I had no peace of mind. I went anemic for a while. Every day from then on, there was something new. Maybe I was dramatic, I don't know. I couldn't tell you because I was a teenager. I did not have a mother that could tell me, "It's going to be okay."

Sonia: What emotions were you going through with the loss of your mother? It seems like she just walked away like, "I need to move on with my own life." She assumed you guys were okay.

Brenda: Well, she left us with my dad, but her intentions were to make a new living and come back for us very shortly. Of course, at that time, I did not understand. I was so mad at my mom for leaving, practically hating her. She did come back for us within a year. I told her, "I'm not going with you. I'm staying with my dad." So my mother took my two little sisters first, because Amalia and I did not want to leave my father alone. She decided to give us more time and went back again for Amalia and me in El Salvador, but I didn't want to leave my dad. I said to Amalia, "You go. I'm staying with my dad. I can't stand a new life and going back to the U.S. where I don't want to be." ... I was so emotional and so angry at life at that time! I was blaming everything on my mother when I shouldn't have. I was judgmental and immature, and I was only a teenager full of confusion.

Sonia: It's when you needed your mom the most, at your age.

Brenda: I was very confused. I was still trying to figure out how the bomb exploded in my face all of a sudden. So I was stuck in the past two years. In the meantime, I was turning fifteen and my father spoiled me to make up for the pain I was living. Every week, my dad would buy me a new dress because I would say, "Dad, I need a new dress," so he went and bought me a new dress. My dad was trying to fulfill that emptiness. I said, "Dad, I want a whole new room set." He went and bought me a whole new room set. My dad did so much for me, but I was still trying to figure out who I was. If you remember, I lost my identity somewhere along the divorce.

Sonia: Wow. He did everything he could.

Brenda: He did everything he could possibly do. I remember repeating, "I miss my mom, I miss my mom," so my dad remarried because he thought that I needed a mom. He put someone else in his life, and unfortunately, it was not working for me. Nothing was working for me!

Sonia: It's not the same.

Brenda: So later he said, "You're going to be fifteen. Would you like to go to England for a student interchange or do you want to see mom? Pick and choose what you would like to do, and it will be your fifteenth birthday gift from me." I said, "I really want to go to Europe," but I was too confused, my self-confidence was to the floor level. It was just not there. If my parents would have been together, I'm pretty sure I would have taken that chance and been an interchange student. So I said, "I want to go see my mom," and so he sent me to L.A. Once I arrived in L.A., my surprise at seeing my mom again brought my anger out. She already had a life and I could not cope with it, so I ran away twice.

Sonia: Wow. Soon after?

Brenda: As soon as I arrived. I couldn't handle her new life. I couldn't handle the change going from a mansion, if you could say that, to a two-bedroom apartment. I just couldn't cope with it. I said, "You left my dad for this? You broke our family for this?" I kept my anger against her because I didn't know better. I didn't know that it takes two. I didn't know that a marriage is about two people in commitment and love. At that time, that's how my emotions were, very confused!

So I ran away and because Jesus has always had control of my life, I ended up in a Christian family home. My friend's mom took care of me, talked to me with love and called my mother to pick me up the same night. As soon as I arrived in L.A., I enrolled in high school because I was considering the possibility of staying with my mother and my sisters. I needed my mother as much as I needed my father. My father said to me, "If you feel comfortable, you can stay." We were to get our Green Card residency maybe within the next six months after my arrival. So it was okay for me to stay, and also my mother already had a Green Card, and my sisters had Green Cards. So it was just a matter of me deciding where I want to live.

My father found out I ran away. I called him and told him. He said, "What's wrong?" and I said, "Dad, I cannot be here. I hate my mother. I don't want to be here," and he said, "Okay. Let's do something. Why don't you go see your grandma?" because his mom used to live in Sacramento and so did his siblings and family. So he said, "Okay. I'll send you money right away so you can go and then tell me how you feel with them. Maybe you can stay and go to school in Sacramento." He didn't want to give up. He wanted me to try a different family environment, so I had a chance. But even though they treated me with love, it did not work for me. I had an identity issue and a big one!

Sonia: You didn't feel like you belonged.

Brenda: I was more confused now. In El Salvador, I felt, "Okay, I miss my mom. I can't sleep." I went back to El Salvador, maybe about three months later. After all this struggling and feeling I'm not coping with this life, and I went back. When I went back, my father said, "You have to change your life. You can't be like this, because you need to move on." I didn't know how, and I cried. I remember sitting in my dad's lap and he was hugging me. He said, "I want you to be happy. You need to go to school, you need to finish your degree." Because my father is a physician, I always wanted to be a doctor so I can take the lead in his practice. He raised me with that mentality, so I made it my ultimate goal. My major issue was that I could not concentrate in school. I felt like a loser for years to the point that my father couldn't handle me anymore. There was a lot of rebellion in me. Now I started blaming my father and mother for my failures and unhappiness.

Five to six months later, we finally got me the Green Card and I remember telling him. "Dad! Don't take me. Don't get me the Green Card! I don't need the Green Card! I want to stay in El Salvador." He says, "Too late. I don't know what to do with you anymore. You need to move on and change your life."

Sonia: How did that make you feel when you heard those words?

Brenda: That made me feel as if nobody could take care of me. Not even my dad. I felt like I was a burden. He brought me against my will to L.A. again and dropped me at my mom's apartment, and I remember crying and telling him, "I don't want to live here! Take me!" He cried too, but he said, "I can't, you have to stay with your mother." I cried every night for nine months straight. My dad kept on sending me preaching tapes from our church in El Salvador. I played them every night and cried while listening. I wanted to go back home. One night, after months of struggling with my new life, one of the preaching tapes transformed my soul and I said to myself, "No, I can't cry anymore. I need to move on, no more crying for me." I was turning seventeen years old.

I knew that I wanted to find a church, and I said, "God, how am I going to find a church that fits my needs or like the one at home?" It happened that one of my friends at school came to the house and said, "Do you guys need to buy anything at Target?" My sister and I both decided to go with him to target, and while riding his car, he said, "Do you mind if I stop at my church to say hi to some members?" When he parked the car, I opened the window, and suddenly I heard the same songs being played from my church back in El Salvador. It was exactly the church I needed. I told him, "It's a miracle! God used you!"

About a month later, my whole family was attending the church. My sisters, my mom, and my stepdad, since she had remarried. I was so thankful and looking at starting a new beginning for me and my sisters.

Sonia: So the moment you heard the song, you thought, "I'm home."

Brenda: Yes, I'm home and I understood that I was in His hands all the time. I understood that He had control over my life from the beginning. I started remembering that when I was a kid, I loved the water and the sea, but I almost drowned in three separate incidents. But someone always rescued me. God had control of my life. I became a youth leader at our new church. While participating in the youth leadership, I met my first husband and we got married as soon as I turned eighteen. He joined the Navy and was mostly away in a battleship, so I was pretty much by myself for a while. I felt lonely for sure.

Sonia: When you first met him, did you feel like that was a ticket to a better life?

Brenda: Yes. I still could not accept my mother's new life nor my father abandoning me, because that's how I took it, so I saw marriage as my way out. Unfortunately, I was looking for companionship and independence from my parents while I was not ready for any.

I had a new life by myself, but that didn't stop me from going to church. I was even teaching Women's Bible Studies. But then my husband was transferred, so we moved to Chicago and stayed for three years. I wanted to go to college, but I didn't know where to start. I didn't know how I would become a doctor in a foreign country. I didn't know how to make it in Illinois, and I didn't have my dad to give me guidance or tell me what steps to take. I was an adult without knowing how to act like an adult.

I felt like a failure at that age, not knowing what to do with my life, what career I was supposed to take, and who I was. What would I be good at? All I knew is I was raised to be a doctor. I lost my identity and my self-confidence in my parents' divorce. I lost my purpose in life. Finally, I enrolled in community college classes even though I didn't know what degree I wanted. I worked hard to get my general education classes, but my heart was still in El Salvador.

I missed everything that was good about El Salvador when I was growing up. What I didn't know is that when your heart is back in your country, and you are physically in another country, you will never get anywhere because your mentality is, "One day I will go back, so I'm not going to do anything here. I'm just going to live or maybe save, and I need to go back." But I couldn't make my husband go where he didn't belong. I kept on repeating, "I want to go back" like a daily song in my mind. This daily song was not helping my marriage.

Sonia: Right, because it was your mindset so nothing else was going to work.

Brenda: Four years into my marriage, my daughter was born. I was so happy that I had someone to fight for and live for. Finally, there was a purpose in my life. Two years later I had my son. They both brought so much purpose into my life; I was finally starting to feel complete. Unfortunately, I was still very judgmental and unforgiving toward my parents; I had mixed feelings about them, even though I knew it was wrong. The judgment and anger were just so powerful in my life. I was not healed and it only brought unhappiness even though I had everything I wanted and needed again.

I was still in college and still trying to figure out my career. I went from wanting to be a teacher, to an engineer, and finally to getting my business degree. I felt like I was betraying my father's dream if I didn't become a physician. I was hating myself because I wasn't doing what I was supposed to do. I didn't understand that I had the power within me to overcome anything and move forward and I didn't know how to fight for my happiness. I didn't know how to go get it because as a child I was given everything by default.

Sonia: When you're young and when so much is given to you, the muscle of perseverance is not being exercised.

Brenda: I was now turning twenty-six or twenty-seven, and my kids were now attending a private Christian pre-kinder. At that point, I was still so naïve, I believed everything I was told regardless if it was from a good or bad source. I didn't know how to identify the bad people around me or my family. Due to still feeling unhappy within myself, my marriage expectations were never met, and love was not present in my life because I did not know what love was. My priorities were materialistic because I was still trying to get back the life I once had in El Salvador. My perception of love was very wrong. I was twenty-seven acting like a twenty-one-year-old in a nine-year marriage. I strongly believed my marriage was over, so I went looking for help. I found the wrong help, and I fell into an unplanned affair.

I was dying from the inside. I didn't drown when I was a child, but I was drowning as an adult at age twenty-seven. I couldn't talk to my mother. I couldn't talk to my father. I couldn't talk to my sisters because everybody was looking up to me. Their perspective of me was perfect. They always thought of me as brave, with very high standards, a perfect sister or child. How could I tell them? I was more than imperfect, and I was in trouble. Nobody knew how deep in the hole I was, and I couldn't tell anyone. I was full of shame. I hit the bottom of the ocean but one thing that kept me alive was my children. The reason of me being. I needed to fight to come out of that hole, the depression and confusion. If in my childhood, I lost my identity, at this stage of life I lost it all. I did not know who I was anymore; I didn't recognize myself or my actions.

Sonia: You were dying on the inside.

Brenda: One day, I finally told my husband the truth. I felt liberated, but at the same time, my life changed. I was suicidal but at the same time, the only purpose of life in front of me was my children. I had to stay alive for them. I had to find the courage to fight for my life and liberation.

My husband and I stayed together for another thirteen years, but during that time I can assure you that I knew I'd hit rock bottom. Who would have planned to fail that way? It was the worst time in my life, I can assure you that this episode over-scaled my parents' divorce pain. It did not have a comparison, and this pain I had caused myself. How do you learn to forgive oneself? It was my biggest challenge on a daily basis.

I left with my kids, and we bought a house in another town and started a new life. I told myself, "I don't care if people are talking about me and what they are saying, this is not who I am, and I will prove myself. I will prove to the whole world that there's always a second opportunity to change." At this point, I had to think about myself and the two precious angels God had given me because He knew I would need them to keep on living with a purpose. God transformed and restored me for years and years. All I cared about was to prove who I really was, but for that, I had to find my identity again. Remember how I shared at the beginning, that I had lost it once in my childhood? Well it was time to restore my identity if I really wanted to prove something, right? I was determined to finish college while raising the kids. I earned a bachelor's degree in Business Administration a few years later. I also obtained my notary public and real estate license the same year I graduated. The professional accomplishments started giving me the strength and the power to overcome the way I felt about myself. But I still was having a hard time forgiving myself.

Sonia: Forgiving ourselves is one of the hardest things to do.

Brenda: The biggest challenge was to open my heart and talk to the ones I loved the most, my children. I opened my vulnerable heart to them when they became teenagers. It was very important to me for them to understand how imperfect their mother was, but most of all I wanted them to learn that bad decisions in life have consequences no matter what you do or who you are. It is not an easy practice to keep it authentic, but my lesson in life is that if you are truthful to yourself, you can be truthful to anyone.

Sonia: You shared the good, the bad, and the ugly. The vulnerable part.

Brenda: Yes, my children are everything to me—my treasure. My statement impacted them, but they loved me the same after the fact. They are still with me and we're still good friends. My kids needed to know that I'm imperfect, but that God has been merciful on me and we need to move on leaving imperfection behind. There is no excuse for bad decisions but as long as we learned from our mistakes and God provides us with a second opportunity there always will be room for improvement in our lives.

Sonia: When inner shame burns inside us, we don't realize that it will eat at us bit by bit. That was very courageous of you, as a mother, to let it out.

Brenda: "The Truth Shall Make You Free." Even though my life was never the same again, I can tell you that when one finds mercy in the Lord's eyes, now you have a reason, a "why" to be happy, thankful, grateful, hopeful. After finding myself in the experience of living gracefully forgiven by the Lord Jesus Christ and my children, I understood that we all need forgiveness at least once in a lifetime. Who am I to judge my parents or anyone else? I humbly learned who I was, what I needed to do in life, and how to fight for what I wanted to have. My beliefs grew stronger and stronger on a daily basis. I learned a purpose in life and my priorities involved me wanting my children to get the best of me as a mother and a professional, just like I experienced with my parents and grandparents.

With that in mind, I decided to start my tax business ten years ago in Sacramento. I jumped into the water believing that God was my provider and he was going to provide no matter what. My entire family got involved and ran as fast as I was running with our new business project. I was still raising the kids and taking them to extracurricular activities in the summer, so at the beginning I was only working part-time. I truly enjoyed being involved in my family's life, vacationing with them, and having those bonding, cherished moments that still live in my heart. It only made me stronger and my values grew. I finally had a real purpose in life; my children were my motive and purpose of life and the reason WHY I should move forward. As they continued to grow, I found myself in situations where my clients needed more than just a tax preparer; they needed help with IRS audits. I realized I wanted to do more for them. I wanted to save them from injustice, and to accomplish it, I needed to become an Enrolled Agent.

I pursued the EA for two years and I finally passed the three intensive IRS examinations. The accomplishment and my clientele demand led me to other successful lifetime events such as Univision featuring me on their morning news, and I was invited by several non-profit organizations to do tax public speaking. I very much enjoyed teaching businesses. I realized that mentoring other business owners is the same as preaching. You have to live what you preach in order to set a true example in life. The Lord continuously spoke to me through different sources, and my faith grew stronger because every year he was taking me to a higher step. I very much understood the commitment between God and me.

Every year since then, I have asked Him, "So where will you place me this year? What position am I taking this time?" God has always favored me in a very special way, but unfortunately, I had to hit the bottom of the ocean to understand it. Never again will I doubt His intentions with my family and me. One evening, He spoke to me through a prophesy, "I'm going to lift you among very important people, and you're going to lead others. You will have people come to you because they need help." Although I thought to myself, "What kind of help?" I accepted the prophesy in my heart. It was just so powerful and an authentically spiritual event in my life. I was not certain of the specifics of God's plan with me, but I did know He was restoring me with a great purpose, and He had a plan with me since before I was born.

When my children were about to graduate high school, I finally went through the expected divorce. I never understood what the word divorce meant until I was living it. I don't wish a divorce to anyone or my worst enemy. I held on to my children and my career. My parents and sisters stood by me and my kids. I once again felt lost, but because I had found my purpose in life, my identity and who I wanted to be, I stood strong and went through it like a rock. I did pray a lot. A lot of clients and people that knew me prayed for me for months. God never fails in my life; He constantly grew my career opportunities by opening doors as soon as I started my divorce. I was impacted by His mercy and the way God kept me strong to focus on my goals. He guarded me with love, patience, endurance, forgiveness, and strength.

I was regularly paying visits to my grandparents Ricardo and Hilda's house. In one of those visits, my grandma Hilda said, "I know your happiness is around the corner. God will give you the husband that will make you forever happy." I remember feeling pity on myself because I did not even know what a man should look like or be like to make me happy. My mind was stormy and so cloudy. I literally was looking for a clear sky even though our California sky is always so beautiful and sunny. It was too soon to start thinking about a new life. I was busy enough making sure my kids were okay and running a business full time. Just about four weeks later, I was invited to a birthday party where I met a very handsome gentleman. That night I didn't realize that I was talking to my future husband, but he did, in fact, realize he was speaking to the girl he had been waiting for. Since that night, he made sure to stay connected. My parents, grandparents, and kids loved him. We got married three years later.

After meeting Mahdi, I once again started to believe in love and second opportunities. Love does exist and so do second chances. Mahdi is a person full of talents, love, grace, and a very strong character. He has great leadership skills and he can't stop making me laugh. We can talk for hours and never be bored with each other. He, in fact, was sent by God to make me whole personally and professionally. Mahdi is the friendliest business mind I have ever met in my life. He compliments my career. We spend 24/7 together and we just can't get enough of each other. We are continuously growing as a couple but also as business partners. We take care of the challenges together on a daily basis. Mahdi helped me to put the kids in college and on a daily basis he mentors them. He has built a very strong relationship with Dianna and Kevin. I can now tell you I have met happiness. I finally have understood what love means. Love is empowering others to become a better person, love shares good and bad times without regret. Love grows in a tighter connection among the people that truly care for you.

Everyone has a story to share, it is so important to discover your purpose and identity. Have you asked yourself recently, "Who are you? What is important to you? What is your purpose in life? What drives you to success or failure?" Don't live another day without finding out the answers that will help and lead you to happiness, love, and success.

Sonia: Thank you for sharing your story.

ABOUT BRENDA REJAMAND

Brenda, CEO and founder of BD Tax & Finance Group, Inc is the recipient of the 2018 Latina Empresaria Minerva Hall of Fame Award of California Hispanic Chamber of Commerce, 2018 Business Hall of Fame Sacramento Award Program 2012-2015 Best of Sacramento award on Tax Returns and Accountants category by the Sacramento Award Program. She is also the recipient of 2015 Latina Style Magazine Best Latina Business Owner in Sacramento.

Brenda enjoys giving back to the industry through mentoring other professionals and speaking to groups about her personal and career experiences. She has been a featured speaker for many organizations including: IRS Workshop for Small Businesses, Univision Morning News, and other various Non-Profit Community Groups.

In 2005, she graduated from DeVry University with a Bachelor of Science in Business Administration. In 2010 she completed the three rigorous and comprehensive IRS Enrolled Agent exams. An Enrolled agent status is the highest credential the IRS federal practice can give. They are individuals that obtain this elite status who must adhere to the highest ethical standards. Since then she has completed hundreds of IRS-Approved Continuing Education series, and multiple successful completed courses approved by CTEC (California Tax Education Council). Her practice is about trust during tax time and throughout the year. She's an expert in small business start-ups and management, tax planning, and can represent you in case of an audit, examination, collection or appeal process, whether individual or business.

CHAPTER 3

You Got This!

Jessie Banuelos

Sonia: I am here with Jessie Banuelos, who has a beautiful story. Jessie, please tell us about you and what you do.

Jessie: Today, I am a mother, a wife, and a business owner. I am a mother to four grown young men, and bonus mom to three more. I have a beautiful husband and I have been blessed with my own business since June 2017.

Sonia: Let's start with where it all began. I see you as a woman of courage and power. Someone who has built her strength along the way in her journey. So tell me where you're from and about your family, and let's take your story from there.

Jessie: I was born and raised in Richmond, California. My parents met in the late 1960s just as my dad was discharged from his service in Vietnam. My mom came here from Mexico as a fourteen-year-old young lady to go to school and to babysit to make money to send back home to her family. She is from a large family with thirteen siblings. Her parents were working hard and raising the family, and it must have been very difficult to maintain a large family because when there was an opportunity for my mom to come to the United States to earn money and help her family, she mustered up the courage to stay with distant uncles to babysit for them and go to school. It speaks volumes about my mom that at such a young age she was willing to come to another country, stay with distant relatives, and work to support her family from afar.

My mom told me that when she was just about twenty, she saw my dad for the first time at the St. Paul's Church carnival. He was tall, lean, gorgeous, dressed in his Army greens, and she almost fell in love with him at first sight. At the time, her English was very limited, and my dad didn't speak much Spanish, so it's curious that they found a way to communicate. A true testament that love is the universal language. They were married soon into their courtship, had five kids within six years, and I am the second-eldest of our brood. Jack is my oldest brother, then there's me, Carlos, Tony (God rest his soul; he is no longer with us), and my youngest sister Becky. As the oldest girl, I bore a lot of responsibility for taking care of my siblings from a young age.

My mother was a wonderful caregiver and she worked very hard to keep her home clean, and her children even cleaner. It was not unusual as toddlers for us to have two baths a day. My dad worked at the Safeway warehouse in Richmond and she had dinner on the table, including homemade flour tortillas, fresh chile de arbol, and all five of us as shiny as a brand-new nickel. Whenever we went to family parties, we were the most well-behaved, best combed and best smelling kids there. But I also remember that my mom used to sneak us out to the park when my dad was at work and we got our baths to wash the evidence off before my dad got home. It was a very "controlled" environment. No fuss, no mess, no ruckus—highly unusual for a household with five kids under the age of six.

When my dad worked for Safeway as a union employee, it was common to strike when the employee contracts were up for renewal. I was about eight years old when he was going through a strike that lasted longer than usual, and it was a tough financial burden on my family. It was the first and only time my mom took a job outside of the home, which I believe at that time was uncommon in the Hispanic culture, where the mother keeps the family home while the father works and provides the financial support. I didn't actually realize that it was out of dire necessity that my mom had a job. During this tough time, it fell to my mom to work and provide, and unfortunately for us kids, we were left at home under my dad's care. We were not allowed to play outside like the other neighborhood children, and we were often punished for minor offenses, like not reciting our multiplication table correctly or not staying quiet while my dad was napping. I remember my older brother and I standing on chairs to wash dishes and making sandwiches for the younger ones. It was a lot of responsibility for me, an eight-year-old, to take care of my siblings.

Sonia: Wow. You became like a mother.

Jessie: It's funny you say that because throughout the years I was known as their mother hen. I used to fill out the school forms, helps my siblings with homework, braid my sister's hair. We were in high school and when my brothers would get into trouble, the school counselor would call me out of class and into the office to straighten them out.

Sonia: How did you feel being so young and having such a huge responsibility at home?

Jessie: It was hard, probably stressful to have so much responsibility at such a young age. I was in charge of my brothers and sister, at home, at school, making sure that everything my mom would have done, I did for them. Aside from that, we lived in a very sheltered environment, we didn't see much outside of school and home, and it caused a lot of anxiety. Because of my dad, we lived in fear of making him angry. Our world was only as big as our family, our extended family was pretty much non-existent, we didn't have friends over, and we never went to our friends' houses to play. While the neighborhood girls were outside riding bikes, playing jump rope and hopscotch, I was inside the house with my mom, helping her clean and cook, learning how to needlepoint, sew, and crochet. Sitting there with her, all I wanted was to be outside with the neighborhood kids, roller skating and riding bikes, but I could not say as much because my dad's word was the rule and my mom knew better than to fight him on it. He wanted us at home, inside, under his watchful eye. I just did as I was told and I knew that as long as I did what I was told, I was less likely to feel the brunt of my dad's wrath. We all knew better than to make my dad angry and always tried our best to stay out of his way.

Every day I felt like I was in survival mode, just trying to get through the day without making my dad angry. All my siblings and I wanted was to do the right thing and do what he said. My dad was a scary man and he was a person whose mantra was, "Do as I say, not as I do." In his daily behavior, he was hardly leading us kids by his example. Instead, he reared us in fear. If he said, "Go to bed at 7:30," even though it was light outside in the summertime, we went straight to bed. My brothers and sister tried to hide from him, and with good reason. But I tried to shower my dad with attention and affection because I thought that if I loved him or if I was this good girl, he would soften up. I remember brushing his hair, getting him whatever he needed, and trying to tend to him so that he would feel loved, and that it's okay, he didn't need to be angry or aggressive. This was my way of protecting my siblings from him, shielding them from him and being the first one in the line of fire.

Sonia: How did he receive your attention, and did he give love back?

Jessie: My dad in his own way appreciated the attention, but "the other side" of him usually won over and it didn't take much to tip his emotions over to the dark side. My dad loved music, so I learned to enjoy the music he played. And he used to play his mariachi music, so

I learned how to dance to amuse him. It seemed like I was always trying to give him happiness, and sometimes it worked and sometimes it didn't, it just depended on his mood. My dad does not know how to receive love, although he has changed a lot in his older years. He has not fully accepted and realized that to receive love, you have to give love, and when you give love, you will receive love. Now that I'm an adult, I look back at how my dad was raised and know that so much of what he did to us, what he gave and didn't give to us had everything to do with what he learned from his experiences as a child. His father, my grandpa Joe, was a very sweet man, but my grandpa had grown up as an orphan from a very young age and he himself didn't experience love and affection to model to my dad. My grandma Jessie (I was named after her) also grew up in a harsh environment filled with emotional and physical abuse. Like most parents, my grandparents did their best with what they had and what they knew, but my dad had a far from ideal upbringing, and for that, we as his children suffered.

And so as a little girl, I spent time with my dad, I wanted him to feel loved so that he would make all of us kids and my mom feel safe and loved. I was my dad's shadow. I went with him to the grocery, to visit my grandparents, and wherever he went, he did not go alone. It didn't really work most of the time. He was still aggressive and angry, but every now and then we had a moment or two where we did feel safe and loved.

Sonia: As a young girl, what was the message you were receiving?

Jessie: Even though I know that my dad loved me, I felt like I had to earn his love, his affection, his protection. And even though I worked really hard to earn it, I didn't get what I felt I needed and deserved. But this is the hand I was dealt. I was thankful for the roof over my head, the food on my plate, I was not homeless or hungry and maybe I should accept that this was as good as it gets. I convinced myself that this is just how life is. I was heartbroken and devastated. I couldn't wait to grow up and get as far away from home as I could, convinced that my adult life would never resemble this life that I lived as a young girl. I just needed to survive until I was old enough to get out of there.

When I was in the ninth grade, my grandma Jessie passed away, and it hurt me deeply because I loved her so much, even if she was old and mean-spirited. I visited her every day with my dad, and it was depressing that every day she sat in bed, lonely and miserable, watching television. I loved my grandma differently than my siblings. They never got close to her, but I sensed she was lonely and that all she wanted was somebody to keep her company. She was a difficult person to be around, complained a lot, and she was mean when she spoke of others and that made me incredibly sad for her. My dad and grandma had a love/hate relationship; they were terrible to each other. But when she passed away, it was the first time my dad was vulnerable, mourning the death of his mother, he looked broken, almost human. The way I saw my dad changed after that. He was different and he took care of my grandpa in a way that he had never cared for us. He made sure that my grandpa never felt alone or wanted for anything. My dad as there for him.

It cut me deeply, and I couldn't help but think, "Well, what about us? You are capable of loving and caring, but what do you give us?" During those years, my mom grew extremely resentful of my dad because she saw the same thing I was seeing. It was the first glimpse of my mom's evolution in her role as a parent in our household. How could my dad give care to my grandfather but not to his own children? These thoughts filled my head and my heart with resentment and my feelings were further destroyed.

All these years I worked so hard to earn my dad's love, never fully convinced he was capable of loving, yet he was there for my grandfather, taking care of him. He was kind, patient, gentle, generous. It was confusing for me; it was hard to accept. My dad had spewed poisonous words at me, but he never spoke badly to my grandpa.

I was fifteen, still the mother but needing to shield my brothers and sister from my dad's wrath, and I could see that my time was coming soon and I would be able to leave.

Sonia: What incredible courage! When did you get out of their house, and what did that journey look like?

Jessie: I was always a good student, earning almost straight A's, and I got into UC Berkeley. It was supposed to be the launch to the rest of my life. I envisioned my future self as an attorney living in New York with an apartment in Paris. I would be a smart, successful, beautifully dressed woman, a powerhouse. I would follow my dreams and work hard to make them my reality. Deep down, however, there was always this sense of not being good enough. I was not smart enough for school, I was a nobody, unimportant, invisible almost. My second year at the university, I felt the need to prove that I was worthy, that a man would and could accept me and love me. This need was the result of my dad's constant rejection, of him tearing me down, making me feel like I had to earn his love and attention. And replaying one of the most hurtful things he ever said to me, "No man will ever want you."

Sonia: You believed that lie.

Jessie: Yes, I believed that those words were truth and so I was determined to prove him wrong. I started making terrible decisions that would change the course of my life. The dream of the jet-set New York attorney life quickly dissipated when I had a baby at twenty-one. I became the typical statistic, a young, Latina, uneducated, single mother. I was damaged goods before, but now what was I? Rejected by my father, rejected by the father of my son, I was on a mission to find a man but this time around it would be different, or would it?

I wanted to find that person who did want me. I convinced myself that it could happen for me. I met someone who also had a little boy just a couple of years older than my son, and it seemed like a match made in heaven. He was a single dad. I was a single mom. He was Latino, I was Latina. I fell in love and we got married. Mission complete! Turned out that he was very much like my dad. It was far from a match in heaven, he played mind games, he was emotionally withdrawn and passive-aggressive, going days on end without speaking a word to me. This scene was all too familiar.

Shortly after we were married, we started our own family. Our first son together was born just after our first wedding anniversary, and then I found out I was pregnant again. Our second son was born very premature, at twenty-six weeks' gestation. The stress level in our home and stress on our relationship was through the roof. We didn't partner well together, and my life was at an ultimate low. I was in survival mode again and asking myself, "How did I get here?"

Still, I was totally convinced that there was more to our story, this couldn't be the life me and my kids deserved, so I pushed forward, determined to make this work. I would not fail this time, I couldn't. I had four boys and a full-time job, I was making it work, and hard as it was, at least my family was together. I was working in an insurance office and one day I said to him, "I want to do something more, I feel capable of so much more. I have a vision for myself and I just know that I need to make a career move." His response cut me like a knife. He said, "What do you know how to do? All you do is answer the phone all day." And I thought, "Wow, is this all he thinks I do all day?" It resonated of my dad. They both basically made me feel like I was nothing.

Sonia: There's that invalidation again.

Jessie: At that point, I realized, "This is not the life that I want, this is not the life I choose, this is not the life I am meant to live." Every day I was in survival mode, trying to get through each day, trying not to make him mad, so we could have a peaceful night, only to wake up the next morning and do it all over again. I needed to make a change.

I put a plan in motion. I was not yet thirty when I realized I had the power to choose and make my life what I wanted it to be. I wanted to buy a house, I required a better job, I needed to stand on my own without a man and in that order. The wheels were put in motion when we bought a house and I got a new job. Still, I held the slightest bit of hope that our marriage would improve, but nothing changed. In fact, it got much worse. I was working, making great money, and taking care of my kids. My home was impeccable, I felt like superwoman. It was work, home, work, home. I thought if I could just keep my house clean enough, and my kids tidy enough, and do everything perfectly, then I would have this perfect home and husband and life. But it didn't matter what I did or how I did it, nothing was ever good or right. It was such an unstable and unpredictable environment. What was I doing? I was putting my kids in the same environment as the one I had growing up.

Deep in my heart, I knew what I needed to do. Of course I wished it weren't so, of course I prayed for our relationship to work out and I searched for signs to prove that we would be okay. It was around this time that my second son started showing signs of being sick, and he was in and out of the hospital. With my other premature baby going through his health issues, it was the perfect storm to tear us apart. We couldn't weather the storm together and even though it seemed like this was not the time to make life-changing decisions, it needed to be done. I mustered up the courage to tell him, "We can't do this. We have to go our separate ways. I want a divorce. I don't need anything from you, I just need you to get out of my home and let me raise my children." It was terrible, it was hard, lots of tears, lots of arguments, and plenty of rationalizing his way back into the relationship, but it was over.

It was one of the hardest chapters of my life, but it was the best thing for me and my kids and gave us the opportunity to create the life that we deserved. Our home was peaceful, it was fun, and we made the best of our situation. I worked long hours and the kids got to spend time with their dad and grandparents. It was, at the time, an ideal living situation.

When I was ready to "move on," I thought about the fact that I had four kids and it would be challenging to date. It wasn't long before I found someone who I thought was my knight in shining armor, my prince charming, the man that would once and for all make it happen for me. The romance was overflowing, there were flowers, jewelry, fancy dinners, and many vacations and weekends away. He filled me up with the compliments I had so longed to hear, "You're so beautiful." "You're wonderful." "You're the best." I got caught up in the romance. I thought, "Oh my God, I have put in my time, and it is finally happening for me."

We quickly got married BUT when we got home from the honeymoon, the honeymoon was over, literally. The minute we walked into our new home together, everything switched. I was duped. When his true self surfaced, I found that I had married someone like my dad again. I worked so hard to get him to go back to the person I fell in love with, the romantic guy that pulled out all the stops, and if only my house was perfect, and I'm taking care of my family and helping him—it would all be okay. I was still working in insurance and succeeding with a rewarding career, allowing me to be the provider of my family, and it just had to work out. My kids went to Catholic school, played all the sports they wanted, took music lessons, we went on great vacations, and I did everything for them that I had wanted for me as a child.

No matter what my life "looked like" on the outside, inside I was dying, little by little the flicker of light that people once saw when they looked at me was fading. I realized I was in survival mode again. I didn't feel good about myself. I didn't feel like I was providing my kids with the home environment they deserved. He was always watching TV and drinking. All the stuff I saw growing up with my dad was repeating itself in my home. This relationship dissolved as quickly as it began.

Taking a huge step back and looking at where I was, where I've come from, what I've lived, the decisions I've made that have resulted in this life in which I was so unhappy, it was a life-defining moment. I asked myself why I was struggling, what was I trying to prove, to whom, why, and at what cost. I had to be honest with myself and see that there was so much work that needed to be done. And so the journey to reclaim my life, my soul, and my dreams began.

Sonia: Wow, what a courageous moment. What were the first steps you took?

Jessie: I took inventory of where I was coming from. I cataloged my situations, incidents, and choices. Sometimes we think things just happen to us, but that's not true. We are making choices. I took a hard look at where I was spiritually and mentally. What was I lacking? What was I thinking that I needed? I needed to learn who I was. I didn't have any friends. I didn't have a social life. I had my children and my work. I wanted my life to be fun and I wanted to laugh. I was not the type of person who smiles a lot and I didn't exude happiness, joy, or positive energy. I did not love or respect myself. How could I expect others to love me and respect me if I didn't give that of myself to myself. I needed to break down all the negative thoughts and feelings, the resentments and failures, let it all go and allow myself to create the person that I was destined to be and show herself.

At the beginning, I was focused more on my outside appearance, berating myself with criticism, telling myself, "You're so ugly, your hair is frizzy, your nose is too big." I'm going to make a confession. I don't usually admit, but I had my nose done.

Sonia: I was just going to say that's a beautiful nose!

Jessie: I had it done but it cost a heck of a lot of money and the recovery process was not cute. I have a little nose now but before I had a big kind of puggy nose. My kids' dad constantly criticized my looks and told me countless times that I had frizzy hair, a big nose, and I was ugly. Although I had heard these same criticisms and comments when I was growing up, it really hurt me to hear that from a person that should have loved me and respected me for being the mother of his children. So yeah, I had my nose done and guess what? Life did not suddenly become perfect, everything that was wrong did not suddenly fall into place, because it wasn't my nose that was holding me back!

There was this other amusing moment when I was taking salsa dancing lessons and I just could not master the timing and rhythm, so I thought if I just had the pretty dancing shoes, I could dance salsa. It made sense to me, but much to my chagrin, I bought the shoes and put them on, and I still couldn't dance salsa. It is funny how we perceive certain things to be game-changers.

It is almost comical thinking that if I just fixed this or tweaked that, then life would be perfect. Over time, I came to the realization that it takes effort, time, and honest check-ins with yourself to make the changes you want to see come to fruition. I needed to dig deep. I needed to love myself. I needed to look in the mirror and be able to tell myself, "You are beautiful. You are amazing. You have so many gifts that you've been blessed with."

Lots of work on the inside and well as the outside. And after many, many dance lessons, I am a salsa dancing queen, with or without the sparkling dance shoes!

Finally, I was in a good place, with my four beautiful boys and our warm, loving, beautiful home. My career was gaining momentum, I was achieving my goals and earning accolades. I developed wonderful friendships for the first time in my adult life and enjoyed amazing times that shaped me and have given me memories of a lifetime of happiness and joy. I take pride in who I am, not because of what others see in me, but because now I love myself.

Sonia: You finally had to embrace the power of belief in yourself and your abilities, and that's when the world around you started seeing the real you, too.

Jessie: I've been through a vast transformation, and forty was the magic number. That's when I realized I was probably halfway through my life and I needed to make changes. I still work on myself constantly. I'm always checking myself and trying to live my best life every day. And I am totally embracing the power of believing in myself, the power to become the woman I am now, the woman that I know I can become, the woman that my kids can look up to, appreciate, and respect.

In my early forties, single life was rewarding, I was focused on me, my kids, and my life was the life I created that made me happy and my kids were happy. I honestly was not looking for a man because life was good! Sometimes I found myself thinking that it would be nice to have a dinner companion or someone to go with on a weekend getaway. A companion, not a husband. I was on my own, financially independent, emotionally strong, and my cup was full. But one night I was out having dinner with a couple of friends and one of them asked me, "If you could choose your ideal partner, what would he be like?"

Sonia: Wow, great question!

Jessie: We were having pizza and beer, and I remember saying something like, "Well, I would want someone who accepts me for who I am. Who loves every part of who I am and embraces me and my quirks, and just loves every piece of me. That's what I would want." And he said, "Wish it into the world. Throw it out into the universe." At first, I thought that was just silly, but after some time, I sat down and I wrote out the characteristics of my ideal partner.

There were no physical characteristics on my list. Gentle in his touch. Kind with his words. Thoughtful in his actions. Generous with his love. Loving father that appreciates his children. College educated, strong career, funny and fun spirited. Not the complete list, but you get the idea. And so I wished him into the universe, and I asked that if this man is out there that we find each other. I am so happy that we found each other! A couple of weeks ago, my aunt asked me, "Where did you find him?" And I said, "I asked for him and the universe brought him to me." I know that this is true!

On our first date, I looked across the table from him and midway through our date, I knew he was the love of my life. I didn't tell him this for a long time because I didn't want to freak him out, but that night was the first time in my life that I had been my true self with a man. Not once did I doubt myself, "Am I pretty enough? Am I smart enough?" I was just myself. We laughed and talked and shared stories for two and a half hours. And at that point in the night he said, "I could talk to you all night, but your children are home waiting for you, so I'm going to walk you to your car. I would love to see you again." He hugs me and puts me in my car, a total gentleman. He said, "Call me when you get home so I know you got home safely." And I thought, "This is the man I'm going to spend the rest of my life with."

And here we are, seven years later! We've created a beautiful life together, and alongside my husband Alden, I continue to be the best version of myself. Each role that I hold, each relationship I have, I feel that I am the best person I can be, as a mother, wife, daughter, friend, colleague, etc…

Together we are awesome. Once he even confessed that when he met me, I made him feel like he wanted to up his A-game. We truly bring out the best in each other.

Sonia: Oh my goodness, you both brought each other up.

Jessie: I had been on a whole journey of wrong decisions and bad relationships, never realizing until now that the key to being in a successful relationship is bringing out the best in each other. We respect and love each other, and he is an amazing parent to my children, and now I have three bonus kids. Together, we have seven boys! Our life together is amazing but far from perfect. We have our challenges, our struggles, but we know that together we can handle it and come through it on the other side.

A big part of our life, obviously, is our children, and my husband and I are very involved with all our boys and their activities have kept us busy with football games, band concerts, fundraisers, proms, and graduations.

It was a big deal to me when my husband helped me move my son Damian into his college dorm and Alden was a big a part of this experience. My husband planned the whole trip, flights, car rental, hotel, the shopping logistics. We had an incredible time and he wiped my tears as we left my son in Southern California, the first one of my boys to move far away.

But that spring we had a terrible scare. I got a call one night from my son that he was in the ER after having a stroke. He was nineteen. How did that happen? What is going on? We flew down to San Diego the very next morning to be with my son, and for six days the doctors were testing him to find out where the blood clot came from, but there were no indications of what really happened. My son recovered quickly and went back to school, and gratefully he stayed with a good friend and his friend's parents. That was the only way I let him go back to school because I knew that this wonderful family would be looking out for him and would keep me informed if his health declined. After that stroke, my son and I would talk every day on the phone to make sure he felt okay.

Our life, however, would be turned upside down. On April 29, 2016, my husband and I were getting ready to have friends over for a dinner party when I got a phone call from the campus police, who told me to call the ER. The officer couldn't tell me what happened but urged me to immediately call the ER and I would know more. The attending doctor told me my son had arrived via ambulance, he was in a coma and they were prepping him for surgery. I will never forget him telling me, "Anyone important to your son needs to come now." I went numb, I was dumbfounded, I couldn't comprehend what he was saying to me and all I could tell him was, "We live in San Francisco but we're going to get on a plane and get there now."

Sonia: What was happening with your emotions at that time?

Jessie: Anytime anything happens to my kids, I immediately go into warrior mom mode, doing what has to get done. My husband was on the computer booking my ticket. I got off the phone and said, "Oh my God, Damian is in the ER. I need to get there NOW!" My husband said to me, "I have your ticket, go pack a bag." He wanted to drive me to the airport, but I needed to drive myself. We had guests arriving for our dinner party and our other children at home to look after. So I get in the car, my heart is pounding, my mind is racing and who do I call? My dad.

Sonia: Wow, what was going on in your mind at that moment that made you want to go to your dad?

Jessie: As many difficult times as I've had with my dad, there have been many other times when he's given me great advice. He is a smart man and in my adult years he has given me great advice and he is very proud of me and my accomplishments. When I called my dad, I just lost it, I felt out of sorts and I was crying uncontrollably. I said, "Dad, I need you to talk to me. I don't know what is going to happen with my son." I was shaking and crying and all he said is "Mija, put it in God's hands and everything is going to be fine. Have faith that our Lord Jesus will keep Damian alive and that's all you can do." He told me to relax, get to the airport safe, get on my flight, and call him when I got there. He told me to put it in God's hands but I'm not a religious person, I'm more a spiritual person, but at that moment I prayed hard for my son.

I arrived at Palomar Medical Center just as my son came out of surgery, and as I was headed to his room the neurosurgeon stopped me and very pragmatically said, "Your son had a stroke. He may not live. If he survives these first two weeks, he will be completely disabled for the rest of his life." I don't remember what else he said, and I looked at him and said, "I need to see my son NOW!"

Nothing can prepare you for this moment. When I opened the door, he had bandages on his head, tubes everywhere, and machines beeping. He was on a breathing machine and it was so scary to see him like this. I put my hand on him and said, "Mommy's here." And I physically saw him relax. I promised my son, "I'm not going to leave your side until I can bring you home."

He was at this hospital for five weeks, and I didn't move. My mom came, my sister came, my brothers came. My husband was flying back and forth, working and taking care of our family while I was with my son. There was a lot going on and the uncertainty of his fate was killing me. My son was fighting for his life and two weeks later he was breathing on his own, slowly showing signs of improvement. Five weeks later, we were able to fly him via air ambulance to northern California.

This whole situation was surreal. I was in total shock and disbelief that my beautiful, healthy, thriving college boy living the dream in southern California almost died and the road to recovery seemed dismal. We had no idea what was going to happen, this was crazy, but I knew that our lives were forever changed and we would never be the same. In between driving to and from hospitals, working and trying to keep our other kids in the loop, I realized that the life my husband and I talked about, our dreams, our future, was not to be our reality, and so I thought I was doing the right thing by giving him an out. I wanted him to know that I didn't expect him to deal with it, and I didn't expect anything from him. This was not part of the plan when we married, this is not what he signed up for, because our life is completely changing. He looked at me and said, "Are you kidding? This is what marriage is. Don't you know? When things get hard, we don't walk away. This is exactly what I signed up for. I would never leave you or our family."

That right there is a family man, with integrity, with heart, with compassion. A man who appreciates his family and who understands the meaning of life. This chapter of our life has brought our family closer together. It has resolved my relationship with mom, repaired my relationship with my sister, and my brother's relationship with our family.

Our family landscape looks so different and with it, we have received so many blessings. After four months in different hospitals and rehab, we made the decision to bring my son home. He lives at home with us and requires twenty-four-hour care. He can't walk, he can't talk, he can't eat on his own. But he is here with us every day. We're Latinos. We bring our loved ones home. Every day, we have another opportunity to kiss him, to laugh with him, to joke with him, and to take care of him. We do it as a team between me, my husband and our kids. My mom comes to our home four days a week, and she helps me a ton.

Life goes on, it just goes on differently. Four months after my son's brain injury, I lost my job. I worked for the same insurance agency for fifteen years, and I had to make the decision to sever our work relationship and take care of my son. I was unemployed, trying to figure out how to take care of my son, how to pay bills, take care of my family, and my husband said, "I got you. We got this. Don't even worry about it. Do what you need to do. And if you don't want to go back to work, you don't have to." It was what I needed to hear, and it really made this ordeal easier to deal with, having his loving support.

After I stopped working, it took about six weeks to get my bearings, accept our situation and learn how to take care of my son, but my days were mostly keeping watch, making sure he was comfortable and giving him encouragement to fight his way back to health. With so much on my plate and the stress of my son's disabilities, I found myself itching to work even just a little. I had too much idle time and I wanted to stay busy.

As soon as I updated my LinkedIn, I got a phone call almost immediately, and within five days I had a contract to work for another company. It was ideal, I set my own hours, and I worked from home.

We were able to video and teleconference, and I was content. I felt like I was normalizing. My son's health was trending in the right direction, albeit the recovery is very slow and hard to really see improvement day to day. We had a new rhythm and we were moving along with our new life.

A few months into my new job, I got a phone call from a Farmers Insurance district manager and he said he'd like to talk with me, so we set up a meeting. When I shared the news with my husband, he asked why I was taking the meeting, and questioned my satisfaction with my new job. He reminded me that I already had my go-around with this company. I told him that when I was nineteen, my dad gave me this piece of advice, advice that has always proved to work in my favor: "Take the meeting, always take the meeting." The first time my dad told me this, I took a meeting that greatly improved my employment opportunity, at the young age of nineteen. So now I take every meeting. You never know what opportunities will be presented.

The District Manager had an opportunity to present! He told me that there was an insurance agency in Orinda, California, and he wanted me to take it over. The retiring agent and agency had a solid reputation and Farmers wanted to try a new program bringing in someone from the outside to take over the operation without disruption. The District Manager, his team, my husband, my family, and so many others were so excited for this amazing opportunity. We got a caregiver and put our home situation in order, and my husband said, "Whatever you need. I'm here for you." I took over the business, a great office, wonderful location, fully furnished and my personnel in place. I had reached the pinnacle of my career!

Thirty days into this new endeavor, everything fell apart. My employees quit and I was by myself. In a deep panic as I drove to my district manager's office, I called my dad and told him what happened. He said, "You got this. You've been here before. You go in there and do what you do best." Holding back my tears, I said, "Okay. If you say so." I put my big girl pants on, and I went back to my office to regroup and strategize. One of my sons came in to help me answer phones and complete the administrative tasks. A couple of weeks later, I hired an amazing team member. In a matter of six months, we completely turned the business around. We are on a mission to succeed and we work hard every day to make that happen. I always had this vision of a successful life, and even though it didn't come to fruition as I had envisioned, even though the landscape changed during the process, and at times the journey has been challenging, I'm still living the dream and new visions of my life are becoming my reality.

I'm very forward-thinking and my business is growing. I just made my one-year anniversary, we moved to a bigger office, hired new teammates, and we are growing and learning. My son Damian is at home thriving and we hope that one day soon he returns to complete health, for him to walk and talk and go back to living his life independently. That is our dream for him. He inspires me every day to give my best, do the most, and to try harder, because in spite of the deficits he has been left with, he smiles and laughs and continues to give us joy.

Sonia: Yes, absolutely, vulnerability leads to strength.

Jessie: As hard as the obstacles have been, as many tears as I've cried, and as many years as I spent fighting my way through the darkness and into the light, they were all building blocks. This is why I tell my kids that life experiences are building your character and paving the way to where you're going. Life is not a straight line and if it is, you haven't taken enough risks and chances. I've taken lots of risks and lots of chances and as many times as I failed at relationships, I'm so happy that I risked it one last time and met the love of my life. And together we have created a wonderful life for each other and our family.

Sonia: I just love that—so beautiful. When you were growing up, it seems you were looking for your dad's validation. But instead, he gave you harshness that cut into your soul and caused a negative belief about yourself. And now it's turned into something beautiful. There was a transformation in him that caused him to change.

Jessie: My dad has experienced tremendous loss, the loss of his parents and the loss of a son. Those losses have caused him a great amount of pain and I know that even though it might be difficult for him to acknowledge the pain and what that has done to him, he now realizes that he has to live in the present and that he has to love us and appreciate us now. He has softened a bit over the years, as I guess that comes with old age. My fondest moment with my dad and when I felt he changed a lot toward me is the day that I came over to see him after I had taken a new job. I knelt down next to where he was sitting and I remember feeling so humbled because I had never graduated from college, I dropped out, I was a single mom with four kids. I didn't look successful on paper, but I had grit and a strong work ethic. I had a drive, a vision, and my dreams, and it didn't matter how often I got sidetracked or my dreams got squashed. I shared with him my ambition for my new job, the goals I set, and the timeframe I allowed myself. I was able to achieve my goals in half the time. In that moment, he told me he was so very proud of me and the milestones I was making. And since then, every time we talk, he says he's proud of me.

And I know my mom is super proud of me too. It is curious, coming full circle. In telling my story, in remembering how I did not want the life my mom chose for herself and us, I wanted to be so different, I did not realize until now that my mother was a warrior herself. She powered through a terrible marriage and raised us kids on her own because my dad was not an effective parent. She did it because she felt it was the right thing to do for her children. The blame, the resentment, it never had a place in my heart and in my mind, and now I see where I got my strength, my grit, my courage.

I am so grateful for the relationship I now have with my parents. The painful memories have faded and now we are enjoying the love and relationship we have.

Sonia: What would you say to those women who had a bad father experience and they're still stuck because their father didn't transform as yours did. How do they start bringing positive affirmations to themselves? Those women who are aspiring to be successful but still have a little girl crying on the inside? Those women who have not yet had a positive affirmation from their fathers? How do they move forward and succeed in life?

Jessie: It's important to realize that it's not about the external validation. It wasn't my dad's validation that changed me, it was my own validation. My realization that I needed to look inside myself and accept myself and believe in myself. I needed to love myself, and I needed to do it for me. My validation was not about finding a husband or getting my dad to accept me and hearing his words of praise. Sometimes it is easier to place blame somewhere else, make excuses and allow yourself to wallow in your sorrow, because doing the hard work, being introspective and taking an honest inventory of your heart and soul, that's painful. It's difficult to own it and even harder to move on.

I needed to do the work on myself first, and say, "Who am I? What am I? What do I believe in? What do I need for me?" How can we give our kids advice when we don't even believe in ourselves? And I realized that loving myself had nothing to do with what size pants I wear, or what designer bag I could afford. It had more to do with how I feel when I wake up in the morning. Am I grateful for life? Am I grateful for my abilities? It has a lot to do with believing that we have so much more power in deciding what our life is going to be.

It's easier to blame things on external forces, but the reality is it starts by believing in yourself. Believing that you have every right to ask for and work for what you want. I compromised in life because I felt I should just be grateful for what I had: grateful that a man loved me, grateful to have a job. We don't need to compromise. We can choose to love ourselves every day and use our power from within. I decided I was good enough, smart, capable, and ambitious, and it was a fundamental moment of changing my mindset when one day my dad said, "You don't need me to tell you these things, you already know."

When we get to the point of loving ourselves, we don't need someone else to tell us anything, because we already know.

Sonia: Right, and it's a fulfilled feeling. It's not a prideful knowing; it's not ego. It that you know your worth and now you can embrace life.

Jessie: My brother told me one time that the light within me glows. I think there is a light within our hearts. Sometimes we keep it covered if we are afraid, but if we peel back the layers and do the work to love ourselves for who we are, the light glows brighter and brighter, and soon enough people will see it on the outside. So ask yourself, "Who do you want to be?" And then believe in yourself and your power to change your life and become the best version of yourself.

Sonia: That's incredible. I love what you said about how the power is within us, and it doesn't come from outside validation. Of course, we may have difficult circumstances, but they don't define us. We can learn from them and know that it takes courage to change them. But we have the power, and everything we desire is within us.

Jessie: It's easy to blame our circumstances on other things or people, losing a job, your spouse abandoning you, being in an abusive relationship, lacking enough money to pay bills, or whatever the trying and difficult situation may be. But if you realize that you are smart enough, you are brave enough, and taking a leap of faith, going back to school, not accepting the abuse in a relationship, walking away from bad situations, and giving yourself the power to make changes and move on. There were many years in my life when I was afraid to leave my job because I believed I had to make a certain amount of money to support my children or I wouldn't be able to provide and survive. And I was forced to take a leap, it was scary, and I was unsure, but I believed in myself and it worked out. The bills got paid, and our lifestyle changed a lot, but we had what was most important.

I hope that every woman who finds herself in a place of not having self-love and zero self-confidence takes a deeper look at who she really is, deep down inside, where she's never given herself the chance to even venture, and that she finds and appreciates her gifts and becomes who she wants to be and have the life that she wants to live.

Sonia: And look in the mirror, and figure out what she loves, what her dreams are, what her strengths are, and who she wants to become.

Jessie: It doesn't happen overnight. My inside joke is that I am like about a bottle of fine red wine. You have to age it to appreciate it. For me, forty was my year, and I continue to work on myself to become a better wife, mother, daughter, friend, business owner, and mentor.

When I was growing up, I wanted to be so different from my mom. And now I can see our lives have so many parallels; we've battled husbands and been in the trenches of war with our families. We've both suffered the loss of a child. It took me all these years to realize that she made her choices because she was alone, she didn't have her parents or siblings here, and I'm so grateful that I do. I just have a deeper appreciation for the woman she is. Now I could only hope to be as good of a mother as she is, and that my children would love me as much as I love her.

Sonia: You realize now that your mom was a woman of strength, but you had to have your children and a tragedy to appreciate your mother.

Jessie: I have realized that I come from a lineage of women of strength. My grandmother shares similar life events and parallels with my mother and me. It is incredible to realize that.

Sonia: I love the quote, "Hurt people hurt people, but healed people heal people." Thank you so much for your story. It is empowering and encouraging, and very deep. The one word I would use for you is "grit." You are a woman of grit. You are a superwoman. Your story will impact thousands of women.

Jessie: The quote speaks truth: healed people heal people. I hope that my story will help heal women that struggle to love themselves and I hope that my story gives strength and courage to become who they are meant to be. There's nothing more beautiful than a woman who loves herself and graces the world with her gifts. Thank you so much.

ABOUT JESSIE BANUELOS

Live every day in gratitude, live every day with purpose, give it all you've got and when the cards are stacked against you, dig deep and realize that the answer is within you and you will overcome. "You got this!" I am a mother to 4 wonderful young men, bonus mom to 3 more. I am the daughter of a strong immigrant mother that has been my rock, my strength and my role model. Wife to an amazingly loving man that has supported my endeavors to be who I am and who I want to be. I am a business owner with a vision to grow my organization to the number one Farmers Insurance Agency in the nation. I am a woman that believes that through the ups and downs of my life, I am wiser, stronger and the best version of myself today because of it. I am humbled to be recognized by Sonia Hassey as a woman with a story to share and hope to inspire other women to realize the woman within has the power to be who she wants to be.

Jessie Banuelos Insurance Agency, 324 Village Square, Orinda, CA 94563

www.famersagent.com/jbanuelos

Facebook: https://www.facebook.com/JessiesBanuelosInsuranceAgency/

Linked In: https://www.linkedin.com/in/jessie-banuelos-cic-107a097/

Instagram: jessiebanuelosinsurance

CHAPTER 4

Do It or Die!

Rosemary Viramontes

My chapter is dedicated to my two beautiful children, Gabriel and Alexandra, my two inspirations that gave me the motivation and the determination to find my spark within and to never give up!

Have you ever asked yourself – why me oh Lord?

How did I get here?

A life shackled by my own accord

How did I, could I put myself in a place of despair?

Inside of this nightmare

Is this how it is?

Is this my life?

How do I get out and steer?

Out of this misery and fear?

Will, I ever see the light?

Will my life could my life ever be bright?

~Rosemary Viramontes~

Sonia: Hello, I am here with Rosemary Viramontes. She has a powerful story to share. Rosemary, tell us about you.

Rosemary: Let me start by telling you about my upbringing so that you may get a sense of who I am at the core. My parents are of Mexican descent, and I was born in California, raised in Richmond and San Pablo, twenty miles northeast of San Francisco. My father was a first-generation Mexican American who came to the US when he was three years old. My father, Augie, barely finished sixth grade, and he had to go to work like all his brothers in order to help support their mom and the rest of the family. My mother, Mary, became an orphan when she was eight years old, and up to that point had grown up in a very small town called Magdalena in New Mexico. She became a Catholic nun at a very young age and was also a Catholic nun school teacher in Panama for fourteen years. After many years as a nun, she decided to leave the convent and return back to her hometown; she felt a strong desire to fall in love, get married, and have children.

Augie and Mary lived a few states apart and met through the "Lonely Hearts Club," a matchmaking letter-writing service for singles. After a short courtship, Augie proposed to Mary over the phone and they both met each other for the first time when he took the train to New Mexico to pick her up and bring her to California to marry her; they were both thirty-four years old. Mary and Augie were very strong in their religious beliefs (mom a Catholic and dad a Baptist). They raised my brother David and me with spirituality that was based on both religions, and most of all they instilled faith, courage, kindness, and strength in us.

As a child, I was very shy and timid. I never spoke up in class because I was just unsure of myself to the outer world—inside, though, I was very sure of myself—confident with a wild and vivid imagination. I was a bit mischievous, for example, at five years old, I had this bright idea to try to drive a car, me at the steering wheel and my friend Laura pressing the gas and the brake pedals using her hands and feet below me. The car rolled out from the driveway unto the street. I'm not quite sure how that happened, but luckily, we got caught and we were not hurt. I was also a bit of a tomboy, and I could be found playing in the creek collecting tadpoles and fishing with my dad, yet I was also my mom's little princess, dressing up in cute dresses and playing with my dolls; I had the best of both worlds. I grew up very naïve in large part due to my mom being sheltered as a nun for nineteen years; she did not have a lot of life experience, she was very innocent herself and still a virgin at the age of thirty-four when she married my dad. She spoiled my brother and me, not with material things, but with a lot of love, affection, and attention. We were her greatest accomplishments, she once told me. Our parents sheltered us tremendously and they were both very kind individuals. Growing up, I really thought that the world was a beautiful safe place, and that everything was supposed to be perfect and loving, and that harm, evilness, hurt, and pain were nonexistent.

Sonia: Perhaps your parents just wanted to protect you from all the bad things in life and instead they only chose to focus on the positive. How did that affect you as you grew up?

Rosemary: Both my parents had experienced many tragedies in their lives, as I had later discovered as an adult. And yet somehow, their empathy, compassion, and kindness were so strong that it became strong within me. It was difficult for me to see anyone hurt, physically or emotionally. For example, whenever I saw a classmate being picked on or bullied, my heart would go out to them and I would befriend them and try to make them feel better. I felt the need to protect others and the need to always be the peacemaker in any given situation. By the time I hit seventh grade, I had to learn to become tough, and develop a resilient rough edge in order to adapt to those teenage years and to my environment. I realized that life was different than what I had believed and what my parents had taught me.

Growing up and being a teenager in my community at the time was challenging; there were racial tensions and I remember carrying a knife to school in case I had to protect and defend myself. Drugs and alcohol were plentiful, and there were just so many distractions that made it difficult for me to focus on my education. I focused instead on the strong friendship bonds that developed; my friends were a lot like me in many ways. As that saying goes, "birds of a feather flock together." Having a good time with my friends was a great distraction from all the chaos and woes in high school. Cutting school, partying, and showing up to class drunk or high was the norm for me; I was even suspended a few times. During my senior year, the school counselor told me that I was not going to graduate—when I heard that news all I could think of was how disappointed my parents were going to be and how disappointed I was in myself—that I would not be walking across the stage with my friends at graduation. I remember praying about it and a few weeks later that same counselor called me into his office and said, "I have good news for you, that summer class you took at Contra Costa College gave you the two credits that you needed to graduate." Hallelujah! I thought within myself, and thank you, God!

Sonia: Were you confused because you came from a sheltered life and all of a sudden as a teenager, you saw what was really out there and experienced culture shock?

Rosemary: I felt completely tormented and confused during my teenage years, I wanted desperately for the world to be free of all the negative things, and I wanted to be a good kid who made my parents happy and proud. I was so conflicted that I even ran away from home one time because I felt so ashamed, ashamed to face my parents. My parents sheltered and protected us maybe a little too much, and didn't teach us about the bad things that can happen in life, and that there are some really bad people out in the world. I had no idea about reality and was so trusting and gullible; I had to learn about reality the hard way.

At the age of nineteen years old, I fell in love and thought I had found my handsome prince and that we would live happily ever after. I became pregnant, and we were excited and talked about our upcoming marriage. Since he was in the military at the time, we were planning on getting married during his leave. The simple wedding that we planned never happened; he was a no show. My son Gabriel was born with my mom by my side. Gabriel's dad was nowhere to be found. I was completely devastated and heartbroken, but I refused to lay with those feelings—I knew that I had to be strong inside and I knew my life would be an upward battle in order to make a good life for my son and me.

I had no idea how to be a mom, like most of us don't for the first time. I still lived at home with my parents. I remember my son would cry and I would cry with him. I didn't know how to comfort him. I remember my dad telling me when my son was one year old, "Mija (my dad always called me mija which means daughter in Spanish), you have to talk to him." And I said, "But why? He doesn't talk back."

Sonia: That's the naivety of it.

Rosemary: Exactly. I was a child raising a child, and I had no clue. I was now twenty years old, and I was even younger emotionally. I was like a little kid. I didn't know how to do a lot of things because my parents did them for us. I thought to myself that I needed a father for my son, and that I really needed to grow up. At home, my mom was still making my bed, doing my laundry, and my dad would be feeding and changing Gabriel's diapers. I just felt so helpless and needy and thought to myself, the answer is for me to start dating and hopefully meet a man I can marry and a man who will love my son.

And so, my quest began and just like that—I met a man through my brother, and thought that he must be a good guy because my brother was hanging out with him. I remember our first date was to Great America, an amusement park, which was my choice. I wanted to ride the roller coasters! Our relationship got serious and I got pregnant again; I thought it was going to be great. "I'm going to have a father for my son, and this man treats me like a queen, and he wants to marry me." I knew I had to get married because I didn't want to shame my parents once again. It was very shameful for them at that time. They wanted to hide, and they felt embarrassed that their daughter had gotten pregnant the first time without being married, and now here she goes again.

We got married and moved into a tiny apartment behind a bar; the only thing separating my kitchen and the bar was a thin wooden door with a flimsy lock. My husband's aunt owned the entire property and lived two doors down from us in the same small apartment complex. The day after we got married, my husband comes home from work and I had made hot dogs for dinner because that's all I really knew how to cook. I told my husband that I cooked dinner and I remember that I felt so proud of myself. He goes into the kitchen and he said, "Hot dogs? Really? I am a meat and potatoes man." And he slapped me.

So, what did I do? I tried to fight back with all my might, me a petit pregnant young woman. I socked him with my fist and scratched him on his face as hard as I could, and as his bright red blood dripped from his cheeks, he then started to beat me, hitting me as hard as he could, socking me in my face, my head, and my body, and all I could think of was, "Here's my son, my little baby son, he's sitting on the high chair. I have to protect him. I need to get out of the kitchen because I don't want my son to get hit." I went into the other room, trying to get away from this madman, and he threw me on the floor and started kicking me. I laid face down on my stomach with my arms curled and tucked against my sides near my belly trying to now protect my unborn child. As he continued to kick me, I laid still in silence hoping he would think I was unconscious and stop. I also could not believe this was happening to me, "Can this be real?"

Sonia: You couldn't believe it. You were dumbfounded.

Rosemary: I was in shock! I thought, "Am I in a nightmare? I have to get up. As soon as I'm able to, I need to get up, grab my son, and we need to run." As I was thinking those things, he told me, "If you think you're going to run out of here, I will kill you and your son." I was blown away, like how could this be? He was so nice to me before. He treated me like a queen. He would bring me gifts all the time, and tell me he's so happy that he's going to be a father to my son and that we are going to have a baby. I thought, "Who is this person?"

This went on almost every day. And it just was not me that was terrified, my son Gabriel was also frightened and was subjected to the violence, as I later found out that the bruises on his cheeks were caused by my husband, not from Gabriel falling down. We felt like prisoners, we didn't have a phone, and I was not allowed to leave the apartment unless I was with my husband. He made it clear to me that his aunt would inform him If I left the apartment while he was at work. It got to the point where he would tell me, "If you tell anyone what I've done to you, I won't just kill you, I will kill your parents and your friend Linda" (she lived a few blocks from us), and I believed him. All the time in my mind and throughout every day I thought about escaping and had made a few attempts to do so, and each time he would always find out. I even thought that maybe if I took my own life, I would be free, but I knew I could not do that because I had a baby inside of me, and I had my son to take care of, they are what kept me going and kept me strong. Then I thought that maybe I should kill him, but I knew I didn't have it in me. There were times when he was asleep when I thought that I would take my son and run. And those times it's almost as though he slept with one eye open; he would wake up and he would take the gun out from under his pillow and point it at me, and say, "Don't even think about it." I lived in fear, so much fear.

One day my mom came over to visit while my husband was at work and I was experiencing false labor pains at seven months, and she immediately took me to my doctor; I was stressed out and very weak from not eating. When we got to the doctor's office, he told my mom, "Rosemary needs somebody to take care of her, it appears that she is not eating and not gaining weight, she is very anemic, she needs bed rest for the remainder of her pregnancy, otherwise she is going to end up in the hospital."

When my husband came home from work, my mother waited there with me and I told him my doctor wants me to stay with my parents; my mom will be taking care of me all day and I have to be bedridden or else I will end up in the hospital and lose the baby.

Sonia: What was his response?

Rosemary: He actually was okay with me going to stay with my parents and I was so relieved to know that my son and I were going to be safe away from him, and that's how we got out from under him for the time being.

One month later, my daughter, Alexandra, was born, and I continued to stay with my parents. My husband would come and visit, and he wanted me to come home with him, and I said it was the doctor's orders for me to continue to stay with my parents because I was so very weak and needed help with Alexandra and Gabriel. He seemed to have mixed feelings about it and a few times he would become angry with me and was very careful not to hit me while he was in my parent's home. He would leave feeling very frustrated.

One spring evening in April, just a few weeks after my daughter was born, my mom and I were running errands, and I saw my husband on 23rd Street in Richmond with a girl and a few other people. I thought to myself, "What's going on here?" My mom did not see or notice anything, and I did not mention that I saw my husband. When we got home, I told her I needed to borrow her car so that I could get some alone time for a few hours. I left to go confront him and wanted to warn the young girl he was with. I asked her if she was seeing him, and she said, "Yeah, he's my boyfriend." I said, "Well, you know, he's crazy." She walked with me toward the car I was driving, and I said, "I'm going to take you home." When he saw this, he pulled out a knife and came after the both of us as we were getting into the car; we locked the doors and as we were driving off, he jumped on the hood of the car, staring at me and waving the knife making slashing movements in one hand and the other hand holding on to the car while I am driving down 23rd Street. I told the young frightened girl, "Listen to me, don't be scared, nothing is going to happen to you, we are going to stop at the next public place or store, and we are going to get help. We're going to call the police."

Sonia: So, she's seeing all of this, and she's realizing that the truth was told.

Rosemary: We were both terrified and when I found out she was only sixteen years old, I felt compelled to protect her. As we approached a red stop light, I went through it hoping the police would also notice a crazy person on top of the hood of the car and pull me over, but that didn't happen. I told the young frightened girl that we were stopping at the store on the corner. I said, "Okay, as soon as I pull over, I am going to get out and move toward the back of the car while he gets off the hood of the car and I'll come around and get you. Get ready to open your door while I come out to grab you, and we will run into the store." As I stepped out of the car, he was faster than I and he grabbed me by the hair and proceeded to beat the crap out of me behind the liquor store.

The beatings that he inflicted on me as time went on were usually not on my face anymore, instead, he was strategic with his blows so that my bruises would not be apparent for others to see. They were usually to my head and all over my body. The police were called on that terrible evening from the liquor store (I found out a few months later), however, we were already gone from the scene.

I was now in the car with him as he was driving and he said, "I've had enough of you. It's time for you to go. You've created too many problems for me." He took me down to the railroad tracks in Richmond and told me, "Get out of the car." He was holding the knife in one hand and then he pulled out a gun from his pants. He said, "Get on your knees. This is it for you. Say your last prayers." I was on my knees with a gun to my head and a knife at my throat. I could see a house about a block away, and I thought that if I could just get up and run, I'd go to that house and tell them I needed help. But I knew he could run faster than me. I had to figure out a way out of this.

My life began to flash before my eyes. I thought about when I was a child, then growing up, being such a mess-up in high school, and disappointed on how my life was playing out. "How did I get to this point? Who am I?" I started asking myself these questions while I was down on my knees, thinking "I hadn't done anything. I hadn't accomplished anything. I was nothing. I was a nobody. Who was going to remember me? My kids were going to grow up without a mom, a mom who had done nothing with her life." I had all of these thoughts and I was praying inside my mind, feeling it inside my heart and soul, "God, please help me get out of this. I want a better life. I want a better life for myself and my children. I want my parents to be proud of me." And the answer came to me as this madman was telling me he was going to kill me and cut me into pieces and scatter my body parts so that I would be unrecognizable. He then said, "If I get caught, I will just plead insanity, but the clever thing is—I'm not really crazy" and I thought to myself, "He really is crazy. He is sick!"

And that is when I started to tell him that I was still in love with him, that we could make this work, that I would help him do whatever he wants to do, that I would be there for him. I asked if he wanted his baby daughter to grow up without a mom. I said, "She's going to know something. She's going to see you as a bad person." I said, "You need help and I'm going to help you. I'm going to do whatever it takes, and we're going to get you some help. This is not the right way, because if you kill me, you're going to eventually get caught and you're going to end up in prison, and your daughter will grow up without a mother and without a father. How could you do that to your child, an innocent, little baby? Do you want her to have that kind of life? Do you want her memory of you as a no-good evil person?"

And as I was telling him these things on my knees, he started to pull back on his weapons. I was keenly watching his body language, his demeanor. I slowly started to get up and I was still talking to him. And my words became relentless, I said, "You're taking a huge risk. I love you. I'm going to help you. It's gonna work. We can make this work." I told him that what he was doing right now could be forgiven and forgotten. I said, "We need to focus on trying to be parents to our innocent baby daughter. Imagine us holding Alexandra's little hands together as she begins to learn how to walk, imagine seeing that and experiencing that together." It started to sink in. I could see it sinking in slowly; I could almost see the harshness in his eyes turn to gentleness before my own eyes.

Sonia: What were you thinking as that was happening? You started seeing relief, but what were you feeling inside?

Rosemary: Complete fear, the worst kind of terror inside of me displayed outwardly through my body as it was shaking profusely and yet somehow, I knew I had to try to not show fear and instead show calmness and strength. I could hear in my mind, "Do not be afraid for I am with you," and "Just as dogs sense fear, do not show it." I needed to get away from him, but I thought that at that very moment the goal was for us to get back into the car. I began to see and sense his calmness and I knew that he was not going to kill me that day. As we got into the car, I kept talking to him and continued with the only weapons I had: my words and my faith. At those moments, the air between us stood still; I felt that I was guided by God and safely brought back to my parents' home. As we drove up to the driveway and parked the car, he said he would leave me alone and he walked off and I went into the house. I couldn't even tell my parents (he was always telling me he would hurt them if I ever told them about him hitting me), I felt I had to protect them. I couldn't tell anybody what happened for fear of putting anyone in harm's way. I hugged my babies tightly, cried softly in my bedroom while my babies slept.

Sonia: You believed what he said about your parents?

Rosemary: Yes, I believed him because I experienced first-hand what he was capable of. I kept that horrific terrifying event to myself as I feared that if I went to the police or told anyone, he would kill my parents as he so threatened to do many times. Some weeks later, I had borrowed my mom's car to go do errands while my parents watched my son Gabriel at home, and I had my baby daughter, Alexandra, with me. I was beginning to feel some normalcy in my life as I had not seen that mentally unstable person that had tried to kill me. It appeared that he was finally leaving me alone.

As I was driving to go home, this car abruptly pulled in front of me that forced me to slam on my brakes, and from the driver's side I saw him walk toward me, that madman of a husband—who was now pointing a gun at my face through the closed window. He told me to open the window. I did so, and he began to spit on me and told me to get out of the car with my baby. He continued to spit on both of us. He took us by force into the car he was driving, and I could see that he was not alone; he had a friend with him, sitting in the passenger seat. We drove over to my husband's sister's house and he dropped my baby off with his sister. He told his friend to drive while he sat in the back seat with me. I said, "Where are we going?" He said, "Shut up, just keep your mouth shut, no wait, open your mouth now, I have all these pills that I want you to swallow." While he was trying to force them in my mouth, his friend said, "Come on man, leave her alone." My husband said to his friend, "Drive over to the Richmond pier." When we arrived, we all got out of the car and my husband said to me, "I thought about this and you're still a problem to me. I'm just going to throw you over the pier. I know you don't know how to swim. It's gonna look like an accident, like we're playing around and you slipped and fell over the pier into that icy cold water. Heck, I might even jump in to pretend to save you, but no, I think not, I don't want to freeze."

Sonia: Was his friend listening?

Rosemary: His friend was standing several feet away from us and he was listening. As I looked his way, he saw the fear in my eyes. That's all it took. His friend came over and told my husband, "Why are you bothering to do this? This is just taking too much time. We have a job to go do. Why don't we do this afterward? We'll do it together. But right now, we have to focus and we have this job to do, so let's just take her back." The kind of job he was referring to was a robbery; as I had found out later, my husband was involved in many robberies, burglaries, and home invasions.

Sonia: Did you know at that moment that his friend was protecting you?

Rosemary: Yes, I knew at that moment he was trying to protect me, so much so that when my husband was trying to throw me over the pier, I pretended to faint, and as my body fell down on the wooden splintered pier, his friend bent down to help me get up and he said to my husband, "We need to take her back to your sister's now and focus on doing the job we need to do." So, they took me back to his sister's, and they left. As soon as they left, I told her what had happened as I was shaking and crying, she then said to me, "I'm going to take you and Alexandra back to your car and you need to tell your parents to get you to a safe place and hide. When my brother gets back, I will try to stall him as long as I can." When I got home, I finally told my parents that my husband wanted to kill me

Sonia: What compelled you to finally tell them?

Rosemary: I told myself that he would never hurt me again, he would never lay his hands on me nor my babies. I would do whatever it takes to get away from him. In addition, the fear that I saw in my sister-in-law and her adamant words to me to tell my parents also pushed me to do so. I wanted to protect my parents, but they made it clear that they would protect themselves and for me not to worry, that they were going to call the police; most importantly, they needed to get me and the children to a safe place. We called my godparents, Mike and Pinkie, and they came and got me and my kids, and I went to live with them in Fairfield. When my husband found out, he called over there to my godfather and said, "I know she's there. I'm letting you know that I'm coming to get her. I'm going to kill anyone who's in my way." In that moment, my godfather took me to his brother Jack's house. My godfather told my husband over the phone that he and his brother would be waiting for him and if he dared come there, they would kill him first. They had already informed the police, and as my husband got to the toll at the Carquinez Bridge on his way to Fairfield, the police caught up with him and pulled him over. They saw that he had a gun, and they arrested him and found out he was wanted for all these other crimes. He went to jail and eventually ended up serving time in San Quentin.

I now felt a sense of relief; I felt safe and secure and most of all my confidence and well-being was sparked up. I started to change my life. I wanted to do something to better my life, and thought about a career as a cosmetologist. As a teenager, the neighborhood girls would come over to my house and I would style their hair and do their makeup. I loved the feeling when they saw themselves in the mirror after I had finished their hair and makeup. I would think, "Oh wow, I did that. I helped them feel good about themselves." Their spark sparked something in me, and I knew that's what I wanted to do. I enrolled in Universal Beauty Academy, and after several months, I received an esthetician license to do facials and makeup. I was a freelance makeup artist and worked for Macy's giving facials, and I loved the work, but it was not enough for me to get off of public assistance and to be able to support my children, or for us to be on our own.

I wanted to build a comfortable, independent life as a single mom with two small kids. A few years later, I made what I had considered a bold move, I decided to enroll at Contra Costa Community College and had to take beginning math and beginning English. At that time, I could barely write a sentence or a paragraph, and multiplication and even simple math problems were a huge challenge for me. My first semester proved to be what my mind craved for, and I became hooked on school. I loved it for the first time. In the past, I had only gone to school to socialize and hang out with my friends. This time, I fell in love with school, I fell in love with learning. Although at the time, I didn't even know what a bachelor's or master's degree was or stood for; and I thought a doctoral degree meant that you were a doctor in a hospital and that was the only type of doctor there was. I had a lot to learn, that is for sure.

Sonia: So, you had a gut feeling, a paradigm shift, that there had to be something more. You knew you were a single mother. What was that nugget that caused you to say, "I'm going to school and this is what I'm going to do"?

Rosemary: It was what you call, "whispers in the wind." For several years, off and on, some acquaintances that I would meet who had professional careers would say college education is the key to success. And as I was working as an esthetician, many of my clients would mention to me about college. They would tell me I was smart and wise and that I should consider going to college. I thought to myself that I had not done well in school and I didn't think I would like it, but maybe I should try it out. Finally, I said to myself, "Okay, I'm going to go. I'll sign up for a few classes." I ended up signing up for four classes because the advisor, Mr. Hernandez, suggested it. I said to him, "Four is too much and I only want to take two classes." He said, "You'll get financial aid if you take four classes." I didn't know there was financial help. After he told me, I said, "Really? Somebody's going to pay me?" I ended up taking four classes, and because I had to take beginning English and math classes, it would be a while before I could take classes toward my major, plus I changed my major along the way and ended up spending four and a half years at Contra Costa College.

Sonia: Did you work while going to school?

Rosemary: Yes, I cleaned houses. Every day after my classes were over, I would go straight to a client's house with very little time to do anything else. By the end of the week, I couldn't even clean my own apartment; I was exhausted. Sometimes I worked more than one job because it was hard to make ends meet. I was always struggling for money, and it was a difficult time. I had a lot of moral support at the community college, and people who would inspire and encourage me and tell me to apply for scholarships. I remember thinking, "Why me? Do I deserve something like that? They must see something in me that I don't." One of my counselors, Mr. Chavez, told me, "I want you to go to Stanford." I said to him, "Stanford is too far and too expensive! You really think I have it in me to go there?" He said, "You can go wherever you want." In that case, I said, "I want to go to UC Berkeley, that is the school of my dreams." It was the only university I applied for, and I remember thinking I knew I would get in; I prayed that I would get in. I was determined to get in; I could feel it. And I did. That day of receiving my acceptance letter was one of the proudest moments of my life.

I was awarded two scholarships to attend UC Berkeley and my major was psychology. That need to help others, help people with their problems, help them feel good about themselves, was very strong inside of me. I am very much an optimist and I wanted to spread that to others. It took a lot of determination and perseverance during those two years at the university. There were times I wanted to give up. I mean, really! I would tell myself, "Never give up, never surrender." As a single mom living on my own, I had to learn to become resourceful and juggle parenting, work, and school. I did have support from my mom who would help watch my kids, and that was a huge help. My brother and a few friends also helped to watch my kids especially when I had to study for finals. Overall, I did it pretty much on my own and it was challenging and so difficult. Most days I would survive on three or four hours of sleep, studying and writing papers while my kids were asleep because that was the only free time I had.

Sonia: I can see that. In those moments when you thought that quitting would be easier than moving forward, what was it that made you say, "No, I'm going to push forward"?

Rosemary: The desire inside of me, my self-determination, my motivation was lit. I had discovered that spark within me, and I learned how to spark it up! That Nike motto, "Just Do It" was in my head. And I came up with my own motto: "Do it or die"—if I don't do it, I will die inside, and I couldn't let that happen. I had to do it for my kids and for myself. There were times when I had flashbacks from that living nightmare that I escaped from, and sometimes I would wake up and feel that gun to my head. I would think to myself, "Do it or die." I could not give in. I would tell myself to never give up, and never surrender to those feelings.

Sonia: Would you say that your big "why" was your kids?

Rosemary: Oh, most definitely. My children were my inspiration, my motivators, my reasons for wanting to do better. I wanted them to have a better life; I wanted to get out of poverty. I wanted to be able to share my blessings because I felt my life had been blessed. I had been given a second chance to make a change, and perhaps not just for myself and my children, but for my whole family, I wanted to be a blessing to others.

Sonia: That is so powerful. It was so courageous of you because when you look at your life, it was almost against all odds. Beginning with your parents sheltering you, and you popping out of that bubble and learning everything on your own, then you hit a hard spot, a do-or-die hard spot, and now you were at UC Berkeley and you were graduating. Tell me about that.

Rosemary: It was such a proud moment from that day of receiving my acceptance letter to my first day of classes at UC Berkeley; I couldn't believe I was there. Like, "Pinch me, is this for real?" At graduation, I remember my whole family was there, including my two small kids, and they all were so proud of me as they looked on, watching and witnessing me walking across the stage. I got a degree from UC Berkeley. Oh my God, wow, was it for real? Or was it a dream? For once, it was a good dream that came true. It was a huge, wonderful accomplishment and also a relief because I had struggled so much over the years in trying to see that light at the end of the tunnel. I told myself, "It's coming, it's coming. I'm going to do this. I'm going to finish. It's taking a long time, but I'm going to get there." I did a lot of self-talk and a lot of praying. And most of all, I had faith and determination.

Sonia: That's incredible. Who would you say were your mentors in this journey?

Rosemary: My parents, but especially my mom. She had gone through so many difficult times in her life, yet she always remained optimistic, happy, strong, and kind. After her mother died, she went to live in an orphanage, and at the age of fourteen, entered into the convent to become a Franciscan nun. She also suffered a lot of heartbreak when our family was in a tragic car accident that left my brother a paraplegic, and when several years later, my dad lost his battle with cancer. My mom had struggled and suffered a lot, yet through it all, she always persevered. She had that special strength and dedicated determination that I admired. I remember at her memorial service, her dear friend Mike said, "Mary has a heart of gold, she is as strong as steel, and yet soft and kind." I thought, "That's what I hope to aspire to. I am my mom's daughter." I can still see her smile and that proud look on her face when she saw me get my bachelor's degree, and her saying, "That's my daughter." My mom was my rock. She was an angel on earth, and now she's an angel in heaven. I was thirty-two years old when I graduated, and I remember feeling pretty old because all the other students were so much younger than me and I felt out of place. But I told myself, "I don't care. I'm me. I made it."

Sonia: What an honor. Your mother became your driving force. What would you say to those women who are feeling that they are pregnant with destiny, with a dream, but it hasn't worked out yet?

Rosemary: It is absolutely never too late. There are always obstacles, there are always excuses that we sometimes tell ourselves. It doesn't matter what you have going on in your life, it doesn't matter how old you are, whether you are eighteen or eighty years old, if you have a dream, do it. As a matter of fact, I have been in my career now for over twenty years. I enjoy my career and have worked and strived hard to get where I am today, but guess what? I still have dreams of doing other things. Life does not stop just because you're older or you are experiencing distress or doubts, or perhaps you are thinking about retiring—look at retiring as a time to now devote to something you have always wanted to do but never had the time to do. You want to still keep striving. You want to still keep doing things. Like that old saying goes or from that old school song, "Keep on Trucking." Keep it moving. Life is just what you make; that's what makes life beautiful; you have a choice, so make it!

Sonia: What would you say to those women about mentorship? How important is mentorship?

Rosemary: I would also say that it is important to have a good support system. It's valuable to have that belief within yourself, but you also need others around you who believe in you and are cheering you on and saying, "You can do this. You've got this." I've had wonderful teachers, counselors, and professors in college who would tell me, "You can do this." Having other people around you to believe in you and inspire you makes your journey much more enriching and powerful.

Sonia: I agree. If I didn't have mentors and coaches in my life, I probably would have quit, because it's hard. Sometimes just one word from somebody will bring a paradigm shift in your life and cause you to go in a new direction.

Rosemary: Definitely! That is so true! My first semester in college was rough; I had previously thought that I was not book smart. But here I had teachers telling me, "You're so smart, you can do anything you want." They were cheering me on and providing moral support. Just like that counselor who wanted me to go to Stanford. I thought he must be talking about somebody else. He saw my potential, and that is just it: every single one of us has potential and I believe it's imperative to have good people around you to influence you. Mentors and coaches make a huge difference. And most importantly, you have to believe in yourself and be open to positive influences in your life.

Sonia: What did you do after college?

Rosemary: I started applying for jobs and landed a job in workforce development. I was then recruited by Mr. Vaca, a manager with the Employment and Training Department for the City of Richmond. We met at a working business event, and he witnessed my work and saw my potential. I have now been with the City of Richmond for the past two decades. I started off as a career counselor, helping people figure out what they wanted to do for a career. I loved helping others figure out their strengths, skills, and interests. I provided them with mentoring and guidance and enjoyed helping them to find their spark and their dream job or career. I worked hard to help make a difference in people's lives and learned all I could to advance my career. Currently, I run most of the employment and training programs that help make a positive economic impact on the Richmond community by providing training and job opportunities to adults and youth. I also create and implement innovative strategies and programs designed to benefit both community residents and the business community. I really enjoy and thrive off of helping to make a positive difference in people's lives.

Sonia: Does your own journey add meaning and purpose to your work?

Rosemary: Yes, I want to do more to help others; I want to share my journey with others to help them to overcome some of the life challenges that may be prohibiting them from following through on their dreams. The journey does not stop, and I'm thinking about my next venture. I want to do more in my life. I want to continue to be a benefit to others on a much broader and global scale. Remember how I had gone to cosmetology school? Now I want to develop my own skincare line. I love learning about taking care of my skin and I want to help educate others on the importance of taking care of the largest organ in our bodies, our skin.

Over the past two years, I have taken weekend courses every several months at UCLA in cosmetic chemistry and science, and learning about ingredients, because I plan on formulating my product to focus on maintaining and creating healthy, vibrant, and youthful skin. I hope to find that "fountain of youth." I am excited about it. I am still in my professional career at the City of Richmond, and cosmetic science is a hobby and something I enjoy learning about. In addition to that, I have a passion for writing, and I am creating a blog focused on providing a welcoming space for women to visit and read helpful and inspiring topics that will promote their spark inside and help guide them in other areas of their life; a dose of encouragement and a spoonful of dessert. You'll have to check it out and visit my blog so you can see for yourself.

Sonia: That's so exciting. It's the next step. And after that, it's another step. We don't have to figure everything out at once, but definitely take action in something that is sparking inside of us. What do you see for yourself five years from now?

Rosemary: Five years from now, I will be retired from the City of Richmond and enjoying the next chapter in my life with a successful product line and a successful blog; I will also be looking at other ways to give back and touch other people's' lives in a positive manner because I know the hardship and I know the desires of wanting a better life. I have encountered struggles and setbacks before; I know that any journey requires determination and perseverance. There will always be roadblocks. You just have to know how to go around them and why you need and want to get past them.

Sonia: What do you want women to walk away with from your story?

Rosemary: I want them to feel inspired, but also to know that everyone is different. Everyone has their own battles that they are dealing with, and I hope my story can help women and men as well who are going through struggles and hard times, to say, "Wow, maybe I can do it too. Maybe I can do something with my life. Maybe this is an opportunity and my chance to do something that I had always dreamed of doing." I encourage everyone to stay determined so nothing and nobody can stop them. Surround yourself with positive people, stay away from the naysayers, believe in yourself. You can do it! Dig deep down inside and find your spark!

Sonia: I love that. We can't succeed without determination. Life is full of setbacks, but determination will drive us to move forward because of our big "why." I love your story of determination and overcoming setbacks. It's incredible because we don't know what it takes until we're in a situation when we're forced to know what it takes. As women, we can come out of any situation, no matter how dark it is. What would you say to an abused woman who is deathly afraid to run away?

Rosemary: Don't let fear cloud your judgment. You can get out of this. They (your abuser) will manipulate you and instill fear in you for a reason: to keep you there. You have to know that there's help. At the time I went through it, there were no organizations out there, but now there are. You have to tell people. That was one of my mistakes. I kept it to myself because I was in fear of other people getting hurt. But understand that's not necessarily the case. You have to share it to get help. You have the power to do so and the more people who know, that helps to build your forces of more power.

Destiny Talks

Sonia: We have to have that courage.

Rosemary: Yes, we have the courage to stand up for ourselves and to believe that there is a light at the end of the tunnel. There is a better life.

My motto: Do it or Die

Die inside if I don't

Light that fire

Get that burning desire

To get up, get out and sparkle on

I can I will I must

Do it or Die

I have it in me

It's there deep within

Waiting… No, you wait!

I make my life, my fate

My spark is lit

Inside of me and inside of you

Power and true grit

Spark it up I say

Starting today!

~Rosemary Viramontes~

Sonia: We have to know our worth. How can we impact anybody else's life if we don't feel worthy ourselves? Thank you so much, Rosemary. Your story is powerful in so many ways, in courage and perseverance. You felt so much lack, but you kept on going, and now you've graduated, and you have a wonderful job and you're still dreaming. I love it. And everything you're doing is to impact people's lives so they also have meaning and purpose. You have a powerful voice, and this is just the beginning for you.

ABOUT ROSEMARY VIRAMONTES

Rosemary Viramontes serves as Project Coordinator and Manager for award-winning workforce development programs at the City of Richmond's Employment and Training Department in California. Her very successful career in city Government has spanned over two decades; during that time, she has developed and implemented several innovative programs that have made a positive impact on both Richmond and area residents and the business community. She holds a bachelor's degree from the University of California, Berkeley and has been recognized as a leader in the workforce development field and in her community. In her spare time, she enjoys traveling, writing and spending time with her loved ones.

CHAPTER 5

Think Global Act Local

Cherise Melton Khaund

Sonia: I am here with Cherise Khaund. Cherise, why don't you tell us your amazing story?

Cherise: My story starts with my dad. He grew up in California in a family that didn't have a lot of money, and he became the first in his family to go to college. He had a few people who believed in him, teachers and mentors who helped him figure out how to be successful. He worked his way through community college and UC Berkeley, and graduated with a degree in engineering. Because of that, our family was able to travel overseas and have incredible experiences and opportunities.

I was born in New Jersey. Halfway through my kindergarten year, my dad got his first job overseas and we moved to Venezuela. At age five, I felt totally bewildered being in a new school where I didn't speak the language. I remember a moment in PE when we were outside on the grassy field, and all of a sudden, I looked to my left and my right and all these kids had started running, and I thought "Okay, I guess I better start running." They touched the fence and then they all turned around and ran back. And I followed along, "Okay, I'm going to touch the fence, and run back." And those were the kinds of things that were happening as a kindergartner. I eventually learned some Spanish, but really struggled to master it and to this day still cannot trill my "r."

I feel deeply for kids in U.S. schools who don't speak English. They could be facing the daily struggle of, "Wow, how do I even figure out what's happening when I don't speak the language?" My personal experience is the root of my passion for education.

We lived on the edge of a community and behind our house as far as you could see there was a desert with cacti. On one side of our house was a cliff. My childhood there was pretty carefree. I would just strap on an orange plastic canteen and say, "Bye, Mom, I'm going to go hike out in the desert." I would pick cactus berries by myself or with friends or with my brother. We'd catch lizards and find snakes in our house that became pets. Things like that.

I got comfortable there and made a best friend, Daniela, who was half Venezuelan. But when I was in the fourth grade, my parents decided to move to Saudi Arabia. I thought, "How can I leave Daniela?" I couldn't imagine living anywhere else.

We moved to a gated community in Saudi Arabia where everyone who worked for the company lived—people from all over the world. It had an on-site, English-speaking school. We learned some Arabic, but I did not have many opportunities to interact with the Saudi people.

In Saudi at that time, women weren't allowed to drive, so we depended on our dads to drive us when we wanted to leave our community. One time, my dad took our Girl Scout troop out to the desert sand dunes and gave us a list of compass points to reach the campsite. He dropped groups of us off in different places with different directions and then drove away. He said, "Use those compass directions to find the campsite. I'll meet you there." I led my group and loved the feeling of knowing survival skills, especially as a girl. For me, that independence was so valuable.

Another time I went camping with my dad, a friend, and her dad. We parked the car in the middle of nowhere off the side of a road and backpacked out a few miles to pitch camp in an oasis area with palm trees. Then we hiked back to the car for more water. We were carrying these heavy jugs of water in our hands, and a truck rolled up and stopped next to us. I heard "Ahlan wa sahlan" as my friend's dad and the truck driver spoke with each other in Arabic. And the next thing I know, we're climbing into the back of the truck with the sheep. We stood up and held the roll bar as the truck bounced over the sand dunes. We arrived at a Bedouin campsite, with camels dotting the edges, large tents, and a falcon sitting on a stoop.

It turned out that the truck driver invited us to his tent because of a rule the Bedouins live by in the Saudi Arabian desert, a hospitality rule: "If you come across any stranger in the desert, you have an obligation to invite them to your tent for three days and three nights."

I remember going back behind the tents and seeing this giant pot with a whole lamb boiling inside. They were preparing a feast. There was even a generator with a tiny little television back there that the kids were watching. We stayed for dinner. We all sat on a big, circular mat on the ground with a huge tray filled with rice and then the whole lamb was brought out and put in the center.

Sonia: A whole lamb with eyes and teeth?

Cherise: Yes, and we were sitting on the ground and leaning on pillows. We ate with our hands, even the rice. You just ball up the rice in your fist and eat it. They picked off the best pieces of lamb and tossed them onto the rice right in front of us. It was so generous of them. We ate and then we drank very strong tea in little tiny glass cups, just like in the book, "Three Cups of Tea." After the meal, they drove us back to our campsite.

When I look back at it now, I realize that the rule of the desert is what community is all about, right? It's a sense of community to depend on each other and to have an obligation to each other.

Here I was, an American who thought the United States was the land of opportunity and equality and freedom. But here I was having this experience half a world away, where no matter what you look like or what language you speak, you're included and taken care of as part of this community. I've tried to take that with me wherever I go.

Sonia: You were welcomed to the community. That's incredible. Where did you go from there?

Cherise: In Saudi Arabia at the time, the international schools only went through ninth grade. So it was normal to go away to school for tenth, eleventh, and twelfth grades. I went to a boarding school in Massachusetts starting in tenth grade. It was an all-girls school which gave me a lot of opportunities to be a leader at an age where oftentimes a lot of girls step back and don't take those opportunities. I flew back to Saudi Arabia three times a year. In the summers in Saudi, there were organized activities for "returning students," probably designed to keep the teenagers busy so we wouldn't get into trouble. That's where I learned to scuba dive and to train other people to scuba dive in the Red Sea.

From there, I went to college in California. Science and math had always been my thing growing up, and my dad was in engineering, so I thought, "Of course I could be an engineer, I'm going to explore that." There were very few women in electrical engineering, and there'd be situations where people would assume that I wasn't smart enough or capable enough to be successful. I proved them wrong, I graduated and earned my engineering degree from Stanford University. Women can do it!

But I think about other girls or minorities who don't feel confident in the subject they want to study. I want all students to feel confident and capable in whatever it is they want to learn.

Sonia: That's beautiful. What gave you that compassion, that drive, to help students?

Cherise: When I was in college, I felt frustrated and angry that people would even think that I wasn't capable of something. And for me, it wasn't nearly as bad as it was for a lot of other people. I still had the opportunity to be in engineering and to be successful. But I struggled with that sense of, "Well, if I don't do well on a test, is it because I'm a girl or is it because I just need to work harder?" Back then, people thought you either had it in your genes, or not. And at least I had the peace of falling back on that because my dad was an engineer, so it was in my genes, right? But not everybody has that. There were so many situations where I could see that if I hadn't had that support along the way, I might have given up.

Sonia: Your story is unique because you were favorited in a lot of ways, yet you looked at ones who were less fortunate. You said, "Wait a minute, what about them?" You were able to experience different cultures and see that not everybody has that opportunity, even here in America.

Cherise: I learned that over time. Living in Saudi Arabia and looking back at the United States, I was thinking, "Well, everything's great in the United States. Women can't drive here, but in the U.S., women can do anything they want to do. And if students study and work hard, they can be successful. That's what the American dream is all about. That's what public education is for. Everyone can get a public education in the United States, and all you have to do is work hard, so they say."

After I graduated with my engineering degree, I was trying to find my passion. I figured out that I wasn't super excited about engineering. I proved that I could do it, but there were people who could study those big computer programming books for hours on weekends, for fun, and that really wasn't me. So I went into the AmeriCorps*VISTA program, which is kind of like Peace Corps. You get placed in different communities to make a difference for that year. I was placed as a community organizer in affordable housing in the Sacramento area.

That's where I had a wake-up call about the inequities that exist in our education system. My job was to walk around the apartment complex and knock on doors, listen to people, hear what they needed in their community and then work with them to make those things happen. I was trained specifically to not come in from the outside to tell people what to do. Instead, I was carefully listening and trying to connect them to each other and to community resources, so they could be leaders of their own destinies—their own neighborhoods—moving forward.

I met a girl who was in the fourth grade and struggling in math. Her older sister asked me if I would help her, so I said yes. I met with her and saw how much she was struggling, and I thought, "I wonder if she has a learning disability because she's way behind, like grade levels behind. She didn't know her multiplication tables and was having trouble with subtraction—basic things. So I went to the parent-teacher conference with her mom. It was at the same school in her neighborhood that her mom had gone to, and her grandparents had gone to.

Her school was nothing like the schools I attended growing up. Was this the American dream? I walked into the classroom and noticed a lack of supplies. I said to the teacher, "I'm a math tutor. What do the kids need to know by the end of fourth grade?" And she couldn't answer the question. She pointed to a set of drawers with some blocks in them, and said, "Well, they gave us this new program. I don't know what to do with it. I have an old math textbook I could give you." And I thought it was a pretty basic question: "What does a fourth-grader need to know?" And she said, "Maybe you could help her out with reading instead." Wait a second. I was trying to help this kid with math.

We went back to the apartments and her mom was very quiet because the whole neighborhood felt like teachers were supposed to do their job, and it wasn't the parents' job to go in and tell the teacher what to do or advocate for their children in some way. I ended up tutoring her on my own. And turns out she was smart, really smart. We went back to second-grade math and started from there, and she picked up on it. She was amazing. She learned stuff so fast. I gave her a set of Brainquest flashcards, and a week later she had learned them all.

Her family said, "Oh my gosh, she memorized everything!" Word got out that she was smart, and she started teaching other kids in her math class. I realized that it wasn't as if the kid wasn't smart before. It was simply the lack of opportunity in that school for that child and for the whole community.

What if that had been my dad? He happened to have good enough schools that he was able to get through and go to college. But these kids were being completely left behind. I remember a high school student in the same community that I knew was smart. He started to get into trouble in the community because he was bored. I asked him, "What classes are you taking?" and he said, "I have PE, PE2, and

ROTC." And I said, "Wait, you're not taking a math class? Why not?" He said, "I don't know. It's just what the counselors gave us."

Again, a situation where a parent doesn't know to go into the school and say, "Why isn't my child taking math class?" The whole community was being left behind.

I had found my passion in community organizing, hearing from people, and bringing them together to lead their own destinies, and I really wanted to focus on education and making the promise of public education real. I never went back to engineering after that.

Sonia: It was a paradigm shift for that fourth-grade girl you tutored, and for you. What happened to her and did you keep in touch?

Cherise: I was the VISTA volunteer for just one year, but I stayed in touch with the community because I ended up working for the nonprofit organization and overseeing community organizers at multiple sites. I worked for that organization for six years and then I got married, moved to Seattle, and lost touch with everyone for years. But a couple of years ago the girl's sister, who was always so resourceful, found me on Facebook. She told me that her younger sister was now a mom with two little kids, that she hadn't earned a college degree but now she wanted to go back to school. She was done struggling with minimum-wage jobs and aspired to work in healthcare. She was taking online courses but had some trouble in economics and finance. Could I give her a call? We caught up over the phone and even held a mini-tutoring session reminiscent of the old days.

I wish she'd had more opportunities, but she made the best of things and had the persistence to eventually go back and succeed. I was glad to be one small part of it, along with her sister and other members of the community. It takes a village. Our public education system needs to provide a base level of quality for all kids. It shouldn't have to depend on whether you get lucky and happen to meet a random person here or there who can help. In our country, we like to think we have a level playing field. "Just study hard, work hard, and you can succeed. And if you don't, it's your own fault." Right? That's what our country says to us.

But in this Democracy, we are the country. So, it's on us to make sure that our communities and our public schools provide an education for all kids. It could so easily have been my family, your family, or anybody's family that gets left behind. And that's not okay.

Sonia: Where did you go from there?

Cherise: After moving to Seattle, I decided, "Education—that's what I want to focus on. I earned my master's degree in nonprofit management and education policy at University of Washington while working for a wonderful grassroots nonprofit called League of Education Voters. This was a way to connect my community organizing experience with my passion for education. We traveled across the state of Washington—organizing school board members, parents, and people who wanted to make sure that public schools are fully funded. It was exciting. We ran a statewide initiative that would have been a one-cent increase in the state sales tax to fund preschool, K–12, and higher ed across Washington. And my master's degree project was writing the formula for how the funds would be distributed to the school districts. Instead of just giving it out in equal amounts per child, we created a weighted formula that would have given more funding to schools that had high numbers of students in poverty, English as a second language, or special education.

Unfortunately, the statewide initiative did not pass. It's hard to raise taxes in general, even if it's one-cent. But that investment would have been incredible for the state. The people who continue to advocate, League of Education Voters, are still there making a difference every day.

Throughout that whole time, people were saying to me, "Why are you driving all over the state trying to improve schools when you don't even have kids? You're not even a parent."

Well, I was motivated not by my own needs but by my sense of community and the serious problems I felt obligated to try to fix. And a few years later our first child was born.

Sonia: You were like, "Alrighty then."

Cherise: Yes, I guess it was time! When my daughter was a year old, my dad was diagnosed with a brain tumor, and all of a sudden, we picked up everything and moved back to California to help my mom take care of my dad. My husband got a job in San Francisco, and then our second child was born the same year that my dad passed away.

From there, I figured out how to get involved with schools again. I was invited to join a group called the Assistance League of Diablo Valley where a group of volunteer women organized a program for kids who were struggling with reading. It was called Buena Vista Auxiliary and was in ten of the local schools. We fundraised to pay for teachers to stay after school for focused reading intervention time: with a ratio of one teacher to two students each. We measured the students' before and after reading scores, and at the end, we'd hold a community celebration at that school. Parents and the community were invited, the students would stand up and read, and then we'd give them a gift bag with school supplies and three books at their new reading level. My kids enjoyed helping. The younger one would count out the pencils: 1, 2, 3. And the older one would pick out the books. "Well, maybe she'd like this book about animals." And so they were right along with me during this whole process.

It was important for me to have my kids involved, too. They may not have been able to go camping in Saudi Arabia, but I wanted them to feel that obligation, that sense of community, even though they also have had many more opportunities than so many other kids.

After the 2016 election, my girls had stayed up late the night before because they wanted to see the first female president get elected, and I said, "Oh don't worry, go to bed." The next morning, they woke up and wow—we were all surprised. And our family went through a bit of a dip, you know, just disappointed by the whole thing. My husband, Sandy, and I thought, "Well, what do we do now?" And we ended up saying, "So many things are beyond our control. But each of us can control what we do in our own local communities. So let's think about what we can do."

Sandy said, "Well, why don't we bring Inventors University to other kids?" Inventors University up until then had been something our kids made up because they liked to read Harry Potter books. They used to put on their Gryffindor robes at home on the weekends and say, "We're going to have our own university like Hogwarts, but call it Inventors University. Dad, can you teach us Python?" It was a beautiful way for them to have special bonding time with their dad. And eventually, I joined in too, teaching a bit of Excel.

Sonia: Oh, I love it.

Cherise: Because my husband and I are both techies, it was based on technology and computer programming. And because my husband Sandy's business was in technology, we had a lot of computers around our house to play with. We had been doing it at home just for fun, but our daughters loved the idea of bringing it to other kids just the same way that we help other kids learn to read. Because not everybody has parents who know how to program computers.

Iris was in sixth grade and Robyn was in fourth grade at the time. Iris designed a logo and Robyn designed the website. They even created T-shirts with the logo on the front and a quote from Hillary Clinton on the back:

> "Never doubt that you are valuable and powerful and
>
> deserving of every chance and opportunity in the world
>
> to pursue and achieve your own dreams."

I thought, "Oh, that's a nice idea." But I wasn't sure we could pull it off in reality. But my younger one, Robyn, started asking me every week, "Mommy, have you talked to the teachers yet? I know you know teachers. Have you asked them to find us some students for Inventors University?"

I was thinking, "The teachers are busy, everyone's getting ready for the holidays, I don't know if I really want to." But Robyn kept pestering me. I connected with a teacher, Karly Moura out at Sun Terrace Elementary in Concord. I'd heard that she started an after-school Mouse Club, you know, like a computer mouse. Kids learning technology after school.

I told her the idea was for my kids to teach other kids. Girls teaching girls computer programming.

They wanted a two-hour block of time after school, but my daughters couldn't get over to Sun Terrace very quickly after school, and two hours was hard to fit in. We decided it needed to be on weekends, but schools aren't open on weekends. Here's where community comes to the rescue.

Karly said, "Let me talk to the librarian at the Concord library, and maybe there's space at the library we can use." Turns out, there was a little room. It didn't even have a door, just a side room with glass windows. We started that January with eight girls who came on a Saturday. Their families brought them every Saturday for twelve weeks from ten a.m. to noon to learn computer programming. They learned on little pocket-sized Raspberry Pi computers. We as a family had purchased the Raspberry Pis, and at the end of the program, each girl got to take home her own computer that she had already been using to program. We had a graduation ceremony and presented the girls with their computers. It was incredible.

Sonia: That is incredible coming from your kids, at that age, too.

Cherise: They've graduated one class in 2017 and they graduated their second class in 2018.

Sonia: Wow, that truly is amazing. Are they going to continue this?

Cherise: I think so. Robyn's new idea is to make it like the TV show, The Amazing Race, where you go around and compete on different challenges. She wants an Inventors Amazing Race. They have new ideas all the time.

In terms of my own time, I was learning how schools work from the parent perspective and leading my kids' school PFC (like PTA). But I felt the need to go back to helping the whole community and school district. I realized that not every school has a PTA or foundation, so in some ways what I was doing was making the inequities between our schools worse.

Many parents donate to their own kids' school, but there wasn't a way for people to donate to an entity that provides for students in all of our Mount Diablo schools. I felt there should be a way, because I know there are a lot of people who truly believe that public education is the great equalizer, the basis of our democracy. We needed a district-wide foundation. There had been district-wide entities raising money for specific things like alternative education or instrumental music, but no overarching nonprofit organization to enrich the whole district overall.

The need in our schools is so great because our state has completely underfunded our schools. California public schools used to be one of the top-ranked of all states, and now we are at the bottom in terms of our per-pupil investment in education, and we have some of the largest class sizes in the nation. I would like for that to change. A group of us in 2017 started the MDUSD Education Foundation with a vision for quality education for all students in the school district, regardless of their zip code. We raise money to provide STEAM (science, technology, engineering, art, and math) enrichment and career technical opportunities for kids as well. I'm so excited about it.

We shouldn't have to be all the same income, or all the same anything, to benefit everybody. I truly believe there are plenty of people in our community, in our businesses, who want to give to our schools and connect in some way. This foundation creates that conduit to connect with the schools. Even those who don't have kids in our schools or whose kids have aged out, and local businesses and community groups, love to help out. But they haven't known where to start because there are so many schools. We aim to make sure that all kids are getting the education that they need.

Sonia: Are you building this program one school at a time, and one community at a time?

Cherise: No, we're looking at it as a whole. The idea is that we want to be a community organization that talks with the superintendent and the schools about what their needs are and where we can help, and also listening to teachers and parents from the communities. We make sure we listen to all voices, so we can be strategic about what we fund and where.

We first launched with a $30,000 donation specifically for the arts—the "A" of STEAM. We created a survey and sent it out to all thirty-one elementary schools, principals, teachers, and parent leadership, and asked, "What arts do you have? What arts do you need? Do you have a model arts program that another school might replicate?" We learned so much. We got hundreds of responses, and we found out that there were fantastic programs in our schools, but each school didn't know about the other.

We set up discussions and said, "How can we work together at that larger level? And can we get a bulk discount?" So rather than an individual hoping that an individual teacher would find the money and take the initiative to apply for this, school by school, we started looking at it as a big picture and creating that opportunity for all our schools.

At one school, a chalk artist had come out, stayed for a whole two days, and led an incredible hands-on art program for all students in the whole school. He starts off with a school-wide assembly to show his chalk art and teach students the different aspects of shading and mixing colors. Then he goes out to the blacktop area and he stays there while, classroom by classroom, the students come out for hands-on time doing the chalk art. In the end, there's a huge chalk art on the ground that every student has been a part of, and it comes together in one big piece, right? Our foundation was able to provide funding to bring him to our other schools. He's creating the Largest Illustrated Story on every elementary school campus in our district, about our connection to Mount Diablo and what it means to us as a whole unified community. There's just so much that we can do when we all come together, it's incredible.

Sonia: I'm amazed that you work to combine all of these ideas. There's nothing more impactful than being a part of a community, in any capacity. What would you say to people who want to help but they don't know how?

Cherise: Everyone is welcome to join the foundation to benefit the Mount Diablo school district. Anyone who believes in public education for all kids can go to our website, www.mdedf.org, and donate or sign up to volunteer. You can follow us on Facebook and Twitter and LinkedIn. We're creating partnerships with community groups. And we're launching an honor-roll realtor program, with sign riders and logos that recognize realtors who donate. Realtors are just one example. There is a way for any business to get involved and be recognized, too.

Sonia: What is your big dream five years from now?

Cherise: I have lots of dreams for the Foundation. Right now, foreign language in middle school is just another elective that students choose between like band, leadership, computer programming, or art. That's why a lot of kids don't take a foreign language until high school. I heard about an education foundation in another school district that raised enough money for their middle schools to add a whole extra period to the day to ensure every middle school student takes a foreign language. We're in a global economy; this is real. Our kids will need to be able to communicate to compete with students around the world. I would love to see us do that too. And if we're really serious about improving our math scores, how about a math coach at every school?

Sonia: Let's make it happen. That's incredible. What else do you see for the nonprofit?

Cherise: At the high school level, a lot of kids have trouble taking all the right classes to be able to finish within the four years and be able to have everything they need to transfer into college. So that's another area where we should have more electives and opportunities for kids to explore, not just for going to college, but also for going into lucrative career fields. We have incredible apprenticeship programs in our area where the only requirement is that you're eighteen years old and you pass a basic math test. The Plumbers and Steamfitters in Concord run one of these programs right now. And when you get into the program, you're trained in the field while getting paid, with a future of high-paying plumber or welder jobs that include a pension and health benefits. Those jobs can't be shipped overseas because we will always need them right here in our communities. More families need to know about this, and more students need access to it. One issue right now is that a lot of kids can't pass that math test. They're eighteen years old and they can't pass a basic math test (math at about an eighth-grade level).

My overall dream is that our state and our country will value education and invest in education from the youngest age all the way up. There are studies that show that for every dollar you invest in early education, you save $7 later on in remediation—things like jails, and the costs to get someone caught up when they're already behind.

Preparation is cheaper in the long run. We need to prepare these students because they are our future leaders. We tell people that our country has a level playing field, that if you work hard and play by the rules, you will succeed. We need to make that a reality by ensuring that all of our schools are truly providing a quality education.

Sonia: I love your dream and it's honorable at every level. We need thousands of you. Thank you for sharing your story. You have given us your heartbeat for community, and your heartbeat about not leaving anyone behind. Your story could easily make me cry. I hope that many people get behind what you're doing because you are making a difference. And it began with that one little girl. That one seed!

Cherise: Una chiquita!

Sonia: Is there anything else you would love to share?

Cherise: I do this work, but I can't do it alone. It really does take a village. You were asking me what my motto would be and it's, "Sí, se puede" (Yes, you can). But it's really, "Todos juntos sí, se puede" (Together we can). That's what it's going to take. If we all look into our hearts and remember that community, if we are obligated to other people in our community, they will be obligated to us and we'll all take care of each other. And that's how we'll succeed, together.

Sonia: I love it. Thank you so much for sharing.

*In November 2018, Cherise Khaund was elected to the Mount Diablo School Board. She also worked with a coalition of volunteers on a campaign for Measure J—a school bond for Mount Diablo school facilities & safety—which passed with over seventy-percent Yes votes.

Sonia Hassey

ABOUT CHERISE KHAUND

Cherise Khaund's mission is to ensure quality public education for all students. She is President of the MDUSD Education Foundation and was elected to the Mt Diablo Unified District School Board in November 2018.

Cherise's experience includes working as an engineer, community organizer, education policy analyst, and nonprofit manager. She earned her bachelor's degree in Electrical Engineering from Stanford University, and soon afterward joined AmeriCorps*VISTA as a community organizer in affordable housing, launching tutoring programs and connecting parents who didn't speak English with their children's schools. That experience was pivotal, changing the course of her career to education. She moved to Seattle and worked for the League of Education Voters, organizing parents across the state to improve statewide funding for public schools. There she earned a Master of Public Affairs from the University of Washington with a focus in Education Policy and Nonprofit Management, where she designed a weighted formula for how the dollars of state Initiative 884 would be distributed to K-12 school districts. After moving back to California, she led a successful reading program for struggling students in the Mt Diablo school district. Her children began attending the local schools, and as President of her children's elementary school parent group, Cherise led a coalition with the city and neighborhood to create safe routes for kids to walk and bike to school. That community success inspired her to run for the local school board, and to start a districtwide education foundation.

Cherise lives in Walnut Creek with her husband Sandy, two daughters, and their dog Tigerlily. You are invited to join in supporting quality public schools for all at www.mdedf.org and to follow Cherise at www.cherisekhaund.com .

CHAPTER 6

Soul In Power: From Trauma To Triumph

Tina Marsan

Sonia: Hi, I am here with Tina Marsan. Tina, tell us your story and a little bit about what you do.

Tina: I've been a certified massage therapist for thirty-one years. I've been practicing massage and holistic health, and I'm very much into holistic health advocacy. I'm a speaker, author, and a life coach. I facilitate workshops for Soul In Power, an organization I originally founded for women, but it's now for women, men, and youth.

Sonia: Beautiful! Go ahead and share with us who you are and tell us your life story.

Tina: I was born in Portola, up in beautiful Northern California. My story is unique because I was born to parents who separated early on. My father went to Vietnam when I was about two years old. Even though I was told, "You look like your daddy," and "Your daddy's in the war," I was hazy about what that meant. I didn't get to see my real father again until I was around seven. Shortly after he left, my mom met a man, and he became the person I considered to be my daddy. We moved in with him, and he was my stepfather until I was thirteen years old.

It was a small town, predominantly white, and my family was white, but I was brown. Being brown in that small community at that time was different for some of those around me, but I didn't really see the difference because I was colorblind. However, one of my first memories was when I was going to kindergarten one day, and I was walking up the street to go to the bus stop.

My mom had let me venture alone on this short little hill, and so when I got to the bus stop, a boy who was about my age met me there, and he started picking up ice balls and throwing them at me and telling me to go home, calling me a nigger. I was traumatized and I was hurt physically and emotionally, and I did not know what to do. I went back home, and I was in tears. My mom was surprised to see me, and she asked, "What happened? Are you okay? What are you doing here?" I blurted out, "I'm a nigger." And she looked at me and said, "Honey, you're not a nigger; there's no such thing as niggers."

I became very aware at that moment that I looked different and there was something different about me. I kept hearing the word, and other words—dirty spic words that I didn't know at the time but that followed me through my life.

Despite the story, fortunately, I started fighting for people who faced prejudices of all kinds.

Sonia: Can you truly say that when people are affected by prejudice, that you can understand where they are coming from?

Tina: Absolutely I do, and I don't tolerate it. I will stand up for anybody in that situation. I have no problem calling people out when they're speaking in prejudiced ways, because it's just completely unacceptable.

Sonia: Wow, and when you decided to fight for people experiencing prejudice, were you still about seven or eight years old?

Tina: Yes, I was about seven at that time.

I also remember around that time, my mother and stepfather sat my brother and me down. My brother was four years younger than me, so he was about three years old. They told us they were getting a divorce. I remember sitting on my daddy's knee, and my mom was facing me, and she said, "Your daddy and I don't love each other anymore." I remember the feeling that coursed through my body. It felt like a dagger and a fire at the same time, because I could not comprehend not loving somebody anymore, or not being loved anymore. Even in that moment, and in the short time following, I just remember thinking that if Mommy and Daddy can stop loving each other, then they could stop loving me, too.

At that point, they separated, and my mother moved away and left my brother and me with my then stepfather, so she could get on her feet for the first time in her life. She had had me when she was seventeen years old. But she was there every single weekend, and she sent cards, and she was very present in my life without fail, and has always been my greatest cheerleader. But from the time I was seven until I was thirteen, my brother and I stayed with my stepfather, who was in his own right a very dynamic, beautiful spirit.

He was a naturalist, he loved the outdoors, he was an artist, he could draw, do stained glass, make and build things, and create amazing living spaces and horticulture. He was truly a hippie at heart. It was the '70s, so while I was with my stepfather, I lived in a very free-spirited, loose environment. He allowed us the freedom to paint whatever we wanted on our walls. He taught me how to plant gardens, and we spent time creating a garden the size of a house. I remember sticking my little finger into the soil just far enough up to the knuckle to plant a seed, and top it with a little fertilizer and pack it down, and then water it.

He brought into my life the knowledge of where our food comes from, how our food comes to be, and the appreciation for the process that it takes, the nurturing and the love. After Mom left, we used that same skill set, which manifested into a little different twist. He actually grew marijuana in the basement of our home. The walls were lined with black polyethylene plastic sheeting, and there were grow lights, and we took the growth process from seed to pipe, I should say. We grew it all the way to cultivating it, pulling it, taking off the leaves, cleaning out the seeds, and even smoking it.

Now, I do want to interject at this point that I know most people would think that's a horrible thing for a parent to do, and I understand that viewpoint, but for me, it was a very fantastic thing. I don't think it was healthy, and I wouldn't do it with my own children, and I don't recommend that other people grow and smoke marijuana with their kids, but it was a time in my life where not only did I learn how to grow plants, but I learned the medicinal benefits of it, because it was calming and it was in conjunction with doing art.

I witnessed how marijuana affected people around me, as far as stress and mood alteration, which has positive and negative sides. Fast forward to today and I am an advocate of using it with treatments for patients who are in pain. I believe very strongly in the medicinal aspect of it when utilized correctly, but at the time, being brought up with that, it was very confusing and it became something that was a habit in my life, and that habit was difficult to break, especially in my teenage years. I would have to say, in hindsight, that the negative aspects of that experience outweighed the positive aspects in my younger years.

Sonia: In what way?

Tina: Well, without a doubt, I believe that it had an effect on my brain and now that I know it's a neurotoxin, I believe that it inhibited my ability to learn and to even have certain forms of memory. I also learned that you use it as a vice to deal with uncomfortable or challenging times.

Sonia: That's pretty incredible and I'm glad that you were able to share that there was a good side of it, but there are bad effects too. Was it a daily or weekly habit?

Tina: When I was a teenager, it was a weekend thing, because it was a habit. But I didn't use it very much. The model for me as a child was not positive, and I believe that adults do not have as much respect for our youth in how they represent drug and alcohol use in their lives. I believe that children see it as being a fun, necessary thing that they get to do when they finally reach the age, and oftentimes, will go sneak to do it because adults do it and it's all good; it just isn't allowed. I'm just not an advocate of the irresponsible use of drugs in the face of children.

At thirteen, I decided that it was time for me to be with my mother. It wasn't anything negative on my stepfather; it was that I was becoming a woman and I needed to have a woman's touch. My mom had wanted me to live with her over the years and I was given the choice, but I chose not to because my dad's house was a little more liberal and I had more freedom than at my mother's house with her new husband who had come into the picture.

I was in no hurry to have constraints put on my freedom, but I did choose to go live with my mom, so I moved in with her and my new stepfather and my stepsister. I entered into a new life in Lake Tahoe, and my social life, my education—everything—started to firm up and be a really wonderful experience as far as school and environment and people go.

To finally feel I got traction and had grounding at my mom's house was really beneficial and necessary. I did get held back in seventh grade, which was heartbreaking, and it had a huge impact on my self-esteem and on my sensitive soul. I made it through the rest of that year, and here's the other side of the coin: even though it was a challenge to go through that year the second time around, I'd done half the classes already and I excelled, and I became a much better student, and it ended up building up my confidence.

I was able to transform that pain into my power, and fulfilling my purpose. I began to love school and had a great network of friends. I did use marijuana on the weekends, and experienced the turmoil of blended families, and God bless my parents, because we were not easy trying to merge my brother and my sister and me. We were hellions, to say the least. We had our troubles and our pains, but what ended up happening through all of that was I gained a foundation and I gained traction and I started to aspire to greater things that I knew I was capable of.

Unfortunately, one night when I was sixteen, I ventured out with some girlfriends. I told my parents I was staying the night at my girlfriend's house, which we were, but I left out the part that we were going to go to a party in between.

We went to this party, and I don't have a memory of the whole thing, which I believe is a result of trauma. What I do remember is sitting on the floor playing caps, where you throw one cap into somebody else's glass, and if you make it, you drink. I had been made to drink several times, so maybe a total of two or three wine coolers. I don't know how long we were there, maybe no more than a couple of hours, before I needed to use the restroom. I left and I went down the stairs to find the restroom, and pretty much the next thing I knew, I woke up in the morning to a voice yelling from the distance that the phone was for me. There was a phone next to the bed I was in. The call was from my mother, who was crying, upset, and frantic, asking where I was. I didn't know where I was. It took me a minute to come to and look around, and realize that I was somewhere I wasn't familiar with. I concluded I was at the house where the party had been.

I had a shirt on but no pants, and so immediately I knew that something bad had happened. I got dressed. There was somebody in the house, I don't remember who, and the person told me where I could go to another area to use a phone. I called friends who came and picked me up, and it took me two days with nightmares and a very fuzzy brain and phone calls from people to piece together what had happened. Two of the perpetrators called me, very upset, begging me not to tell. That was the first time I figured that something had happened with them and they said, "Please don't tell. One of us is already on probation." I believe he was eighteen and a senior. I didn't know what to do with that information. I went to school the next day, and as I walked around the halls, everybody was making train noises and I thought, "What the heck is that all about?" People were giving me funny looks, and the energy and the vibe were off. I figured something was going to go down.

I was pulled aside at lunch by a girlfriend's boyfriend, who asked me if I knew what was going on, and I said, "Not really." He informed me that I had been raped in a "train" by numerous people on the football team at the party. I had to leave school because I was consumed by shame. When I returned home, I received a phone call from another boy from my high school. He told me that he attended the same party and had heard screaming coming from the room I was in. He had pushed himself through the door and had put the head of one of the perpetrators into a wall to stop the rape. I couldn't tell my parents once I knew what had happened. I was very fearful of what their response might be. I got grounded for not coming home the night of the party, and I could not defend myself because I couldn't ... I didn't know what it was I was defending. For several days, I contemplated and even began to plan out suicide before I realized that I couldn't do that, and so my next thought was hurting other people.

I knew there was a party coming up the next weekend, and I actually thought of getting a gun that I knew was available and taking it to that party. And then I realized I couldn't kill myself or harm other people, so the only option left was to run. I called my real father, who had not been in the picture other than one visit sometime when I was around seven, and I asked him if I could go and live with him, and he said, "Of course." I told my mom I needed to leave, that I was not doing well in school, and I was unhappy, and she still didn't know what happened and she supported it, so I left.

I moved to Arizona for the remainder of the year and the summer, and finally decided to come back and see if I could live in Tahoe again. I went back, but I could not be at the school, so I went into a continuation school. That was one of the best experiences I ever had. The continuation school was actually a better education and more attentive than my whole experience in high school. Unfortunately, I could not remove myself from social exposure. The pressure became too much to handle, so I dropped out of school and made plans to move to Sacramento to get away and attend junior college.

Even at that time when I moved away, and then years later when I came back, I never owned being a victim because I felt life just happens, and I'd had so much of life just happening in challenging and adverse ways that I knew it was just life. Life is a little bit bumpy, so I wouldn't allow myself to be a victim, and I used all of my skills that I had known since I was a child to heal myself.

The very first time I remember using those skills of self-awareness was after my mom had left and I was lying in bed alone in the house with my younger brother. I was about eight. I was lying in bed with the covers pulled over my head, thinking that if anybody came in, they wouldn't be able to find me. There was a branch scraping the window outside, and with the sound of the wind, my heart was racing. I was literally paralyzed with the fear of something happening. And somewhere in there, I started thinking about my mom and my mind went off track from being afraid to thinking about my mom. And at that moment, I realized that my thoughts were creating my emotional state. And my emotional state was affecting my body physically. My heart was racing and I was clammy, but the minute I quit thinking fearful thoughts and being afraid of what might happen, and I started looking forward to my mom's visit and thinking about my mom, my body calmed down and my emotions shifted. The denominator was my mind.

I was like, "Oh my gosh! I can control my thoughts? My thoughts don't just happen? I'm thinking them and I feel this way. This is the experience that I'm having with other people because I feel other people and their emotions. I'm feeling their process of thinking and seeing how it shows up in their body language and their body. So how I think, how I feel, and how I show up with my body is evident to other people like it is evident to me in those other people." So, getting that piece at the young age of eight years old was profound.

Sonia: I would say most definitely profound because that is something, even for me at my age, I didn't realize until ten years ago. I love what you said about our thinking and what goes into our mindset. And for you to be at such a young age is pretty incredible. What happened once you experienced the awareness?

Tina: I took the big leap to, "Wow, can you move things with your mind?" and the power of it all just started making sense. The power of manipulation, like I can control how I appear, I can control my body language, I can think powerful thoughts, and I believe that even transcends my body. It becomes like an ethereal palpable thing between people, because that's what I experienced in feeling from others. I started realizing that people do manipulate that, in both very loving ways and very hating ways. That started bringing me to the awareness of the light and the dark, the good and the evil, and the choice that I had as an individual to direct myself accordingly.

I carried that with me all the way up into the experience of the rape, and through that experience, I was able to regulate my breathing and shift as best as I could out of that traumatic experience. So it took a lot of work on my part to heal the many layers of pain that were like a meteor hitting my heart and shattering my life. And then I got to take that shattered life, and create a mosaic out of it, and put the pieces back together to create myself. That took me into and out of the conditioning of my childhood, and I started developing Tina, as her own unique individual, character, and soul.

Sonia: That's so beautiful. So how old were you at this stage, in this awareness?

Tina: I was very aware when I was a teenager of relationship and interaction and the law of attraction. It was from when I was sixteen until I was twenty, and going through a lot of growth.

Despite my efforts, I managed to put on a lot of weight. I couldn't get a size sixteen skirt past my knees, and I just kept getting bigger. I was eating my emotions; I was eating the pain that I had not resolved yet.

When I was eighteen, I moved from Tahoe to Sacramento for a short stint, and then down to Santa Clara, where I decided I was going to be an entrepreneur and start a business. I worked in a consulting firm for the Minority Business Development Agency. I was a secretary, and I saw these business plans come across my desk, so that was my education. That's where I learned how to start a business and grow it, and what to do. Six consultants were there, and I learned. I took that information and did a survey around the Marriott area, asking if they would like to have a doughnut delivery service.

I started a company called Executive Treats, and it was pre-ordered every Friday. I brought in the doughnuts you needed for your office, and it became a little catering business. It outgrew me within about a year and a half because I didn't know as much as I should about business.

I left the business and took the money I had earned at that point, and I put myself through massage school. I was certified in 1988.

Sonia: How did you choose that path and go from entrepreneurship to massage? Did you always have a passion for massage?

Tina: I always had a passion for massage. So when I was a little girl before my mom moved out, I would have these episodes in bed where I would have this uncontrollable nerve pain. My feet were tickling and I would bend my knees and race my feet on the sheets to try to get rid of this nagging pain that would go from my hips to my feet almost nightly. My mom would come in and massage my feet for an hour until I would go to sleep. If I did not fall asleep, I'd wake up and I would cry, and she'd come back until I fell asleep. I loved touch. She would use her nails to scratch my back. When she left, my therapy stopped.

So as an adult, I started trading people: I'll massage your back if you massage my back. I'll massage your feet if you'll massage my feet. And so that was my life.

Touch was part of my life; massage was just part of my family and my life. My first stepdad was also very into holistic health and eating healthy smoothies and doing chiropractic and karate. And judo was his thing. I was raised with touching and eating right, appreciating and respecting the body. So it wasn't a leap to go from selling doughnuts and thinking that I was going to put this hat on to be some executive success story in the Marriott Silicon Valley area, to really following my heart and becoming certified and nestling into what my true purpose was.

Sonia: That's amazing. Were you self-employed or did you go and work for somebody and learn from them?

Tina: I was self-employed and at a time when the industry was new. So after I got certified, I moved back up to Tahoe and lived above my parents in their studio apartment. I told my mom, "I'm going to open a business," and she actually told me—sweetly, I must say—"You can't open a business; you don't have an education." That's just how she thought about it, but that's all it took. I was like, "Oh, watch me." I found a spot to rent above a hair salon, next to a psychotherapist and catty-corner from our family chiropractor, and I opened Cloud Nine Clinical Massage Health Care, which I kept for almost four years.

Sonia: All by yourself?

Tina: Yes, all by myself. It did well until I decided to get married. That only lasted about eight months, and through that turmoil and lesson, I decided it was time to leave Tahoe again and moved to Sacramento. So I closed shop and moved to Sacramento and waitressed at Black Angus while I built a practice inside of a hair salon.

I had a serendipitous meeting with a chiropractor who had recently moved to the area, and he and I decided to open a space together as independent contractors. So I opened A Healthy Touch in the Pocket area of Sacramento, and stayed there for about six years.

After my first marriage ended, I was single and dating. I met my second husband and we hit it off right away. I got pregnant shortly after, and we got married when I was eight months pregnant with my first child. She arrived ten days before my thirtieth birthday. We ended up having two beautiful children. Before that, I thought I was not going to have children because I wanted a business and I wanted to travel.

When my youngest daughter was five and my oldest daughter was seven, I discovered that my oldest daughter had severe scoliosis. She was on the massage table, and I was running my hands down her little back and spine. I could feel and see a significant S-curve in her back. So, I had her get off the table. I dotted her spine and had her bend forward, and sure enough, there was a huge S. We went to an orthopedist who confirmed that she had scoliosis. He told us we needed to have a full spine MRI in case there was an underlying issue. In the meantime, I did my research because there was no way in heck I was going to put my daughter in a full torso brace for the remainder of her school years.

I found Spine Core, a company in Canada that had just designed the first corrective brace for scoliosis. We were going to do whatever it took to keep our daughter out of a hard, turtle-shell brace for the rest of her juvenile years. Sadly, her MRI revealed an underlying cause known as Chiari. Chiari is a condition where the cerebral tonsils of the brain right at the base of the skull have descended into the spinal cord, impeding the spinal fluid that flows up and down. Our daughter was diagnosed with Chiari, severe idiopathic scoliosis, and syringomyelia—a cyst inside the spine. Normally they're about the size of the tip of your pinky. Hers is from the base of her spine to just below her shoulder blades. She needed to have brain surgery.

A decompression surgery was performed, relieving the pressure from the herniation. Her scoliosis improved a lot; however, we opted to have her wear the Spine Core brace. She had to wear it for twenty-one hours a day. It was a movable brace worn under her clothes, but for her, it was like having a straitjacket on. She was supposed to wear it through high school but the toll it took on her mentally and emotionally required us to relieve her of it after two years.

Not even two years after my oldest daughter was diagnosed, my younger daughter started presenting with different symptoms of Chiari. And so we took her to have an MRI. As it turns out, she has Chiari also, but hers has not created syringomyelia or scoliosis, so she was not a candidate for surgery. Now they look for Chiari in utero. But when my daughters were young, it was extremely rare and the medical field was just beginning to collaborate regarding treatment. We had to make difficult choices with little information or statistics. In a sense, we were on the frontier of change.

Thankfully, my life had afforded me the opportunities to face tremendous challenges and to overcome those challenges in a holistic way that worked. Because of this, I was able to assist my daughter and family through this trying time by using my varied skill sets. Prior to her surgery, her diet was clean and vital, and she took natural supplements aimed at helping her heal well. She learned the value of visualization, meditation, and massage therapy, but most of all, she endured the process with love and trust in those who were there to support her. In a sense, all that I had endured enabled me to optimally serve my daughter. Life happens. There are no mistakes or do-overs, because odd as it may seem, the perfection of life is often revealed in its seemingly imperfect trials.

Sonia: Does it still flare up and how is she doing now overall?

Tina: My oldest daughter is doing great. She still has lasting results of the scoliosis. She always will have syringomyelia. They both have to do activities that are brainstem-friendly. Chiari can cause dizziness, weak upper body strength, and it can mess with your organs. It is the central nervous system, so anything in your body can present as a symptom. It's hard. Most people go about seven years before they are even diagnosed. And if they don't get an MRI to determine the cause, the current medical system causes people to suffer tremendously because they overmedicate people, and people suffer from a lot of pain before they have any answers.

My daughters understand the symptoms and they are fearless. They're good with it.

Sonia: That's incredible. Thinking about health, let's talk about your life. I would love to know your journey on how you lost that weight. Was it an emotional journey as well? How did you do that?

Tina: The last time I saw the scale I was 169, and I went up from there. When I decided there was a Tina inside my body that needed to come out, I knew that I could physically be a different person. After my massage training, I became a vegetarian, and every single day for three months, I hiked from Kings Beach in Lake Tahoe up into a lookout tower in Tahoe Vista. I also went to a gym. I lost the weight in three months from the hiking, being a vegetarian, and practicing meditation and visualization. I went down to a low weight of 103. At that point, options in my life opened up and I became more empowered and less burdened by my body image.

Sonia: Wow! Were you able to sustain that weight loss?

Tina: Yes, absolutely. I stayed a vegetarian for thirteen years until I became anemic. Thankfully, my first stepdad had provided me a healthy foundation regarding food and nutritional awareness. Becoming a vegetarian was not a huge leap for me. I have not had red meat since I was twenty. It has been thirty-one years now. I eat a little more dairy than I used to. But for the majority of my life, I've had a clean, simple diet and habits that have helped me to sustain my physical health. I love science—I've always loved science—so I've learned about how the body uses food and how the mind, emotions, and body can work together to create health or keep people unhealthy.

Sonia: What has the weight loss done for your whole physiology?

Tina: Well, even though I lost weight along the way for years, even up to a couple of years ago, I still felt like I looked in the mirror and saw myself as being heavy. It's just the weirdest psychological experience to know that I just put on a size two pants, and the mirror tells me that I look 160 pounds. The curves still looked too big. It's something I've struggled with. What finally broke this for me was turning fifty. I thought, "I'm done. I'm done being concerned about what people think about me, and I'm done thinking so negatively about me. I'm just going to love me with all my curves and everything about me." I laid down the sword and haven't picked it up again.

Sonia: That's incredible. It's freedom. I have experienced what you experienced after I gained weight after my pregnancy, then I went down to ninety-eight pounds, and still looked in the mirror and thought I was overweight. The power of the mindset is so incredible. We can have a negative belief, no matter what the reality is, until we understand how to shift it.

Tina: Absolutely. Something else I want to touch on is that when I was thirty-five, around the same time Chiari was happening, I decided to test my armor and attend a class reunion that had been shared on Facebook. It was an interesting frame of mind. I look back at it now and think it was silly to have the mindset of needing to "test" my armor rather than recognizing that I needed to learn how to remove the armor. The fact is, armor is heavy and limits freedom of movement and expression! I went to the reunion and when I went down the stairs, the first person I saw was one of the perpetrators who had come forward at the time of the rape event twenty years ago. I was very surprised that it didn't trigger me, and I was able to look at him and move on. And so in my mind, I was like, "Check one, I'm good." And I went on down to the beach and other people greeted me with open arms.

I continued through the event at the beach, just saying hi to people, and then later everybody joined together at a bar. This person showed up again at the bar. This man who had participated in the event had been watching and making me feel uncomfortable. I was like, "Why is he watching me like this?" It wasn't a bad watch; it wasn't evil, but he was just watching me. So somewhere in the course of an hour, he started to move across the room to approach me, and the bar quieted down because everybody knew about the train, and they were obviously surprised I showed up.

It became a moment, and he started crying, saying he had been looking for me all these years and he thought I had taken my life. As it turns out, even though he was present at the event in high school, he hadn't physically done anything to me. He said he had just wanted to fit in, so he told others that he had partaken in the act. My heart went out to him because truly I had healed quite a bit at that point. But this man had carried a burden from a lie, thinking that I might have killed myself as a result. He needed my forgiveness so he could forgive himself. His testimony and my witness helped us both heal. Isn't life amazing!

But what happened for me was that it cracked open the deepest part of that wound that I didn't even know existed at the time. I cried for three days straight after that and had quite a nervous breakdown. I literally remember feeling an energy pouring out from inside me. And I thought, "Where did I keep all of this?" I just sobbed and let it go. Finally, I realized that in that moment, what I had done back in high school and through my twenties and early thirties was deny myself the right and the need to embrace being a victim.

When I got that piece at thirty-five, and I realized, "Oh my gosh, I was a victim!" all over again, suddenly I was able to become a true survivor of that victimhood, and because of my maturity, I understood that it was just symbolic of many pains. I knew how important it was to understand and really own being victimized by circumstances or people in your life. Once you own that, you can truly survive it. So I did. Shortly after getting that piece of "Now I'm a survivor," I realized it wasn't enough. I didn't want to just survive. The image of just surviving was like being destitute on a deserted island and surviving, and that didn't sound very good or fun or joyous. So I thought, "What's the next step?" Well, the next step was to be a thriver.

At thirty-five, I was able to go from victim to survivor to thriver, and all of a sudden, I realized all of that story that I have shared of pain and circumstances and people was about to serve me. And I was about to step into my greatest purpose, which is to transform the experience of my life into an opportunity for other people to learn and grow from so they can overcome their pain and become thrivers and joyous souls.

Sonia: You were on your way to healing already, but it still came full circle with that guy. He was convicted all those years of playing the part. What happened after that?

Tina: Ironically, over the years, I had people from that time come back into my life on social media. Each one tested my armor again until I didn't need the armor anymore. I shed a lot of those people who I decided didn't get to have access to me because it didn't serve either of us. I have not stayed in touch with anybody, really, from that time. That time of my life was shut off, and it took me years to be able to go back to Tahoe without feeling like, "Is somebody going to see me?" and fear what people would think.

So with the whole story said, everything from my kindergarten experience to the divorce of my parents, to the Chiari with my kids, to the rape, and my weight loss, I wouldn't change any of it because not only did it serve me, but along the way, it has served everybody who participated in those things with me. Sometimes I think, "What if my healing of moving from victim to survivor would have happened in my twenties?" But then I realize that I wouldn't have been able to impact other people in that amount of time in that way, and I needed me to be the person who I was at that time to be part of their stories. There are no accidents and no wrongs in the process. I wouldn't do any of it over, and I wouldn't change anything in my life. I tell people all the time, "If you're going to make a decision or a choice, do it without guilt and without questions. Just move forward. Be powerful."

Sonia: Your story is profound because you were able to turn things around in your journey of pain to be on a journey of courage. Greatness was rising up in you. So now when people see you, they don't see a victim, they see a strong woman. Why? Because you've learned to understand life. Life isn't perfect. Now your desire is to impact not only yourself and your family, but the world around you. Share with us what you're doing now to make that happen.

Tina: This past year, with the loving support and encouragement of my husband, Russell, I have been able to flip my business model.

I left a thriving massage practice in Sacramento and opened a much smaller part-time practice in Yuba City. This has enabled me to focus my energy and use my time to create a solid foundation for my speaking, coaching, and workshop interests based on my practice and advocacy of holistic health care. My "Soul In Power" work is now my primary source of focus. It is the brand and umbrella for all of my entrepreneurial interests.

I am working with youth, especially troubled youth, and with women and men who can relate to and identify with the many pieces of my story. Six years ago I wrote a book, *Experiencing Serendipity*. It is back in print and will be used in conjunction with my Soul In Power work.

I have lived through such a wealth of experience. My platform can be anywhere. It can be in the school system, it can be in corporations. I'm finding that people are all of a sudden saying, "Hey, I would like you to speak here." My Soul In Power work is part of a mindfulness program in a local continuation school for at-risk young women. My life in a sense has come full circle. I am back in a continuation school, this time as a facilitator for health and wellness, serving youth that I can identify with and who likely identify with me. I feel I am involved in promoting the wellness of the community. I am designing my life on purpose with power while assisting others to do the same.

Sonia: I love that you're going to design your life. You will not live it by default in any way. That's so powerful. I personally had no idea that you had a heart for youth. The need is so great for us to get out there and impact these young women's lives, and youth in general.

What would you say to all those women who are victims? Who are overweight, who are pregnant with destiny but don't know what to do? What is their first step?

Tina: I'd say, first believe that you are worthy, valuable, and powerful. Embrace your pain. Go get it. Allow it to be present. Feel it to its core and push through it because the pain is just a symptom of being dis-eased. You're dis-eased and you want to be in ease. You want to live a life of ease and joy and grace, and anything that impedes that is not serving you. Unfortunately for all of us, it happens to exist mostly in the mind. It's about perception and fear. You've got to work with the way that you perceive—not just what you perceive, but how you perceive. Question what you believe that supports unhealthy perceptions. And that is very personal and individual, and it takes a lot of work to change your personal perception. That can't be done from the outside of you. People and life may support your process, but you have to do the work from the inside out.

Seek healing support in the environment and with people. Acknowledge and value the holistic nature of all things. Everything is connected right here, right now. Know you are a 100 percent an organic being, a life force like no other, that there is only one of you in existence—in the entire Universe. You are literally a miracle! Your presence matters. What you do, just you being here, has an instantaneous impact on everything else. Know that who you are is instrumental in creating our collective experience and overall progression as a human race. Take responsibility for your life and the way in which you have an impact on the lives of others. The first step is to believe you can transform pain to purpose, and go from being a victim to a thriver. The next step is to do it.

Sonia: I admire you so much as a beautiful woman of strength, a woman of power, because you've learned to embrace you. You have learned to embrace your pain, but you've also learned to give grace to people. And now you understand the power of forgiveness. Everyone needs forgiveness because no one's perfect.

Tina: I would like to acknowledge the honor I feel for having participated with all of the people in my life. No matter how those relations showed up, no matter how challenging or painful they've been. Life isn't easy, and we're not doing it alone. We are only part of the whole. We're all in life together.

Sonia: That is so powerful. Thank you so much.

Dedication: This chapter is dedicated to my family, by blood and by marriage. You are my love story, my "Once upon a time …" and my "Happily ever after!" I love you all beyond explanation. Thank you for supporting me in sharing my story.

ABOUT TINA MARSAN

Tina Marsan is an entrepreneur. She became a certified massage therapist in 1988 and has been in practice now for the 31 years. Tina has owned and operated several holistic wellness businesses. She is the author of *Experiencing Serendipity*, and a speaker who has been featured at Sacramento State University, UC Davis, The Learning Exchange, Sacramento Police Academy, various Sacramento schools, and other organizations. She is a certified facilitator for Lightness to Dark, working to educate adults on how to recognize, prevent, and report childhood sexual abuse. Tina is a life coach and the founder of Soul In Power, created to provide experiential workshops for those seeking healthy, sustainable, vital change in their lives by transforming confusion, chaos, and pain to plan, action, and freedom. Tina believes her success comes from helping others succeed. Just for the Health of It!

Social Media

Website: www.SoulInPower.Com

Facebook: https://www.facebook.com/SoulInPower/

Instagram: SoulInPower

Book *Experiencing Serendipity*: www.ExperiencingSerendipity.com

E-Mail: Tina@TinaMarsan.com

CHAPTER 7

Grace – The Ultimate Gift

Lucy Garcia

Sonia: I am here with Lucy Garcia Robles and she is going to share a little about her life story and her passion for the Mexican culture.

Lucy, tell us about the foundation of your upbringing and passion from the beginning.

Lucy: I was born in Mexico in Ciudad Guzman, Jalisco, to very traditional parents. My Mom and Dad got married when they were young at the tender age of seventeen and twenty; and less than a year later, I was born. Then they had another child within a year. They soon realized that Mexico was not going to provide what they wanted for their growing family, so they migrated to the United States, leaving my sister Mini and I with my maternal grandmother. About a year and a half later, we were reunited when my parents were able to save enough money and send for us. I've been here in the States since I was three years old. I grew up with a mom who was and is an amazing cook. We ate nothing but fresh, authentic Mexican food. She was a housekeeper for many years, and she would come home tired. But she still made us homemade corn tortillas, while listening to Mexican music. My father was a very hardworking man as well. He was a farmer. The best of my culture was the music, the traditions, the food, and the family gatherings. I always recognized that with us, my father was not affectionate and had a Machista mentality, and my mother was the opposite, very submissive, always serving, always catering to all of us. There were five of us kids all together. I have two brothers and two younger sisters.

As I mentioned earlier, my mother was mainly a housekeeper at a hospital when I was growing up. But she told herself, "I didn't come to this country just to mop floors. I came here for a purpose." I saw that drive in my mom when we would sit and do homework at times, and she was also learning English. She now has her own successful state-licensed elderly care business since 1993. But all through growing up, I saw her passion for always wanting to do more than just what people thought she should do or was able to do.

Sonia: It seems that they built a strong work ethic and you saw that growing up.

Lucy: Oh yes. My father, although he was strict, instilled a lot of good in us. My dad was a provider. He was a farmer, but he ended up being a foreman for the farm owner. I believe both of my parents were leaders. Definitely all five of their kids inherited their work ethic.

Sonia: Tell us more about your childhood and what your daily life looked like.

Lucy: I'm the oldest of five. The first four children are less than a year apart. We were all very close. I have a baby sister who's eight years younger than me. But when she was born, I took the role of her second mom. My mom would have to go to work at six o'clock in the morning, so I had to get my sister Maribel ready, and many times I was the volunteer at the school field trips or helping in her class. When I was in school, my mom always encouraged us to pursue higher education. Of course I also grew up watching novelas. My mom was super lovable with us all. I also remember my mom always making sure that we did our homework and aspired to do something professional. My dad always demanded that we only speak Spanish at home. I'm grateful for that because all of us kids speak it very well.

My dad would come home tired from working long hours in the fields under the scorching sun. He was always serious and very strict. Now that I look back, I realize that it was more about him protecting us from the outside world, especially living in a foreign country.

Sonia: How did he display his protectiveness?

Lucy: Definitely, it was not in the most loving way. Now as an adult, I understand with all the stress that we have as adults, that it was more about the stress of him providing for the family, trying to get ahead. He was just grateful to have a job and put a roof over our heads. I do remember when my mom finally decided to buy a home and I had to translate all the documents for them. I was twelve years old when they bought their first home,

They built a business in assisted living for the elderly care home. My mom was the caregiver, providing some of the best care in the industry. My dad would help her where he was able to as he still worked long hours in farming.

Sonia: How did you feel growing up? Because I understand the Mexican culture is very strict and demanding. How was it for you?

Lucy: Being a female and the oldest of five, there were a lot more expectations of me. I was very close to my mother; I was inseparable from her. At times, my mom was having conversations with her adult family and friends, and I was just hanging on her like a little monkey. My dad, I don't know what exactly was going on with him, but there are things that as children we don't know what's going on with our parents' marriage. But for some reason, my dad always took it out on me. I felt a little neglected. My dad was very harsh with words.

I laugh about it now because I think back and realize we always had to be busy. We couldn't sleep in or just sit and watch TV. We always had to be doing something, which explains why I have a hard time staying still now. He was so strict that he would not even let me wear nail polish. I couldn't wear anything sleeveless, let alone anything above my knee. I was so scared of my dad that I didn't have a boyfriend until I was in college. I didn't want to do anything to upset my dad.

Growing up, I didn't have that loving father who I felt protected by. I think about how he had the stress of having five kids and a wife and the bills and then add living in a different country. So I justify his actions now, and I have forgiven him. However, now we're older and think differently, and the day finally came when my father told me, "I love you." That made a big, big, big difference in our relationship and in me.

Sonia: It's great that you have that full understanding that Dad or Mom didn't know any better at that time, but being back in your childhood, what was missing for you?

Lucy: The missing link would be a dad not being supportive, encouraging, or loving. I had the provider father, but I didn't have a loving father growing up, and I think that it carried on into my adulthood and into my marriage.

Sonia: Talk to me about when you became a teenager with all of your hormones and trying to figure yourself out, to then becoming a young mother.

Lucy: I was a late bloomer, very wholesome, always respectful and well-mannered. I was playing with Barbies until at least fifteen years old. I grew up with the "good girl" behavior driven into me by my mom. Constantly, she reminded us that our virginity was what made us worthy as women; and if we lost it out of wedlock, we were not as valuable. I actually accepted that idea.

However, I feel like my whole focus during my teenage years was just surviving to be able to move away and not feel trapped or imprisoned by my dad. When I was able to get out after high school, I had two choices: get married or go to college. I chose college. I didn't have straight A's because I worked since the age of thirteen, but I had enough College Prep credits to apply to Sac State. I was able to apply to the University through the College Assistant Migrant Program (CAMP).

Thanks to my father who was a farmer, I was able to get into the University, because CAMP was federally funded to help first-generation students who worked in farming or had farm-working parents. I had not worked in farming, but my father had. I never picked a tomato in my life, but my father had. Thanks to him, I was able to get into CSUS. Those were my teenage years. I was trying to find myself and thinking, "What do I want to be?" "Who do I want to be?"

I always knew that I wanted to do something to serve the community and help people. I graduated from high school and attended Sac State. I started majoring in criminal justice and government because I initially wanted to go to law school.

For some reason, I had this passion for helping women, especially women who were being physically abused or emotionally abused. My father never abused my mother physically, but I did see a lot of emotional and verbal abuse.

Of course, there was always the idea of Prince Charming, my knight in shining armor, rescuing me. See, proof I watched too many novelas! My mom would make sure to tell me that it was a must I married with my virginity untouched. I knew that I wanted to get married and have children and dreamt of my wedding in a white, beautiful dress. Sounds corny, but I bought the fairy tale story. Well that didn't happen for me.

I met my first love, without having any other relationship experiences except for what I saw with my parents. I had the foolish mentality, "Okay. This is it. He is the first boy that I'm with." I ended up pregnant out of wedlock in college. We had to tell my dad the news. It didn't go so well.

There were two things that have transformed me and that have made a big impact in my life. One was when I became pregnant out of wedlock. I remember the day I found out I was pregnant, I turned to my boyfriend and said, "Oh my God. We've got to get married." He had already asked to marry me three months into our relationship, but I thought it was because he knew I didn't want to have sex out of wedlock, so I said no. Also, he had not even met my dad yet, and I was living with my sister Mini who was still in high school and I felt she needed me.

It wasn't until a year after we were dating that he met my dad, so I was scared as I knew my dad expected us to marry. However, at the time of my pregnancy, his father became ill, and since he was the older male, he felt responsible for his family. He stayed living at home with his parents. I struggled to make ends meet and eat healthy. He didn't make any effort to figure out a plan before the baby was here. My whole first pregnancy, I was left alone. My fairy tale was shattered, and I resented him for that.

I look back now and realize that he was scared too. However, I was not asking him to leave his family, I just wanted him to make me part of his, as my dad had disowned me. I felt abandoned by my ex, he was all I knew, and I feared what my mom had told me that no other man would want to be with me, especially with a child now. I had to fend for myself. I remember asking my sister Mini, "What are we going to do?" She was my only family support during my pregnancy. She was the one to rub my belly and talk to my baby. She was my rock.

It was just her and me because I couldn't go home to my parents and I couldn't go home to my boyfriend's house either, as his family blamed me for getting pregnant and felt I had shamed them too. Yet here I was expecting a child at three months shy of twenty, and frightened for what my future was going to look like as everyone had turned their backs on me. In a way, I have to thank my ex for not resolving our issues or finding solutions because I've always had to step up to the plate and find solutions to whatever life threw at me. That made me the woman that I am today.

Sonia: How did that make you feel? I could only imagine that for me, it'd be like rejection on both sides.

Lucy: Absolutely, it was rejection on both sides. Honestly, I felt lonely. I felt rejected. I felt abandoned and I don't know where I got my strength. I believe that I got my strength from my baby. I just thought, "Okay, I got this. I've got to get out of this negative thinking. I've got to get up even if it's just my baby and me. I can't fall into depression. I can't." I ended up doing what I had to do to survive. And at the time, I couldn't work. Who's going to hire a twenty-year-old pregnant student? I was getting financial aid for school but that was for books and tuition. I couldn't possibly have a healthy baby eating top ramen noodles, so I had a friend who told me there were programs that could help. I ended up getting on welfare, WIC, and Medi-Cal throughout my pregnancy. Getting care for my baby was important to me. I think this is one reason I believe in social programs. They are there when people need them for a hand up, just like I needed it once.

I remember when I went to the Welfare Office, it was so humiliating. The first thing they asked was, "If you want to see a doctor prior to your three months, it would only be to get an abortion." I knew that's not what I wanted. I had a healthy boy, and he became my drive. He became my purpose. I've since been contributing in paying taxes; so I've paid back more than I used those two years from Uncle Sam, and my ex did have to pay back some of the money, too, as I had collected government aid a year after the baby was born. I wasn't sure if he would stick by my side and I wanted to make sure my son and I had a roof over our heads.

When our son was two years old, we ended up marrying and we were blessed with two other daughters. We were married for twenty years, together twenty-three. I had believed what my mom said, that you stay with your first. You just make it work, and marriage is the whole up and down and lots of compromises. So I stayed. He and I grew up together, but unfortunately not side by side.

Sonia: That comes with experience because we don't know about purpose growing up. Coming full circle, he ended up coming back to you after you felt abandoned from your dad and your boyfriend. How did that take place?

Lucy: Once our son was born, I think we both just realized, "We have a child now and we need to make it work." He graduated from college first and then he went to the Police Academy. We were just supporting each other constantly. Then he got hired right after the Academy. He had a new demanding career, we had three kids, a mortgage, and I was still going to Sac State. I wanted to finish school because I wanted to finish what I started. I graduated pregnant with my last baby.

All of that added lots of pressure on our marriage. There was lots of yelling on his part and complaining about housework not being done. I figured this was normal as I saw the same pattern with my parents and his. Culturally, women are supposed to be submissive, do all the housework, and deal with the kids. I tried to fit into the perfect stereotype mold, but as he said once, "You always fought me back." I just felt it was a double standard. The kids and the house were just as much his as they were mine. When I started making enough money, I hired a housekeeper once a week to help me. I tried to take care of the kids, the house, and myself, and it was just never enough.

My drive, my perseverance, and just not giving up started during my pregnancy, when I just thought, "If nobody else does it for me, I've got to do it myself." And so I did.

One day it hit me, I already had my three babies, I was sitting there nursing my third child and I looked up and saw my degree on the wall. I thought, "Oh my God. This is not what I signed up for." I've always been an entrepreneur. I was running a licensed daycare at the time so that I was able to stay home with my kids and help out financially. I just thought, "There's something more that I can do and still raise my children." So I got my Real Estate license and I've been practicing Real Estate since 2002. I was very successful until the market took a dive. We lost rental properties and almost lost our home.

If you have the right partner who will encourage you and pick up where you slack and vice versa, then it's possible. My ex-husband and I were a good team in that sense, but something still got lost or was missing in the marriage.

Sonia: What was that piece?

Lucy: Now that I've gone through counseling, I think it goes back to my upbringing. I felt confined when I was growing up, with my father being so strict. And then all of a sudden, I was married and I felt confined, like I was constantly still trying to be that perfect good girl, wife, and mother. Trying to always be on my best behavior, not upsetting my husband, and at the same time, trying to fit in the American dream, where you're working together, you're building something, keeping up with the Joneses or whatever you want to call it. I feel like the forgiveness was missing. I don't think I ever really one-hundred-percent forgave him for abandoning me.

Although he was there and we were building together, I was always the entrepreneur. "What is Lucy going to get into now?" was always his question. He would resist, but he was still letting me do what I had to do. He had the stable income and law enforcement career. He was very traditional and just like my dad, a hard worker and provider, working as a cop. I feel like I got the double whammy: the Machista and the law enforcement control. But I always pushed back. Until one day the rubber band just finally busted.

Sonia: What caused it?

Lucy: I feel like I had taken control of so many responsibilities, making decisions for all of us. But although I was a strong woman, I still wanted to be taken care of. Not so much financially, but I wanted to feel protected. I never understood how he was out there protecting the world, yet I didn't feel protected by him, especially when it came to his family always in our business. I didn't feel as valued for my true virtues, my servitude, my patience, my perseverance. I was trying to move us together up to a better position financially, and so at times, there were lots of put-downs by him when things didn't go right. To this day, he still mocks me. Telling me I'm no entrepreneur, I'm a farce and that I'm not all that. I don't let it bother me anymore because as they say, the proof is in the pudding.

I think he felt like I could take care of my own. He said once, "I thought you could handle it" when I asked him to stand up to his family on my behalf. I just think that I got disconnected from him and tired of him just being on the sidelines. However, the last ten years of our marriage he was the opposite, as I had tried to leave once after eleven years of being together. Feeling like he was losing me, he kissed the ground I walked on to the point where I got suffocated. I felt owned like I was his property. When that happens, you feel so lost inside. Then you hear it from someone else about how wonderful you are, and how beautiful you are, and you feel connected to someone else. You begin to realize there's something missing. Something was definitely off in my marriage.

Sonia: Do you see a correlation or a pattern from your dad in your marriage?

Lucy: Yes, because I never rebelled against my father. All of a sudden, I found myself at forty years of age feeling like when I was a teenage kid with my dad. I began to tell my ex, "Well, you don't own me. You don't control me. You can't tell me what I think. You can't tell me what I feel." I had met someone and fell in love like a silly school girl.

I told my ex-husband what was going on with me emotionally. I ended up moving out of the house and separating, but sometimes when you're in the eye of the hurricane, you just can't see straight. You're just kind of taken over by the emotions. Now I look back and think, "What was I thinking?" I ran the wrong way and did things wrong. I felt like I was cornered. I felt like, for once, I was making a choice, and even though it was a bad choice in the eyes of many, I was making the choice on my own. This man changed my life too. I never saw him as the cause of my divorce. It was just the wrong timing for us as I was married.

I believe feelings aren't good or bad, it's our actions that are good or bad. I learned that the hard way. Nevertheless, I wouldn't erase my mistakes as they are what have given me more wisdom now. I try to do what they say, "Remember the lesson not the disappointment." I've always looked on the bright side of things. And definitely try not to make a mistake twice.

Sonia: Was there a voice inside that you felt was missing? Like the true Lucy wasn't coming out because you didn't have the freedom to express the truest version of who you are?

Lucy: Absolutely. I felt that I was still being silenced. I was still being put in a box of being that good girl, even though I was not a bad girl. I joke about it now, but I went from being the Virgin Mary to Mary Magdalene in the eyes of some people. That was the worst thing that could've happened to me, because I had been so instilled with the idea that being with just one person made you more valuable as a woman. Now that I'm older, I know that's not what makes us valuable. It's not what's between our legs that makes us valuable. It's what's in our hearts. Despite my shortcomings, my intentions were not to hurt anyone. We are human, and we all make mistakes, and sometimes it's because other people cause them, and other times it's because we cause them. In my life, it was both. Both have brought the same feeling of shame, and that was very traumatic to me.

That shame of getting pregnant out of wedlock and not having that person by my side to be there to pick me up, that brought a lot of shame. But I overcame it because I had my child to live for. Then the second time, when I had the affair and all of a sudden, I found myself broken once again, and it was exactly the same feeling of shame. It still went back to a lot of what I had been carrying.

Sometimes, as women, we think of this fairy tale in our head and we're like, "Oh, our Prince Charming is supposed to be this and that." When our Prince Charming doesn't necessarily involve romance. Whether we have that person sweeping us off our feet or not, I don't want to be a princess anymore, I want to be a queen.

Sonia: There you go.

Lucy: This time the fall from grace and the feeling of shame was more powerful, and it was harder for me to get up. I'd dug my head in a hole like an ostrich in the sand. I couldn't seem to find my way out of that black hole. "Oh my God. Everyone is looking at me like I'm some whore of Babylon, when that wasn't the case. I know sometimes egos get in the way, and that's what happened in trying to reconcile my marriage. We tried, but things were worse with his family, and it was just a plan for him to basically do the same to me. The double standards, I tell you, are real. I'm in a better place now, and a big part of where I'm at now has been to forgive, not only my father and my ex, but myself.

Sonia: I know that many women have been in those situations with affairs, and it takes women to a difficult level. What was it like for you personally?

Lucy: This subject is super taboo for women, especially in the Latino culture. Men can have a fling and it doesn't seem to mean anything. They could come back and say, "Oh, it didn't mean anything." Or sometimes they even get a high-five by their buddies. But when it's the female, we are tagged as a whore, and they quickly slap on the Scarlet letter.

If it was up to him and his family, they probably would've loved to have lynched me from a tree and stoned me to death. I endured so much abuse and bullying from his family during and after my divorce. I am still blamed for everything. When it takes two to tango. So now my big advice in marriage is don't let anyone meddle in your marriage. That was our problem: too many people in our business. We didn't stand a chance, especially when he didn't stand up for me.

As women, we have a lot more to lose. But at the same time, I found my own voice. I'm not perfect. I was open with my children and now the day has come when my daughters understand me more as a woman. To me, my children are what matter most.

Sonia: What specific steps did you take to overcome that situation?

Lucy: I did a lot of counseling and soul searching. I actually ended up crawling back to my mom's home for three months. During that time, I really lost myself. I ended up getting a lumpectomy on my left breast because I was diagnosed with precancerous cells. And so I realized the stress was just making me not only emotionally sick but also physically sick. I just held onto my faith and unplanted all the negative thoughts that my ex would tell me like, "You're worthless. You're no good. You're a cheater." Financially, he didn't help me this time around, either. However, since we were married twenty years, I was able to get nine years of pension. I had thought of giving it up as he pleaded with me, but my mentors advised not to. I had helped him in his career and stayed home with the kids. Unfortunately, as I told him he married an entrepreneur, and of the hundreds of thousands I had contributed to our marriage, much was lost when the housing market took a dive.

He would say to me that once someone found out that I've cheated, no one was going to want to be with me. It was almost the same thing as when my mom was saying, "If you lose your virginity and you don't get married to that person, no one's going to want to be with you." I bought that and then again, fast forward twenty-something years later, now it was him telling me I'm worthless. I had been tainted. When the ironic thing was that he was the one to taint me first. So for the longest time, I couldn't be with anyone. I kept my circle of friends small and stayed closer to my family.

Sonia: What was the moment when you felt in your heart that you were finding your voice?

Lucy: Well, we got divorced. I've always worked for myself. Everyone kept telling me, "Go get yourself a job. You have a degree. You are a smart woman." I knew I couldn't work for someone else. I don't know if it was because of my upbringing and my dad being controlling, and then with my ex-husband being controlling, but I've never wanted to work for anybody. I always knew I wanted to work for myself.

It was not until I actually went to work for someone else, and I was working sixty, seventy hours a week, that I realized, "If I put this much work into my own career, I can rebuild myself." It was 2015 when I jumped back into Real Estate and reconnected with an investor. I've been working with him for the last three years and I've learned so much. He's been my mentor, my client, but above all, he's a sincere friend. His experience as a businessman, for me, has helped me grow and see business as just that, business and try to remove the emotional aspect of it. If it wasn't for his entrepreneur knowledge that he has shared with me I would've had to read many more books in business development. This all led to me regaining my self-confidence as a businesswoman. I thought "Wow, Someone believes in me. I'm not incompetent as I was told. I really started believing in myself again.

Sonia: You were rebuilding from that place of vulnerability and rising from the ashes.

Lucy: Yes, I hit rock bottom. Despite all the heartache, I'm grateful because it has taken me where I'm at now. All of this has taught me that everything can be transformed and renewed. I found love again and now I'm in a relationship. I love my boyfriend very much for many reasons, and one of the main reasons is that he lets me be, he's not judgmental, and he is very supportive of my endeavors.

Sonia: I love what you just said. He lets you be. I believe in relationships we should allow each other to be. Even in the Latin culture where there's a sense of ownership.

Lucy: That's what a lot of people don't understand, because you feel owned and trapped when someone is jealous and possessive. Especially when they tell you how to dress, act, not act, or they go through your suitcase to make sure you're not taking anything cute to wear when not around him, and calling you fifty times a day. This is also a form of abuse. I know that now.

Sonia: From all your life experiences, what would you say you gained from those experiences, and from taking responsibility? How did it build your character?

Lucy: Understanding and extending grace to others who failed me. I came full circle with my dad. My parents are no longer together. I experienced them going through a divorce after forty-five years, and so I was put in my children's place when their father and I got divorced, and how both of us would play our children, and I realized that was wrong. All of a sudden, I was forty-five years old and my mom and dad were getting divorced.

My dad met someone else during his divorce process. Shortly into their relationship, she ended up pregnant. Here they were expecting a child and not married. I didn't abandon my dad in this situation. I stood by his side. He was sixty-six and expecting a child, and remember, once upon a time I was nineteen and expecting a child when he turned his back on me. But I didn't turn my back on him, because I put myself in that situation with an unexpected pregnancy, and regardless of the age, the same feelings of fear of the future are still there. I heard his cry because he felt lost, but I said, "Okay. Well, the baby's on his way. What are we going to do?" I did the opposite of what he had done to me. I extended grace and I've been by his side through thick and thin. I love my baby brother. He's two years old now.

Sonia: Where is your relationship now with your dad, seeing that it came full circle?

Lucy: It was not until I was divorced and found myself alone, the second time when I felt alone and abandoned, and my dad this time said, "I'm here no estas sola ... you're not alone." Five years ago in a little French Cafe in Mexico was when I first heard my dad say, "I love you." We both cried and hugged each other.

Sonia: Wow. What a big difference.

Lucy: I needed to hear that because I had been dragging unforgiveness for the lack of love expression from him. I truly forgive my dad. I've also forgiven my ex-husband, and everybody who has hurt me.

Sonia: That's beautiful. When we come full circle in our journey and say, "I have given grace. I've learned how to extend grace to people." Because in reality, everybody has a story and we can't judge right away because we don't know what happened before. We don't know the fullness of it.

Lucy: Yes. At the time when all this was going around, I felt like I was in chaos. I couldn't take the podium and say to everyone what I'm sharing with you now. "Let me tell you my side." I just couldn't then. The shame and the guilt wouldn't let me.

Don't get me wrong, my marriage had a lot of good, but also bad, and people just didn't know that, and the sad part in divorces is when people take sides. The saying is true, "No one knows what goes on behind closed doors," and there's no doubt my ex and I loved each other, it just wasn't healthy love. With him there was never balance. It was black and white, and it went from one extreme to the other.

Sonia: What were the gaps in your marriage and life at the time? What were you looking for?

Lucy: Validation for sure. Validation from my dad and my husband at the time. I now realize that we don't need validation from anyone but ourselves. We have to get to a place of first loving ourselves, accepting ourselves, embracing ourselves. For the longest time, I didn't embrace my womanhood because I had three kids in my twenties and I thought all I was, was a mother and wife. I had to learn to embrace myself and say, "I'm smart, I'm beautiful and yes I am sexy." There's nothing wrong with that.

Sometimes you have to lose yourself to find yourself. So I lost myself and found myself, but now I am constantly improving myself for sure. My mom always said, "Make a message out of your mess." So here I am transparent in hopes that if another woman feels trapped or find herself in a similar situation, she may learn and know she's not alone.

Sonia: I love what you said about learning to embrace yourself. You have to love yourself first in a healthy way.

Lucy: Yes. It's like when you fly, the first thing they tell you is to put your mask on first before you help anybody else, because if you're not taking care of yourself, you can't give the best to the others. And not to feel guilty about it, either. That's always our downfall as women; we feel guilty for everything we do or do not do.

Sonia: Live your life unapologetically. Now, tell me your passions. You've come full circle, you've learned to embrace yourself, you're learning to love life, you're learning to love people, and you love your culture.

Lucy: When I grew up, we didn't go back and forth to Mexico. I was brought up here, but I ended up venturing out and buying property in Mexico, because I do real estate. In the last fourteen years, I've been going back and forth, so I was able to learn more about my culture. Also, I was living in a neighborhood in Sacramento where there were not a lot of Latinos, and I wanted to expose the Mexican culture to my children.

I became involved with the Mexican Culture Center. I was a director of "Reinas Fiestas Patrias" (Mexican American pageant) which I'm going to start getting involved in once again this year. The organization empowers young women, college-bound students, who are pursuing higher education. It's a tradition in Mexico to crown a beauty queen of the town. I've mentored about one hundred young women and they receive a scholarship to pursue their education, but we also instill in them to give back to the community, communicate with the community, and network with the community.

That's how I started getting involved with the traditions of our festivities, promoting the beauty of our music, food, and culture. I graduated from Sac State, so I was also President of the Latino Alumni back in 2002. I love being part of everything that has to do with encouraging women and higher education.

The culinary passion actually stemmed from when I was pregnant with my son. I wanted to feed my baby healthy food, and growing up, my mom always cooked homemade meals. I would call her up for recipes since I couldn't go home during my pregnancy. I would get together with my good friend Janine and cook dinner all the time. I have my grandmother's tortilla maker and I made homemade tortillas.

I take great joy in cooking and preparing meals for my friends and family. Love is my main ingredient. I love watching their smiles as they taste my food, mainly authentic Mexican food, which comes from my Mommy.

Sonia: I know you have a passion for cooking and travel. What else are you embracing in life right now?

Lucy: Right now I am embracing the idea of just being kind. It doesn't take much to be nice. We're starving for kindness as a country right now, and we need to focus on the good and strive to do something to better our world. You waste more energy being angry and spending your time beating up yourself or others with guilt and shame. That doesn't bring health emotionally, spiritually, or physically, because without that balance we really can't get anywhere.

Just be grateful and thankful and have faith. My faith is what really got me through it all. If you have faith, and mine is Christianity, you know that He has forgiven us for whatever we do. It doesn't mean that you're going to go off and do it again. You have to learn. I had this professor who told me when I got pregnant with my son, "Don't ever see your child as a mistake. He was a surprise." If something happens once, it's not a mistake. I've had many surprises in life.

Sonia: Where do you see yourself five years from now?

Lucy: I see myself back on my throne saying, "That's my castle and I've built it from the ground up, I managed to get out of the rubble." Maybe in five years, I will have grandchildren as my kids are getting older. I see myself financially stable and helping other people, my businesses are taking off because I plan to have more than one business. But Real Estate will always be one of them. Of course, I will be traveling and using my little bit of French and Italian. And maybe eventually open a little cafe spot in Sacramento. You see, I'm no longer in that box anymore. Ever!

Sonia: One last question. What would you say to those women who are still stuck and don't know how to take the next step?

Lucy: Just take a step. You may fall thinking you're diving into a crystal-clear pool, only to discover that it was freaking dark with hard cement on the bottom. But keep in mind that you will always find your way back up.

Paul Coelho is one of my favorite authors, and he says, "Tell your heart that the fear of suffering is worse than the suffering itself, and no heart has ever suffered when it goes in search of its dream." Take that leap even if you fall on your face. You get back up. That's the beauty of it.

Sometimes we work ourselves up and stress about so much but it's all about perspective. I ask myself these two questions when I hit an obstacle in life now:

1. Am I going to die?

2. Am I going to jail?

If both answers are no, then I just find a solution and get on with it, or as the British say, "Carry on."

Sonia: Thank you so much, Lucy. I love your story. It has taught me about character and perseverance and learning to embrace yourself, learning to love yourself again, and how ultimately, there is hope.

Lucy: Thank you so much for encouraging me to share this.

Sonia Hassey

ABOUT LUCY GARCIA

Lucy Garcia attended California State University, Sacramento, and was the first in her family to graduate with a bachelor's degree in Spanish Literature and a minor in Criminal Justice.

She has been involved with the Latino promoting higher education through culture, art and fashion. She served as the CSUS Latino Alumni President 2003-2005. She was the Mexican American Pageant Director and helped organize the Mexican Independence Day in Sacramento for Northern California 2006-20011 and will resume the role as Director once again, this May 2019. Lucy has a passion for helping and has raised money for LLS, breast cancer and numerous other needy causes in Sacramento.

Lucy began her career in real estate in 2002 and rapidly developed a very successful practice, receiving awards for production and service. In her first year, she acquired Masters Club status. Lucy's continual inspiration is the joy on the faces of her first-time buyers when they acquire their new homes. Lucy soon branched out as an International Realtor and received her Certified International Property Specialist (CIPS) designation through National Association of Realtors. She is helping clients across the borders and recently joined ExP Realty and has a team with her friend Anna Padilla and growing their business. She is a California Notary and in the last year has ventured into being an Airbnb host.

Lucy has three adult children who she adores, Andre (27), Izabella (22) and Vanessa (19).

CHAPTER 8

Family, Community, and Faith

Diana Becton

Sonia: Hi, I am honored to have Diana Becton, District Attorney of Contra Costa County, here with me to share the powerful story of her journey and how she has learned to transform and overcome and become the woman she is today. So Diana, why don't you start your story from the beginning?

Diana: There's an educator, Thomas Groome, who talks about the connectedness of time. Everything that happened in the past shapes and informs who we are today, and who we're going to be tomorrow. So I start my story on the St. James River in Virginia. I recently visited Virginia, and I learned that the St. James River was a point of entry where slave ships landed, and it was where my ancestors may have first touched ground in America. My ancestors were transported across the Atlantic, in the hull of a ship, packed in like sardines, for ninety to 120 days. Many did not survive the journey. The "black human cargo" was unloaded in the dark of night, so as not to offend the "good white" people in town. My ancestors were "cleaned up" and taken to the auction block to be sold as chattel. That is where my story in America begins.

My Aunt Ruthie traces our story to slavery in the "Georgia Sea Islands," and then to Louisiana. My grandparents were part of the folks who migrated, leaving the life in the "Jim Crow South," where it was difficult for blacks to live due to poverty, oppressive systems, racial segregation, the Ku Klux Klan, and lynching. Sadly, today, there is a museum in Alabama that documents at least four thousand lynchings in the United States. Wanting a better future, my parents came to Oakland, California. My grandparents came too, and they lived nearby in "Russell City," which was actually in present-day Hayward, California.

I grew up living in almost two different worlds. In Oakland, my sisters, Gerrie, Carol, and I were city folk, sometimes called "the Becton girls." I'm the youngest daughter in my family. My father was an aircraft mechanic, and my mom, a self-employed beautician. My grandparents lived in Russell City on a farm, owned their land, and maintained a lifestyle that was similar to the way they had lived back home in Louisiana. At their home, actually a trailer, we cooked on a wood-burning stove, used an outhouse, and got all our food from the land. There were animals, chickens, cows, and pigs, a hearty vegetable garden, and my grandmother maintained her own bees for honey. We got fresh eggs from the hencoop every morning. We bathed in a big tin round tub, used an outhouse, and had to draw water from a pump. Some of my favorite memories are of my grandmother teaching me how to cook, on that wood-burning stove.

On the weekends, we drove twenty minutes to Russell City to live with our grandparents, and then we'd go back to Oakland to be regular city girls. We lived in a small community in East Oakland. People didn't have a lot; most had come from, and endured the tough times in the South. There was a strong sense of community, however, and people always helped each other out. We played outside, jacks, hopscotch, and street ball. We got dirty, watched cartoons, and our parents yelled through the window when it was time to come in and eat. All the neighbors could tell you what to do, and you knew not to talk back. We had home cooked meals and Kool-Aid for dinner every night. We always had to be inside when the streetlights came on.

When he wasn't working, or tinkering, my father loved to garden, and he maintained a wonderful garden full of fresh greens, tomatoes, corn, and peas. When he harvested the garden, of course, everyone in the neighborhood got fresh vegetables. And when folks across the street went fishing and caught a good crop, we all received fresh fish. So that was the sense of community in which I grew up.

But I'm also shaped by the times in which I grew up—the '50s and '60s. It was the civil rights movement, the black power movement, and I watched little Ruby Bridges take the first steps to integrate schools in the South. People were sitting in, attempting to integrate lunch counters, I watched people get hosed and attacked by dogs simply for trying to get equal rights in this country. The Black Panthers started free breakfast programs, which FBI director J. Edgar

Hoover said was probably the most dangerous thing, because the Panthers were winning not only the hearts and minds of young kids, but also their parents. All those things shaped me, including the death of Martin Luther King Jr, and the death of President Kennedy.

Sonia: How old were you when Kennedy died, and do you have vivid memories of that time?

Diana: I was in junior high school, and yes, I have very vivid memories. I also remember the death of Malcolm X and Robert Kennedy. It was a time when there was so much change, so much turmoil. My parents, still living with the fear of the "Jim Crow South," warned us to stay away from all the "movements," but I was determined to take part in all that was happening.

Besides our close community and our close family, I also had my faith community. My family belonged to a church in East Oakland called Allen Temple Baptist Church, and it was there where I grew up. Along with my sisters, I went to Sunday school and sang in the choir. So much of our lives centered on the church. That's also where a group called the Business and Professional Women that influenced me.

Sonia: Wow. That's wonderful to have that group in the church.

Diana: It was amazing because I didn't have to go looking for role models outside of my family and community. I had these strong women with amazing professions who were doing wonderful work in the community, and who were focused on raising money for scholarships to send young people to college. I think some of the values my people brought from the South had to do with making sure they were giving us a better life than they had. These women had a big focus on education and giving young people the opportunity that they did not have. They played a big role in shaping who I became as a young woman.

Also at the time, the new church pastor, Reverend Dr. J. Alfred Smith Sr., came to town. Later, he wrote a book in which he talked about what he saw upon arriving in East Oakland. It was rough. Men on the corner drinking, prostitutes on the street. He came to church one Sunday and said, "We're not going to sit in the lazy rocking chairs of religion. We're going to get into our community and make a difference."

I was about sixteen years old, and that certainly shaped who I am and why I have such a strong sense of giving back to my community.

Sonia: I love that. That's where you learned that it was up to you to take responsibility to get out and make a difference in the lives of people. You were in high school then. How was high school for you?

Diana: High school was a mixture. Some of it was very really fun. Those years were some of the best. I was involved in student government, and I was on the yell and cheerleader team. I built friendships with women who are still my girlfriends to this day. There are five of us who continue to be the best of friends, and we gather annually to spend time together. When we get together it's just like it was yesterday. We call ourselves the sisters from "the hood."

But high school was also a tumultuous time because we were in the midst of the civil rights movement, the birth of black power, the Black Panthers, and it was all happening in real time for us. I remember going down to city hall where the Black Panthers stood wearing black leather jackets and black berets. My sister Carol and I had to sneak out to the rallies because my parents who still carried the fear of the "Jim Crow South," said we couldn't be involved in the rallies. There were riots and all kinds of things. And we were finding out who we were, and starting to talk about black is beautiful and about black power.

I started to wear my hair in an afro, I was so proud. My mom and dad were afraid of what the afro symbolized, and there was this struggle about my hair. I was eventually forced by my parents to "straighten" my hair and look "normal," which I now understand was the tension between "safety" and "freedom."

With the help of an amazing teacher, Dr. Cecelia Arrington, we developed a black studies department. It was probably one of the first in the country and we began to study our history, our stories, because you know, the history books did not include us. Dr. Arrington was an incredibly strong woman who helped us navigate through this difficult time, and she also helped us build something beautiful: our black student union. This gave us a voice, and a lens through which to filter all the things we were going through.

We began to learn from our own stories, and to learn what an incredible race of people we came from. So that was my high school years.

Sonia: Wow, that's so incredible. You grew up in such an interesting time. Again, this was building a foundation for you. After high school did you get ready to go to college?

Diana: I always knew I was going to go to college, but my family didn't have the resources. No one in my family had gone to college yet, and we didn't know much about it. I knew about San Francisco State because I attended rallies there, so I applied and was accepted. I was an economics major, and I loved working on topics about our economy, numbers, and math. It was my passion, and math is still a strong skill for me. But then I took some different turns. I wanted to be a lawyer from the time I was a little girl, but I didn't know how to get there. The only lawyer I'd ever seen was Perry Mason on television.

During the civil rights movement, I saw how lawyers were able to make changes through court cases, and by passing laws to make things fair and more equitable for everyone. I learned that law was a career where you could make changes in our society. But I didn't go to law school right away because I wanted to work and get out into the world.

After college, I started working at a finance company where I became a manager and eventually made my way into the field of Housing and Community Development. It was there that I was supervising a unit of housing counselors for the city of Richmond, when I made contact with legal aid lawyers who wanted to train us to help the public with questions about landlord-tenant law. The experience reminded me that I still had a dream inside of me to be a lawyer, which I shared with one of the attorneys. He said, "Well, you should just go to law school." And I thought, "Wow, but I need to work; I need to have my job; I'm married now." But I applied to go to law school at night so I could continue to work, and then both of my sons were born during the time that I was in law school.

It was a good time, but a tough time, because I was juggling a whole lot of things at once: family, school, and a full-time job. And all those things were priorities. My last semester of school was tough. I was carrying my youngest son, I was trying to finish up, but it was a difficult pregnancy. The doctor said I could either go to work, or I could go to school at night, but not both. I knew I needed to work, so I missed the entire semester of school. I had to come home and be on bed rest in order to take care of the health of my child. So again, it was a tough time.

Sonia: How did that make you feel during that time while you were trying to pursue your goals?

Diana: I was trying to pursue my goals and I was so close to graduating, but I had not been able to study or attend classes. Shortly after my son was born, I called up my mom one day and said, "You know, I'm going to have to come back to this later. There's no way I can finish school now because I've got two kids. I'm still working, and it's impossible for me to make up a whole semester of school."

There was a long silence on the phone, and I said, "Mom, are you still there?" She said, "We're not quitting. We've worked too hard to get where we are and we're not quitting." I took a week off, packed up my children, and went to my mom's house early in the morning. She was a beautician by trade and her shop was built on to our home. She and her customers literally just put me in a room, brought me food and tea at certain intervals, and the women took care of my children as they were coming in for their appointments to get their hair done. They rocked the babies, fed them, played with them, and did everything that needed to happen so I could study and take my final exams. So that's how I finished law school.

Sonia: What an incredible support system. What an encouragement from your mom! How did that make you feel?

Diana: My mom was always one of my biggest supporters. I miss her; she passed away a few years ago. She was always one of my biggest fans, but she never really had an opportunity to fulfill her own dreams due to the circumstances at the time. She wanted to be a teacher, however, that would have meant going away to college, because she lived in a small town in the south with no opportunity for higher education. And her parents, my grandparents, would not allow her to go to college, out of fear for her safety, because she was an only child and they didn't know anyone in the town where she would have gone to school.

They were like, "No, who's going to watch you? We can't send you there." Eventually, they found a beauty school where she could go to learn to be a beautician, and they knew a woman in town who would watch over my mother as she did her studies. My mother pursued this profession, but it was never in her heart. It was never her dream. Even when she moved to California, she thought she was going to work in an office, so she became excellent at typing and all those things.

Back in those days the job ads were in the newspaper, and my mom and her girlfriend called every single job to make sure each one was open, and they headed out on the train. At the time, you took the San Francisco train. And they knocked on every single door, but once the people saw that they were black, they said the jobs were no longer available. And every door closed, every single door. They must have gone to twenty or thirty places, and everyone said, "We don't have any jobs here for you." So that was tough for my mother.

It is probably why, when we had to face something difficult, she would always tell us to "brace up!" But she had a business and she was good at it, and that's what she did. It's how she helped support our family along with my father, and it allowed her to pretty much be a stay-at-home mom, and a businesswoman at the same time. In a way, it was a good thing, at least for our family, because she was there for us as we grew up.

Sonia: I would call her a very brave woman.

Diana: Yes. Both my parents were great influences. They loved reading, and they introduced us to books and the power of learning early on. For my parents to have a daughter graduate from law school was huge, a really big deal.

Sonia: When you graduated, how old were your kids at that time?

Diana: I had an eighteen-month-old son, Justin, and Kevin was six weeks old.

Sonia: What was your transition from there?

Diana: Believe it or not, at first, I didn't want to necessarily practice law. I'd been doing a lot of work in housing and real estate and community development. I was a real estate broker and putting together partnerships to help people buy property. But one day, I took on a case. In Alameda County, you could volunteer to serve as a lawyer for indigent clients, and I took the case of a woman who was being evicted from her apartment. I had to go to trial on her case, and we won. That helped me realize that it was a good space for me, so I started working at a small firm in Point Richmond. We became partners and grew the firm. We had about five lawyers working for us.

Thereafter, I went solo and opened my own business. A couple of years later, the governor appointed me to a seat as a judge. That came about in such an interesting way. A friend of mine, a judge who, I had appeared before several times, said, "I think you would make a wonderful judge and you should put in your application." This went back and forth for about a year, and finally I did. But I got a message back, basically letting me know that my application was dead on arrival because the governor was Republican and I was not. But I had friends—Democrats and Republicans—pulling and pushing for me, and it took a good long while, but I was finally able to get the attention of the governor's office with their joint support, and I was appointed by Governor Pete Wilson in 1995 to serve as a judge.

I was involved in the community, and doing work that I loved, helping people, and giving back in a powerful way. It was an amazing time for me to be sworn in. I was the third African-American judge in Contra Costa County. Judge George Carroll was the first, Judge Patricia McKinley was the second, and I was the third. For many, many years, I was the only African-American judge in the county. I became the first African American judge to serve the Superior Court of Contra Costa.

My career took off right from the start. I was elected Presiding Judge of the Richmond court, and I moved to Martinez to take on more difficult cases. I supervised the felony criminal calendar department, which was over the plea-bargaining in the county. I went to the civil division and became a supervisor, and I handled Juvenile, and almost every assignment that you can imagine. Finally, I was elected Presiding Judge of the entire court, which means I was over the whole court including the budget. I was the first person of color to serve as Presiding Judge. Also, I led the team that was instrumental in implementing our courts' strategic plan.

I served during a difficult time of court budget cuts, and we had to do a lot of work to figure out how to best serve our community, but at the same time, cut back drastically without cutting staff. We had to close courthouses and make tough decisions about how to keep the doors open.

I became president of the National Association of Women Judges, the nation's leading voice for women in the judiciary, and also served in many state and national positions and became a leader in our justice system.

In 2017, the former district attorney resigned after pleading to felony charges, and my phone started ringing immediately with folks asking me if I would put my name in to be considered, to bring my leadership skills, a fresh set of eyes, and a new way of doing things in the criminal justice system. The Board of Supervisors selected me out of twelve candidates to become the first woman and the first person of color to serve as the district attorney in Contra Costa County, in 168 years, since the office was founded in 1850. From there, I stood for election and survived a grueling race that tested me in so many ways. Every day, I had to really dig down, pray, and find the strength to keep going, day by day. In 2018, the people elected me to a full four-year term. So here I am.

Sonia: That was incredible. You've accomplished so much. There are a lot of women out there who have accomplished one or two major things, but every time you step into a position, it's like you are already ready for the next position and the next position. What has been your driving force? It could mean your "Why." What has kept driving you to pursue something greater for a greater impact?

Diana: It goes back to what I learned growing up, and that is there's a responsibility for wherever you are in life. I've been given so much, and afforded so many opportunities, and there's a saying: "To whom much has been given; much is expected." I've always embraced that saying, and I've always understood it. I know that wherever I am, wherever I've been blessed to be, I have an opportunity to leave things better than the way I found them, and to help others along the way. That's been my driving force: I understand that I'm there to give back, to help others, and to make sure the doors are always open for the next person to come behind me.

Sonia: That is so incredible. I'm proud that you're a woman! Looking back at your journey, I have two questions. Did you have mentors who helped take you to that next level? And if so, who are they and how did they do that for you?

Diana: Yes. Of course, I mentioned the Business and Professional Women, the church women. I love them because they did show me what it meant to be successful, and to always be thinking about giving back. So all of those women were my "she-roes," if you will, from the time I was a little girl. Of course, there is Dr. J. Alfred Smith Sr., the pastor I mentioned, an amazing "giant of a man" who is still in my life encouraging me today. He's always been a mentor and role model, and a man I just totally look up to in so many ways.

Shirley Chisholm is another person that I love, especially as I've moved into this arena of running for office. I so appreciate how she described herself as the people's politician, and how, in her own words, she was "un-bought and un-bossed." I absolutely love that. I strive to see myself that way because I understand clearly that it was the power of the everyday people who got me where I am today, and I have a total responsibility to always give back, to open doors, and to try to change our criminal justice system so that it works for everybody and gives equal justice to everyone.

You asked about mentors, and there were just so many different people over time. In addition to my mom, and of course my sisters, and women like Fannie Lou Hamer, Sojourner Truth, and all the women upon whose shoulders I stand, certainly influenced my life. There are others.

Sonia: I want to talk about the power of community. When I say that, what is the first thing that pops in your head?

Diana: The first thing that pops in my head is a story about my oldest son, Justin. Of course, I have two sons and I love them both dearly and I'm so proud of each of them and what they've accomplished. My youngest son, Kevin, is a college counselor and he helps young people navigate their way through college; it's an amazing position. My oldest son Justin is a professor of neuroscience and loves teaching.

But when Justin was about three years old, he was burned. Talk about one of the toughest times in my life. It was the most difficult period that I've ever lived through. But an entire community came to support us, to support my family, and just to be whatever we needed them to be to help us through that difficult time.

At that time, Children's Hospital didn't have accommodations for families, and so at night, I would sleep underneath my son's bed so that I could stay all night. And then I would go home in the morning to get dressed for work, and I'd rush back to feed him and all of that, and stay with him as long as I could before I left for work. And all through the day, there was generally someone who was with him to help us through that difficult period. My friend Sonia Carter was there every day when I walked in after work. Every day she was with my son.

Sonia: An angel was there.

Diana: Yes. She was like an angel who was at his bedside every day. It's people like her who have given so much to me, who give meaning to the word "community" for me.

I also want to emphasize that community means the power of giving back in whatever way that you can, and sometimes it's not on a grand scale, like being a district attorney. Sometimes it's on a small scale, and it's in those quiet places where people need you and you're just there, being that presence for them.

Sonia: What you just said about community is so valuable. I love that. It's not necessarily about position, but it's the people who are in our lives in the hardest times. We all experience it, and in those moments, we say, "You were there. You were like the mother, the sister, the brother, the pastor," right? We can't do life alone, but our culture is so fast-paced now that it feels like we're supposed to do it all ourselves. But we are missing something. We have a gap in our culture, and we are missing the power of friendships. We can't let that go.

Diana: Family and community and faith are always in the mix of things for me.

Sonia: I believe that in our personal lives, in business, in every area of our lives—relationships and community should be a big part of who we are. It's all about people, and once we can truly embrace that, we can live a fulfilled life.

Diana: Yes, that's right, because in today's time we have so much busyness in our lives, so many distractions. And sometimes we forget the importance of family, friends, and community. But those are the relationships that sustain us. Some people say their business sustains them, but I think friendships sustain me. It goes back to family and faith and community, every single time.

Sonia: That's so beautiful. I see that you're so thankful that your family built that foundation for you. Just like how you talked about your dad gardening and sharing with everybody, that's the beauty of community: sharing and loving.

What would you say to those women who are reading your story and thinking, "Wow, she had hardships, but she persevered. I also have dreams that I have not yet fulfilled. I'm afraid to take those steps." What would you say to those women?

Diana: I'd say to follow your dreams. Always follow your dreams. Every one of us has something inside of us that perhaps we've forgotten about, but the dream still lives inside us. I think my story is a testimony to the fact that we don't have to take the steps in order. Sometimes there are hardships in between, sometimes we get sidetracked or knocked down, but we have to keep getting back up and back on the path, stay in the fight. Sometimes we have to eliminate distractions from our lives, too, that keep us from following our dreams.

Know that if you step out in faith to follow your dreams, even though it seems hard, and you don't know how it's going to come out, there will always be someone there to help. There's going to be a mentor, a friend, a family member, or whole communities that will help support you on your journey. So follow your dreams!

Sonia: I love that. My step of faith was making that first phone call. Just a phone call. And it took me to the next step, then the next step. I absolutely love that because we're all created for a purpose, and when we step out, everything can line up for you. The right people happen to come into our paths. It's an incredible journey when we step out of our comfort zones.

Diana, thank you so much for sharing your powerful story that began with your ancestry and continued as you followed your dreams and built a community. That's what makes you a Woman of Destiny.

Diana: Thank you so much being the leader of *Destiny Talks* and bringing these stories out so they can be shared with others.

Sonia Hassey

ABOUT DIANA BECTON

District Attorney Diana Becton has spent most of her professional career as a judge, lawyer, and manager. In 2017, she was sworn in as the 25th District Attorney for the Contra Costa County District Attorney's Office. Following her appointment from the Board of Supervisors, she was elected to the position in June 2018. District Attorney Becton served for 22 years as a judge in Contra Costa County, where she was elected as Presiding Judge.

District Attorney Becton is Past President of the National Association of Women Judges, the nation's leading voice for women in the judiciary, and Past Chair of the State Bar Council on Access and Fairness.

Her top priority is keeping the streets of Contra Costa County safe from dangerous and violent criminals. District Attorney Becton is committed to safeguarding our communities from crimes that threaten our health, well-being, and livelihood, protecting our seniors, and working on positive outcomes for our youth.

District Attorney Becton leads a prosecutorial office of approximately 200 lawyers, investigators, and staff. She is the first woman, and the first African-American to serve as Contra Costa District Attorney since the office was established in 1850.

A native of California she is a product of Oakland Public schools and a graduate of Golden Gate University School of Law. Most recently, District Attorney Becton earned a Master of Theological Studies at Pacific School of Religion.

District Attorney Becton has received the following honors: Madam C. J. Walker, 2018, Pioneer Award, National Coalition of 100 Black Women, Inc., Oakland Bay Area Chapter, Woman on Fire Award, Ladies In red (2019), Judge of the Year (2017), Black Women Lawyers of Southern California; National Bar Association - Judicial Council, Thurgood Marshall Award 2017 (Toronto, Canada); League of Women Voters, Contra Costa County, "Social Justice Award"; CABL Bernard S. Jefferson, Judge of the Year (2016); California Women Lawyers, "Rose Bird Memorial Award" (2012); Honor for positive contributions to the City of Richmond (2016); National Organization of Black Law Enforcement, "Trail Blazer" for Community Service (2014); BWOPA Honoree 2013; American Business Women's Association (2012) "Women of Distinction"; California Women Lawyers, (2011-2012) Women of Distinction"; KGO Channel 7 "African American Salute (2012); "Judicial Excellence Award," California Association of Black Lawyers, Judicial Section (2011); "Judge of the Year" Alameda-Contra Costa Trial Lawyers Association (2007); "Award of Judicial Excellence, Charles Houston Bar Association" (2006); Black Women Lawyers of Northern California (2011). She was inducted into the Castlemont High School Hall of Fame in 2007, receiving the highest honor, as a "Knight in Shining Armor," and she received the "Dumlao Martial Arts Image Award" (2011) for leadership and character within the martial arts studio.

District Attorney Becton serves is a frequent lecturer and panelist, and she continues to participate in many community outreach activities. She convened "Clean Slate Day" helping individuals to clean up their criminal records. In 2015, District Attorney Becton served as Co-Chair of the "Know Your Rights" Youth Symposium for West Contra Costa County, as part of a national dialogue to educate youth in our communities, and to open the lines of communication between youth and law enforcement. She serves on the Board of Directors for Castlemont High School Alumni Association, and mentors students who are frequent visitors. District Attorney Becton has two adult sons.

CHAPTER 9

Living My Best Life Fearlessly

Roseann Torres

Sonia: Hi, I am here with Roseann Torres and she is going to share her story with us. Roseann, tell us who you are and what you do.

Roseann: I'm the founding attorney of Torres Law Group Inc. in Oakland, California. I started my own law firm after I left my position as a Deputy District Attorney with the prosecutor's office in

Stockton, where I was born. I have been in private practice for going on fifteen years, since early 2004, when I relocated to Oakland, where I am also serving my second elected term on the Oakland school board.

My family on my mother's side has been in Stockton and Lodi for many years. In fact, I was third generation, and my daughter was also born there. She is fourth gen.

My great-grandparents on my mom side migrated to California from Mexico around 1920, and ended up in the central valley, eventually becoming grape farmers in Lodi. It always brings me great joy and pride to think of my great-grandparents story, because when they made it to Northern California, they had no money so they lived in an abandoned train, as many people apparently did back then, on the Islands just to the west of Stockton. They each were very determined and through hard work, they managed to purchase several acres of land in Lodi where they began to grow grapes. This land included three homes that they built, and when I was a young girl, my family lived briefly in one of the homes. My great-grandparents lived on one side of us and my uncle and aunt on the other. It is interesting that today I have made a great life in Oakland, in an extremely urban setting, yet I grew up on a farm and have beautiful memories of spending hours either sitting in the cherry tree eating cherries or running up and down the fields eating dusty grapes right off the vine. I have a dream of growing a small patch of grapes so my husband and I can produce our own wine someday.

Although I had a lot of family in Lodi and Stockton on my mother's side, for the next several years, my parents uprooted our lives to move back and forth to Mexico where my father had all his family.

He would convince my mother how important it was that I speak Spanish, experience Mexican culture but also he had numerous business ideas he would sell her on, these were "get rich quick" schemes. My mom was unable to say no to these constant moves. So this back and forth between two countries went on until I was nine, and usually my mother would get depressed and convince my father to move back to Stockton or there were the times, she simply sent me on a plane with a relative and followed later.

The reality was, my parents' marriage was in shambles because of my father's repeated infidelity and the lack of financial stability. However, an amazing thing happened during this tumultuous time. My mother had become so depressed and even suicidal during a time when we lived in Guadalajara. I was about six. She turned to her sister Chris back in Stockton for advice and desperate help. My aunt had begun seeing a man who was a Nichiren Buddhist and she explained the basic concept is that you chant Nam Myoho Renge Kyo to become happy. My mother found out where the local gathering of Buddhists was in Guadalajara so she could try it for herself, and I recall my mother took me with her to a stranger's home where several folks were sitting on the floor and chanting. I was just a child and did not understand what chanting was, but my mother felt something instantly, so she made a decision then and there to convert and joined the organization called Soka Gakkai International (SGI). This did not go over well with my Catholic father, though he never attended church nor prayed. My mother did become stronger and more resilient so much so that one night, while my father was out with his girlfriends, my mother purchased two Greyhound tickets to Stockton and we left, riding the bus back took over three days. We did not say goodbye or tell my father we were leaving. Interestingly, my mother still chants and that was 1974. I began chanting at age fourteen when I was a freshman dropout in high school.

School was not easy for me because I was never very anchored in academics from missing tons of school. All that shuffling between two countries made me became very shy and it was hard to make friends. Being the new kid in class and late to the start of the school year is pretty disruptive. It was also confusing to go from Catholic schools in Mexico with very strict environments, to public schools in Stockton where things were a lot more relaxed and kids had different manners and things were more chaotic. Finally, my parents divorced when I was twelve after they bought a new home in Stockton at a time when my father was making great money selling life insurance. I was in seventh grade attending middle school in Lodi, and although we lived in a brand-new home in a new development, things became financially strained because my father left and remarried right away, having two more children. This meant no child support or help with the mortgage. My mother had been a stay-at-home wife, so she was forced into the workforce of low-wage jobs with only a high school diploma. I recall that before the divorce, coming home from school my family ate dinner together, both my parents were great cooks, and after my parents split up, I would get home after a forty-five-minute bus ride, my dinner in the oven because my mother got a job that worked swing or graveyard shift. I was a classic latchkey kid and I started acting out immediately. I became a bit of a class clown, often talking back to teachers or classmates, and spent many afternoons sitting in the principal's office. I was suspended repeatedly, and my mother stopped picking me up because she was afraid to lose her job if she kept leaving early to pick me up for getting in trouble. Heading into high school things got worse.

My best friend and I decided to go to the same high school, a local Catholic school that my mother could not afford but my grandmother decided to lend a hand, and within a few months, I found myself alone when my best friend got a boyfriend and spent all her time with him. I was still pretty shy at school and extremely awkward at making friends. Then I began to be bullied by two boys in some of my classes and I did not tell anyone because they were jocks. I dropped out around January of freshman year, at which point my mother forced me to go the Buddhist youth activities on Sundays. I loved the gatherings and quickly made friends, which is why thirty-six years have passed and I am still chanting today.

Sonia: What was that like? Did you just wake up and decide you weren't going to go anymore?

Roseann: I just reached a breaking point. I didn't have my best friend anymore. Plus I had two guys bullying me on a regular basis, while I suffered in silence because there was no "anti-bullying campaign" invented yet. I didn't like the school that I was going to and I only chose that high school because I insisted on following my best friend. My mom was surprised of course, but I had already gone through two years of post-divorce anxiety and anger making me an out-of-control teen. I had been skipping more and more school in junior high; I guess it was inevitable. I used to hide from the bus after my mom went to work, and I'd stay home and watch TV all day. *The*

Brady Bunch, Gilligan's Island, Eight is Enough. MTV was invented around this time, so it was MTV raising me. Nobody was around to tell me to do chores or homework, for that matter. So by the time I got to ninth grade, I already knew that my mom was lenient enough that she couldn't control me. She didn't know how to make an intervention happen. She just didn't have the bandwidth as a single mom with little support. She was a young mom herself, in fact, she had me at eighteen a few months after graduating from high school.

Like kids today, people don't really know the full effect that divorce can have on kids, and the middle school years, twelve to fourteen, are rather brutal. Most people probably did not think that my life was as stressful as it was because I lived in the same home, in a quiet neighborhood, but the house was a skeleton. There wasn't an opportunity to talk to a counselor and we didn't have any money to go to therapy. When my dad left, it was financial destitution for my mom and me. Before, he was the high wage earner and we had a brand-new house, new cars, new clothes, and I remember shopping at Macy's was routine for special Easter outfits. But after he left, my mother had to work two jobs, sometimes three, and my aunt who used to sew was now making me clothes.

Sonia: Okay, so at fourteen years old, you were at home. How long were you out of school?

Roseann: I stayed out of school the rest of my freshman year beginning in January, so half a year.

Sonia: What did you do on a daily basis?

Roseann: I literally continued the routine of what I did in middle school, watching TV nonstop for hours on end. I had no siblings, so there was no one to play with or engage with. My mom was always working is how I recall this period of my life, but she asked me to participate in the SGI Buddhist youth activities. She wanted me to be around young people who were doing something positive. So on Sundays, I was given a ride for two hours over to Daly City where SGI youth gathered all day to chant, to study Buddhism, and to practice for a local parade or some other festival. I was drawn to the drill team then.

I had a new routine weekly, stay home all week, and on Sunday mornings at seven a.m., get in the car with other young Buddhist girls and head up to Daly City to the center for a day of activities. There were hundreds of girls and boys from throughout the Bay area as far as Sacramento, Stockton, and San Jose. The "Youth Division" of SGI was for those twelve to thirty years old, and for the first time in my life, I was exposed to young career women of all races, and I had never seen that in Stockton. It was pretty cool to meet women with cool new sports cars, nice clothes who were also single and had their own money. I made friends with a Chinese woman who was a banker, and developed a very close friendship with a Black woman who was a stockbroker. At that time I had no idea what stocks were. She turned out to be one of my lifelong mentors and close friends after I grew up and was in college. Our friendship lasted many decades and although she passed away in her late forties from cancer, I can attribute many of my strengths to emulating her over the years. We all went through struggles and challenges together and were always there for each other to chant for each other dreams or overcoming whatever was holding us back. So that's where I began to turn things around and I never left the network of SGI family, where today I still find my true inspiration and comradery when things get really hard as they often do.

Sonia: Was that the beginning of your inspiration and your realization that there had to be something better out there?

Roseann: Definitely. I was inspired by new friends in the Buddhist community, these professional women, earning a salary, living in their own apartments without men or kids as a goal, I realized that education leads to independence and financial security. I recall as a teen, I was not interested in marriage, kids, or anything "typical." I think back to when I was in middle school and high school, and although I wish that a caring adult would have intervened at school to ask why I was suddenly acting out and getting into so much trouble, but alas I did return to finish high school, yet that was not a complete transformation yet. In tenth grade, I got into a rough crowd at a new school and started cutting school pretty fast, plus I drank and smoked pot on the regular. Some of my friends were even selling drugs. I ended up in that "cool" crowd but inside I was confused because I knew I wanted to be like the women I saw on Sunday in Daly City. Every Sunday at my SGI activities, I used to ponder this double life I was leading. I finally had this notion that I wanted to go to college and have a career to buy my own way in life, but Monday would come, and I had to fit back into my crowd and be cool, so cutting school to get high or drink was how I scraped by in high school. After I graduated high school, and just barely, mind you, because my grades and GPA were horrible, I wanted to work. None of my friends were talking about college anyway. They were talking about getting married, one had dropped out to have a baby and another one was also pregnant.

Sonia: And somehow you enjoyed both?

Roseann: Yes, I enjoyed both. I completely enjoyed diverse situations, probably from being raised back and forth Mexico and California. I had the ability to traverse two entirely different environments of church services on weekends, to a rough, rowdy crowd at school all week.

In my late teens and into my twenties, my friendships deepened with the Buddhist friends, so that influence won out. At first, I was not headed to college because my mom said we didn't have the money for tuition, so I got a full-time job that I found in the newspaper ads. I found myself working at a printing company owned by a woman named Eleanor who was a tough old broad with three stores. I ran one of the copy centers with her son as the manager. It was interesting to see a woman entrepreneur first hand, especially with the other Buddhist influences of professional women. It didn't take long to see that Eleanor was serious about her business, because she had to fire her son who was never working even though he was paid a nice salary. He was often off golfing, or at Kiwanis, or some other club. I was basically running the whole business at age eighteen, and I was making minimum wage, like $4.75 an hour.

One day, she and her husband came in and said they fired their son and the new manager was starting the next day. I was shocked. The next day, the new manager, Diane Riedel, started, and she was a hard-working, wonderful role model who became my mentor. She was an amazing woman who had run a printing press and had other businesses with her own husband. I truly loved our shop because we also hired a young Cambodian woman to run the printing press, there we were the three of us running Eleanor's printing operation.

Sonia: Wow, so despite leaving school, you still had mentors. What was your next transition?

Roseann: The next pivotal stage was that I was becoming more mature and involved in my Buddhist community. It resonated with me that I was responsible for my happiness and overcoming the challenges of my life, without being in the mode that is common of simply blaming others for our dismal life's circumstances, or lack of opportunities. I was young, eighteen or nineteen and I started letting the messages sink in deeper that it was up to me to create the future by making better decisions in the present. In high school, I was disconnected from the idea of "study hard and get into a great college" because the environment I was in was about "seeking instant gratification." If my friends and I wanted to feel like we were grown up, we cut class and did what we wanted, not what adults or teachers told us. We were not given guidance at home often, nor at school by staff, and sadly, even most of our teachers, who could have been more attentive or intervened, but they didn't.

Another theme that was ever-present in my spiritual world was this concept of "never give up" such that you should keep trying until you succeed at your goals, rather than leaving things half finished. I often did not even try to excel in school, so the idea of giving up halfway was a nonstarter. But one day I realized I had started taking classes at the community college and I wanted to finish, I wanted a degree—what kind, I had no idea. I just knew I wanted a bachelor's degree, not an associate degree.

I was so fortunate that my manager Diane allowed me to shift the schedule around and take morning classes at the community college a mile away from work, which in retrospect, shows me how often my life was protected with positive forces, like a boss who wanted me to be more than a cashier.

Sonia: That's incredible! I love your story. So here you are, working and earning your degree, and you're not married. What happens after that?

Roseann: I had decided that I had to be independent, that I would never get married or depend on a man, and that I wouldn't have children, because it didn't work out too well for my mom. I was just wanting to reflect what I saw in the Buddhist women who seemed happy single. I was excited about the independent women I saw. I transferred to San Francisco State University and graduated with a bachelor's degree in marketing. I put myself through the final stage of school while working full time, since my mother couldn't help with my college. I did live with my aunt and uncle, however. They were very Latino, and they took care of me, fed me, and coddled me a little bit.

I managed to get through community college for over two years, somewhat a mix of my old ways meandering through life, because sadly I took random classes without a purpose toward an end goal, and wasted my own money and time. One day it became obvious to me that it should have only taken two years for an A.A. degree, and I was going on my fifth semester with no A.A. degree in sight. That was when I decided to transfer to a four-year university. The opportunity to move to the Bay Area arose because my aunt lived there, working as a nurse in SF. Eventually, I ended up at San Francisco State University and graduated with a bachelor's degree in marketing. Moving out of my mother's home was what I needed to grow up. Latino families have a tough time with girls leaving home, and sadly I know of many families that refuse to allow a kid to go to Harvard or Yale on a full scholarship because of fear that a girl will get pregnant if she goes away. Lucky for me, I had very little supervision since I was twelve, so I was not too coddled or overprotected. But more so, I think my mother had grown in her faith to know that she should not limit my ability to live in this world, no matter how far I desired to go. Oddly, this helped me later when I lived in New York, then Japan, and then I came home to Stockton briefly as a lawyer, which in retrospect, that parental style of allowing freedom served me extremely well to feel free to move about the world as I saw fit.

Once in SF, I still had to work full time, like always. My aunt got me a job at Clinique cosmetics, I worked for the SF school district, and also at the Hyatt Regency hotel where I ran the business center used by guests. I was in charge of the business center mostly used by conference attendees. I dealt with lots of pushy lawyers and doctors and keynote speakers. I remember thinking, "These guys are really important," since they were so demanding. I was twenty-two and had never worked for these types of professionals before. However, I had a strong personality and was not gonna let myself get pushed around, so they liked me because they could give me something and I would say, "When do you need it?" Even if it was seven in the morning and they needed it in two hours, I would get to work. When I delivered the finished product, it was interesting to see the look on some of the lawyers' faces, a bit befuddled that I managed the task and completed it as asked, with no mistakes. I remember thinking how happy I felt that these important people trusted me with their work, even though they didn't know me like their own secretary back at the office. I once overheard my boss telling a client, "She's really strong. She's dependable and sharp. She just gets it done."

How odd that many years later I would be a lawyer attending a conference at the same Hyatt that my law firm was sponsoring as well. That is some turn of events!

After I graduated with my bachelor's degree, I went into sales for a few years, and began to do some traveling. I took my mother on a nice Hawaii vacation and told her "thank you" for putting up with my BS. A couple of years after graduation, I met a young lawyer in a Buddhist meeting, she shared her story about a major career shift that was profound and touched me deeply, and I was not really sure why. Something just clicked with me, and I reflected on the few courses I took in business and criminal law. I had really loved those classes.

I ended up asking this lady out to lunch, and told her, "I'm doing the sales thing and I'm making good money, but I don't feel truly challenged, especially as it concerns the mental challenge. I want a career that is more meaningful." She convinced me to take the LSAT, which is the prep course for law school. I guess you could say that I did okay. I decided to go to law school, and I also wanted the whole "moving across the country" experience. I attended a small law school, Albany Law in upstate New York, where I had received the most scholarships. It was a great decision that I could never have imagined would transform me forever, both because of the required resources needed to be three-thousand miles away from home, family, and friends, but also because law school develops your abilities to be perceptive as a critical thinker who can effectuate change in the world.

Sonia: When you got to that college, did you know that it was exactly what you wanted to do? Did you know it was your passion?

Roseann: I knew I wanted to do something where I was not only making a good living, but also helping people, so it appealed to me. I knew it would offer endless opportunities to either go back into business, be a lawyer, or teach. I had talked with lawyers through my Buddhist church who said they loved law school but never practiced. I didn't understand why until I got to law school. It changes you so much. It's extremely stressful—like pressure-cooker challenging. Some of the people are detestable and just there to make money, which wasn't my purpose.

Before I began my legal career, however, life took an unexpected twist, because after all, my life has been all about the twists, and turns and forks in the road. It is never a straight line for me. One of my study buddies in law school was engaged while in school and his fiancé was in Japan. I learned that before law school, he traveled there to teach English through the JET program and ended up falling in love. He encouraged me to look into JET and knew I would love it too, which was for me the chance I missed in undergrad—that whole thing of backpacking in Europe, or simply taking a semester abroad. None of my high school crowd was academic, as I recall, and I worked full time in college, so again I wasn't exposed to the semester away. I did apply for the JET Program (Japanese Exchange Teacher) and took off right after graduation. I had an awesome experience meeting people from all over the world: England, Australian, Sweden, India, Turkey, New Zealand, and got a bit of adventure in before starting a career in law that now spans almost twenty years.

There was one other little surprise hiccup in my plan to become a badass lawyer saving the world. When I left for Japan, turns out I was with child. I didn't know when I traveled over there, and it took me a couple of months to notice that something was "off." When I was finally able to confirm pregnancy with the help of a friend who could read Japanese on the home tests, it was a shock. It was hard to be in another country, not speak the language, and be pregnant. I had hoped to be in Japan for two or three years, but I came back early to have my daughter in California then take the bar exam.

Sonia: Incredible! How did you do it, working as a lawyer and being a single mother raising a daughter?

Roseann: Fortunately, I had a co-parenting relationship with her dad, and it was extremely powerful and positive sharing fifty-fifty custody. We tried to make it as a couple to raise her, but it lasted only three years. When we split, we knew that we loved Ajani so much, that no matter what, her needs came first. We had birthday parties and holidays together, even took trips together for her. So over time, we learned to be the best parents we could, and we both moved to new relationships that are also very healthy. My daughter has four caring adults that have her back, and in her junior year of high school, we did a joint vacation to Italy and France. That was a highlight of my life that will be one of my fondest co-parenting memories. Mind you this was not a fake closeness either, I really employed my spirituality practice of Buddhism to get through the ups and downs. Ajani brought out the best qualities in each of us, and sure there were hard times too, we had our share of arguments and fights. After all, she is a teenage girl. Now our beautiful daughter is in her second year of college as a plant biology major on her way to UC Davis.

Becoming a mother was the most amazing blessing I have had but since I had a nomadic childhood moving back and forth from Mexico to California, and attending thirteen different schools by the time I graduated from high school. I decided my daughter would have a stable life. I dreamed that she would have friends that were made in kindergarten and all throughout her life. This is what we did when we relocated from Stockton to Oakland as she was entering school. She went to one elementary school, one middle school, and one high school. No multiples for my girl, and I have enjoyed seeing her friends grow up too, honestly.

Sonia: What a blessing that was. That's probably one of the best scenarios in co-parenting without being married.

Roseann: Always put the child first. And because I only had one child, and the co-parenting situation was almost perfect, it allowed me the space to quit working as a lawyer for the government. I was a prosecutor when she was turning five, and her dad was supportive when I quit and decided to start a business/law firm in this case.

I knew when I was working as a prosecutor that there was a major need for more Spanish-speaking lawyers on the side of clients. Often, a Latino defendant would be accused of a fairly petty crime but struggled to get decent representation due to the language barrier. The court interpreters would often make errors, or they would be really pushy with folks telling them to plead guilty so they can just go home or back to work. This would piss me off, and I knew I needed to be out there helping clients as a bilingual person.

This became an opportunity that I knew was right for me to embark on, and in March 2004, I made the decision to quit my job as prosecutor while we were moving to the Bay Area to get ready for school. I did not look back, even though many people thought it was nuts to walk away not only from a good paying stable job with amazing benefits, but more so the prestige and title were what people thought I would miss. Funny thing, I never cared about titles much. It took me years to look back and realize that indeed I had a lot of power, and people wanted what I had in that job, but for me, doing the right thing is always more important than impressing others. Using my Spanish skills to offer litigants the competency of an attorney they can communicate with directly was what appealed to me more than anything. To this day, the majority of my clients speak Spanish only.

I have been in private practice since 2004, and have had many mentors, some lawyers, judges, retired men and women who have all contributed to my success. I have paid for coaching a handful of times, folks with very different styles, and learned a bit from everyone I ever met. Not all of them were a great fit, but we can always learn from people if we decide to. A mentor can be someone whose life you admire. Growing up, I started reading books about people who were impactful in society. I read two books about Eleanor Roosevelt's life and it made me realize that presidents are often the face, but the muscle is the woman. She was writing policy during the Great Depression, visiting people all over the country who were destitute and looking for some relief from the government at a time of major loss of wealth and housing. She is why we have social security and a social welfare system. Her effort of getting the data and seeing how people were starving. I may have never met Eleanor, but I consider her as a mentor and role model.

Sonia: People came into your life at the perfect time, even books about Eleanor Roosevelt. For me, it was Dale Carnegie who changed my life. He took me out of my comfort zone and into public speaking. He was my mentor, and that's what I'm seeing in your life. You found mentors starting when you were young, and they have impacted your life to this day. It's incredible.

Roseann: Yes, I had mentors who were physically around, and mentors through reading and life lessons. And the simultaneous practice of my faith, which is about cutting your own cloth in life, and having the power and independence, even for a woman of color, a Latina, a woman with a background in poverty, with a disenfranchised upbringing that wasn't expected to go far in life. None of that matters. Buddhism is a proactive state of living where there is no limit. The sky's not even the limit. I didn't come from a family with money and I didn't have the right name or people in high places. In fact, I didn't go to the right schools. But I never worried about trying and looking dumb. I never worried that I might fail as a lawyer. The small setbacks are always temporary, always. Now after fourteen years with a successful law firm, and my husband having his own law firm, he looks at my success and says, "How is it that you thought you weren't very bright, yet you are so smart and handle things well?" As a result of turning fifty and entering a new decade of life, it excites me to think of new mentors for another step up in life, as I say, time to level up again.

Sonia: I love it. We all need to seek mentors to challenge us.

Roseann: I also enjoy serving as a mentor. I've been a mentor to a lot of young people over the past fourteen years as a lawyer and business owner, a businesswoman, and entrepreneur. I would never tell my mentees, "You're gonna reach a plateau and that's it." That would never be true, right? Life is a continuum of growth.

Sonia: Who do you love to mentor the most, and why?

Roseann: I love to mentor high school-age girls. A mentor has to compete with social media, and the fact that they're on their phones the whole time and they don't communicate verbally. The impact doesn't always take effect right away, but later the lessons come back, no doubt, and they grow up. Some of my mentees are in college now at Georgetown, Sac State, UC Berkeley, community colleges, and other schools. It makes me so happy when they keep in touch, reach out for coffee to check in. They know they can reach out and call me if they need a reference for a job or an internship or advice about law school. It's been a blessing to have them come back into my life and say thank you.

Sonia: Do you actively go to high schools or do a type of outreach to find these girls who need mentoring?

Roseann: In the first three or four years of starting my business in Oakland, I got on every kind of board I could. I was on the board of directors for the Alameda Hispanic Chamber, a women's political group, and various other committees and boards. At one point I was with an organization with a youth academy, and that's where I started getting high school students into the law firm. As the law firm grew, we began to host an intern per semester and have done so for many years now. Now that I am in politics as an elected official on the Oakland School board, I have more exposure to students and that is how I also get mentees and interns. I am also on the Board of Directors for Girls Inc. and their work with our girls of color in schools makes a huge impact for graduation and reading levels. It is also where I get interns who are girls that are Strong Smart and Bold, which is the motto.

Sadly, I learn that even now there are teachers similar to what I experienced, who tell students they are never going to college because they don't have the chops, or they didn't do well on a paper, so don't get the hopes up. There are nasty adults saying these things to students. I also had bad experiences in middle school, and when I ran for office, I realized that I had suppressed some of those memories. Teachers can be uplifting, or they can be damaging to a student's psyche and performance. Students need mentors and people to take an interest in their success, because sometimes they're not getting the support from their family.

Sonia: Are you still active with the school district position that right now?

Roseann: Yes, I'm in my second term. It is four years long and I am done in 2021. Being elected has taken a toll on my business and financial success, but I figured out how to balance it so the business would start to grow again with recent shifts in the type of cases.

Sonia: What has been one of the greatest career struggles in your journey, and how were you able to overcome it?

Roseann: When I ran for office, I was told, "Be careful. You could lose your entire business because you'll be giving so much time to your political position." And I thought, "Nope, I can do it all. I always juggle. It's who I am." But I almost did lose my business within the first nine months of being elected. It took so much time, and I had to do some soul-searching about how to be a better person who could work with others. How could I bring on good employees and keep them for the long haul, and be the type of boss that somebody wants to work for? I had to be like many CEOs who read books about how to grow an awesome business, develop the people in the organization and find everyone's talents to nurture, even my own. I learned that you need to know what employees think of you as the boss. You have to know why they quit the job and go to the competition and destroy your business. It can hurt you and your business.

I started reading all these books to learn how to balance the politics with the law firm. I found other people with successful businesses and law firms and asked them how they did it. Ultimately, there is nothing static about business, it grows, it shrinks and sometimes it will coast for a bit, but it never stays the same. I am working to be better and change many of my bad habits as a boss, but have a long way to go. In the end, with every disruption and twist, I know one thing: I AM RESILIENT and weather each storm, to land on my feet no matter what.

Sonia: It's an adventure, a mix of "it's scary but it feels right."

Roseann: It feels right to grow. We're serving more clients and we've added civil litigation, and we're helping small business owners. That is fascinating for me because small business owners think lawyers are too expensive and then they find out that a small retainer can go a long way in helping them grow their business and do things more professionally as far as contracts and employee issues. My vision is that we could add an office in Southern California in the next couple of years.

It's interesting how life plays out. There's never a dull moment! A business has to evolve to grow. You have to listen to your team. I'm big on sending my team members to conferences or classes, getting them out there and mixing at events. I know when I am doing something right, which has nothing to do with what my GPA was, or what college I went to, it has to do with grit, gut instinct, and persistence. I had the vision of knowing that I wanted to serve Latinos and Spanish-speakers as best as we could without overcharging. I am proud of that the most, and even today, my client base has grown beyond Latinos.

Sonia: You're definitely a driven leader, casting a vision not only for yourself, but for your team, and expanding everybody. I remember when I was starting out, I took a successful woman out to coffee and asked her what she thought my next step should be. At the time, I thought she gave me the worst answer. She said, "I don't know how to answer that for you, but you're going to know what that next step is." And years later, I get her now. I knew when it was time for my next step. I had to cast a vision for it. It's incredible that you've listened to your dreams and known when to take the next step.

What would you say to women who aspire to succeed, to live their passion, but they don't know where to begin?

Roseann: I would say to slow down enough to listen to your heart, to see who is doing what you want, to watch them, talk to them if you can, and learn. Listen to your heart throughout the day, whether you're working, not working, or raising children. Ask yourself if you're doing what makes you happy, or just doing what others expect of you? Is it just to pay the bills, because if you can squeeze in some time to do what you love, that may not pay well, then you are balancing out life, there has to be a part of us that is alive, and passionate, not simply the grind for money. We won't get the time back if we waste it.

We are such a busybody society, and our lives are full of distractions with Facebook, the internet, Netflix, and overdosing on watching series after series, right? It's important to get away with yourself and have a cup of coffee without distractions or a device, and just think about how you see yourself, and what you would be good at doing, vision work is key, letting yourself see this new life you want, and how it feels to be living it. It will come that much faster if you have the emotions to match it. Many times I have said to women friends, you need to be more selfish, and I mean to the extent that it's no good for anybody if you're putting none of your needs first. Women are often last on the list of "to do's" and that means not going to the doctor, or reading a good book, or getting a massage! I never miss that chance.

Understand who you want to be, what's going to make you happy, and don't worry about needing approval from others. Don't worry about the money. If we're "selfish" enough to serve our deepest desire, then we're going to inevitably serve society. We're going to be the best barista, the best florist, the best dog walker, best lawyer or whatever your passion is.

I have a friend who's a young African-American woman who I knew growing up. Her father is a surgeon and her mother is retired. When she went to work, she loved her dog so much that she didn't want to leave it at home, so she decided to start a business walking a few dogs. Then she walked a few more, and hired helpers. Now, four years later, she has a successful dog-walking business with fourteen employees. It's morphed into all these things, and it started with the love of her dog. It's a good example of taking the time to step out of your head and follow your vision, be selfish enough to combat the haters, to squash the inner voice that's scared and doubtful.

If you're not happy because you feel stuck in a career or a marriage, it's okay to be selfish enough to go for what really matters to you. It will benefit everybody else in the long run. You can tell people to wait and see, give you space and respect. Saying no to people is easier because it is saying "yes" to me.

Sonia: Yes, until we remove the noise around us and think about what we want, and process it, we're not going to get there. When we're doing what we love and helping people, which brings meaning and purpose, that's called living! We were created for living!

Roseann: We all need to think more, to be alone. Especially in nature. So take a hike, go for a walk, sit by a lake, or take a long drive with the window down. We need time to think and process, instead of just go-go-go. If you just keep going on autopilot, you'll end up somewhere that you didn't plan to be or like.

Sonia: Is there anything else you would love to share with the women who are reading this?

Roseann: Nothing happens by coincidence; everything connects to something else and happens for a reason. Ultimately, people need to see that anything they considered as bad or negative can actually be a source of information and growth. It tells you what you're made of when you use every experience for fuel. If you've been through stressful events, rather than asking "Why does bad stuff happen to me?" you can learn to start saying, "I lived through that obstacle and I'm still standing because I am strong. I'm still here. This shows others they can be strong too." I wish we would all stop comparing ourselves to others because the timing of our success differs. For some it comes young, for others it comes later in life. Our own lives need to matter to us not be based on what others think of our lives or choices!

Sonia: You're so right, and I love it! Everyone's journey is so unique, and we have to follow our own paths. Thank you so much, Roseann.

Sonia Hassey

ABOUT ROSEANN TORRES

Roseann Torres, Esq. is the founder and CEO of Torres Law Group Inc since 2004 and serves as elected official to the OUSD School Board as Trustee since January 2013. Now in her second term, having been re-elected in 2016.

Roseann began practicing law in January 2000. She began her career in government in San Joaquin County, first as a Deputy County Counsel then as a Deputy District Attorney. She moved to Oakland in March 2004 and started Torres Law Group Inc. The firm serves the community with bicultural and bilingual attorneys and staff who are all fluent in Spanish. They represent injured clients in personal injury and small businesses in civil litigation. There is a strong sense of pride helping those who are often underrepresented in legal matters.

Being equally committed to the community in which she lives, Roseann gave back as soon as she became an attorney, helping local high schools with mock trials, in schools with majority Black and Latino students. Showing the students that lawyers are able to be both successful and give back is key, since she attributes much of her pivotal life decisions to mentors in her youth. She was at one point a high school dropout in a crowd headed for either prison or low wage work. But with the intervention of successful role models, primarily women of color, she made choices that changed the trajectory of her life to eventually graduate high school, college from SF State University and finally law school at Albany Law in upstate New York.

CHAPTER 10

Who Am I?

Maria Dominguez

~Knowing who I am and whose I am has been my greatest gift to the world~

Sonia: I am here with my dear friend Maria Dominguez. I love this woman so much. We've been on this amazing journey together and I'm excited that she will be a part of this *Destiny Talks* book. Maria, please tell us your story.

Maria: Where do I begin with my story? Since I have titled my chapter "Who Am I?" I believe it is important to talk about my ethnicity, my upbringing, and what led me to where I am today.

My late father was Puerto Rican and my late mother was Portuguese, Irish, Dutch and Black. Both were fair-skinned and then there was me—brown-skinned with long curly bangs and pigtails. I was born and raised in San Francisco in the '60s in the Ingleside district (right below Hunters Point) in a working-class neighborhood. There wasn't very much diversity there—you were either black or white. And, there weren't many biracial children living there or Puerto Ricans. I was not black enough to be black, and I definitely wasn't white. My childhood wasn't filled with having to choose a race until I entered junior high school. From that point, I questioned where I fit in. I mostly hung around black students and with each year that passed, my circle of friends became more diverse. Oftentimes I was shunned for dating outside my race. I got the "look," or I was followed home after school and threatened. There was always something about me that caused me to question who I was. I was overdeveloped, I had brown skin and freckles, and then this long wild Chaka Khan hair.

I looked different from other women who were my skin color. I didn't want to look different—I wanted to fit in. I wanted the afro. I wanted to be a part of the Black Students Club. It just didn't come easy for me. As I was entering high school, I decided I didn't want to spend my last years in school fighting to be me. I then chose, at the last minute, to go to a private Catholic school. I went from a pretty diverse junior high school in the suburbs to a school that was ninety-five percent white upper middle class. It was there that I met a small group of Latinas and I learned about my Puerto Rican culture, salsa dancing, and the food. I definitely stood out there too AND I loved it. The path to not fitting in continued but I still flourished. I became class president, I was active in extracurricular activities, and I had a great relationship with the students and the nuns, and I went on to attend UC Berkeley.

I went from the fire to the frying pan at Cal. It was the start to a very curvy and dangerous path that led to my demise. No identity. No purpose. No foundation. Drugs came into my life and were a part of my life for many, many years. You name it, I probably tried it. I met musicians in the music scene and/or I danced at some of the gay clubs in San Francisco all night long. And, I hadn't even reached my twenty-first birthday! I never paid for the drugs or the high with cash—but, instead, I paid for it with my body and soul.

So now, the two sides of who I am became three, and I further got lost in my identity.

Sonia: So before you were even ten years old, you were already going through this inner struggle to find your identity, and all these feelings of "Who am I?" were coming out.

Maria: Yes and fortunately for me, I have a big, vivacious personality. I have always been an outgoing person and I've been doing things my own way. I equate it to being a "wild child." I was the only child of my mother and my father, and unfortunately, when you're an only child, you're also labeled as spoiled. There are so many negative ramifications to being an only child and a wild child. One day when I was young, I overheard someone say, "Oh, she's such a spoiled brat. She gets everything that she wants." Even though I was an only child, I didn't see myself as spoiled. BUT … it was in that moment that I changed. My identity shifted and I became a "yes girl."

Sonia: How did that make you feel? Because first you were having a racial identity crisis, and now you're having to deal with the identity of being a spoiled only child.

Maria: When I think back to hearing that, I just remember that it hurt me, and I didn't want to be known as a spoiled brat. So I changed my personality to be a "yes girl"—a people pleaser.

Sonia: What were some of the actions you took when you were trying to please people?

Maria: It's interesting because I didn't realize that, between age nine and forty-five, a lot of my actions were tied to what I overheard that day. The list is long of some of the things I did to be a people pleaser and, even today, I have to watch my behavior. For example, in high school friends would say, "Maria, I need a ride or let's go to the liquor store and buy some beer," and I'd say yes even though I may have had plans, or it was wrong. And "Oh Maria, I'm gonna smoke a joint. Do you want to join me?" And I'd say yes even though I knew it was illegal. And when I started to date—it was the worst. I said yes to too many things because 1) I wanted to be liked and 2) I didn't want to be labeled a spoiled brat or the other "b" word. I lost my identity and my voice during that process because I felt like my identity was whatever everyone else told me it was.

Think of it this way—I didn't know what Puerto Rican or black meant. Each race has traditions and I knew none. I didn't know any of my father's side of the family. And, my mother had a broken childhood with nothing to share culturally. So, if someone said to me, "Puerto Ricans act like this or did this," I had no point of reference.

Sonia: When did you begin to realize what was happening and that you weren't true to yourself?

Maria: It started in my forties when a series of events happened. I was in my second marriage and living in Elk Grove with my husband, my son, and my mom. At the time she was eighty-seven, but she had lived with me for five years before I got married, so she lived with me from age seventy-five on. In my marriage, I had no identity. I was a Christian wife, mother, and caregiver to my mother. Those were my labels. But there was no Maria. There were labels and expectations of what and who I should be. I was dying inside with a smile on my face. I struggled with depression. I put on a lot of weight. I was getting to the point where I was taking Vicodin or Tylenol with Codeine, or whatever drug my mother had, and I was taking it with wine on a daily basis. If one glass didn't do, I got another. I was miserable, and my body hurt. I was tired. I was really, really tired. Like I was tired of this life, my life, and something had to change, but I didn't know how or what to change.

Then one Sunday night that I will never forget, my life changed forever. I was walking up the stairs and I was exhausted. Every joint in my body hurt. My knees hurt, my elbows hurt, I was just in pain. I think my spiritual pain was showing up as physical pain. I remember thinking, "I'm so tired. Can I just get some help (referencing help with care for my mother)?" Sunday nights were my bubble bath nights, so I went in and took a bath with my candles and my wine. I had already taken Vicodin or whatever it was that day. I was just sitting in the tub of bubbles silently crying under the loud television noise that my husband was watching and saying that I couldn't do "this" anymore.

I crawled into bed that night just mentally, physically, and spiritually exhausted. That night I had the worst nightmares. I kept dreaming about death and seeing tombstones and black spirits. I had this vision of my mother next to her bed, curled up in her favorite pajamas like a baby.

When I woke up the next morning I thought, "That was a weird dream." I went downstairs to check on my mom before starting on her breakfast. When I walked into her room, I saw that she was curled up next to her bed exactly the same way that I had seen in my vision the night before. I remember closing the door and saying, "God, this is a joke, right?" I closed the door and opened it again, and she was still there on the floor. I tried to wake her up, but she was incoherent. I couldn't pick her up. My son couldn't pick her up. When the paramedics and firefighters arrived, I told them it wasn't an emergency, she just fell out of bed and with her history of two broken hips, we just needed help to put her back in bed. They then told me she was in cardiac arrest and little to no heartbeat. I thought, "Wait, what? I just needed help putting her back in bed."

Within a couple of hours, they pronounced her dead. My world shifted right then and there.

The blessing after her death was that I was reunited with my father and I found out he was a Christian serving in his church. He was still emotionally distant (and that is the way he is) but we made peace. I also learned that I had a huge family and I felt like I was reconnecting to my roots. Most of us had brown skin with curly wavy hair and were all uniquely made. I fit right in.

Soon after she passed away, and me wanting to get closer to my father's family, my husband of over nine years left our marriage. No warning. Just a note. My world unraveled one piece at a time: I could no longer afford to live where I was, my son moved out on his own, my credit was so bad that I couldn't find a place to live, I lost my job, and my dog ran away.

Where was I to go? I was ashamed, embarrassed, abandoned, and just lost. I ended up moving in with a friend and renting a room. And my thought was, "Here I am, a woman in her forties who is renting a room." Shame. I had to deal with that whole emotional label, which was hard.

Sonia: What brought you to that realization that something had to change?

Maria: Every label that was attached to me—wife, mother, daughter, homeowner, dog owner, employee—no longer existed. I was nothing. Everything about me was attached to the identity of those relationships.

My friend suggested that I go through a Celebrate Recovery (CR) program at our church. I remember saying, "I don't have a drinking or drug problem." She said it was for my hurts, habits, and hang-ups. And I said, "I got those." So I went to the Celebrate Recovery step study for a year. And then I went back and led it for a year. I did the emotional work because I decided that I wasn't going to live the latter half of my life the way I had lived the first part. I wanted freedom from my old hurts, habits, and hang-ups.

At Celebrate Recovery, I used to say, "Hi my name is Maria Dominguez, and I'm on the road to recovery from abuse, abandonment, codependency, drug addiction, promiscuity ... and the list just kept going on and on. I did the work to get rid of the pains of my past so that I could change my future. And, sometimes it was messy, and it was definitely not easy.

Sonia: That's so brave of you. You got to a point where you had to make a decision to bring up all those negative habits, so you could break them. Was that the beginning of your transformation? You also mentioned that you had been a Christian but were not happy with your identity.

Maria: Yes, I started Celebrate Recovery in 2010 and it was the beginning of my transformation. I honestly feel that it saved me. Being a Christian and my identity? What I am going to share may upset people and, honestly, there needs to be a change. I have been saved since 1996 and I have lived fifteen years in bondage as a believer in Christ. I would go to church, sing the songs, raise my hands in worship, go up to the altar for deliverance, get prayed for, and STILL I was stuck in my past with old hurts, bad habits, and hang-ups. I believe as believers we should ALL go to CR.

When I was married, my husband would say, "Oh, you're just bringing problems up there so everybody can see." I have had pastors counsel us, mentor us, and nothing ever changed. His behavior got worse and since we were active in the church, God forbid if we got a divorce or there was any talk of abuse. So I stopped going to some churches and I definitely stopped seeking spiritual counsel. I was tired of hearing that God doesn't like divorce and that led me to believe, well, then He must be okay with being abused.

My vision for what I wanted my identity to look like in Christ appeared one day while at church. I remember watching a young girl up at the altar, praising and worshipping God all-out. Her arms were in the air, she was dancing, speaking in tongues, and I was jealous. I wanted that ... I wanted to live and be in complete abandonment. But, how could I? I was stuck in a deep hole spiraling downward in depression. I was living a lie in my marriage and I didn't want anyone to tell me (especially my husband), "Maria, you're too loud, you're too this, you're too that." I realized I was still looking for permission from someone to let me be me instead of just saying, "I'm going to be me whether you like it or not. You be you and I'll be me."

Sonia: You felt like a shell but deep down in your soul you knew there was so much more to Maria Dominguez. But you didn't know how to let yourself out.

Maria: Yes. I wanted to honor my marriage and be who my husband needed me to be. I wanted to honor my mother and be the daughter she needed me to be, which was her caretaker. I wanted to be the mother that my son needed me to be. But in that whole process, I forgot that I also needed to be who Maria wanted to be. God has been giving me visions for a long time, but because I didn't know who I was, the idea that my dreams would come true wasn't even in my mind. My belief was that I couldn't do things because I was taking care of everyone else. And, honestly, I began to feel that why would He trust me with His dreams? I was damaged. I did bad things. I was unworthy.

One of my dreams was in February 2001. God gave me a vision of me talking to a large auditorium of women, and I thought, "I don't know how that's going to happen." In my mind, I thought about a cosmetic network company I was involved with and I thought, "I'm going to become the highest level I can be so I can be on stage." But I was married, and I knew it wouldn't work. It never happened while I was in my marriage. BUT, once I was divorced, I went through the work to break myself free from my past issues and lived a life fulfilling God's promises for me, AND I shared my story. I ended up on stage in front of thousands of women. I was able to share my mini testimony on stage with Oprah when she came to San Jose for the Live Your Life Tour. Woo hoo! Letting my light shine …

Sonia: You light up the room, and who isn't attracted to that? Even women.

Maria: Unfortunately, unless it's a strong man with his own light within himself, we will not work out. The wrong man I meet would suck that light right out of me. They're like, "Oh we like the light, it's so pretty. But now that I'm with you, shut it down so others aren't attracted to it."

Sonia: It's their insecurities.

Maria: Yes. But I was meeting them one after the other. Thankfully, I could tap into a lot of tools that I learned in Celebrate Recovery, and I could recognize what was happening and decide that it wasn't going to work out early. I also was afraid because both of my marriages started off with promises and love and that they would take care of me, but they both didn't end well.

Presently, when someone makes promises that they're going to do all these wonderful things, I think that it's probably not true. I ask them to be directly involved in my world just to see how they interact with my interactions. And nine times out of ten, it doesn't work out. It's not a fit for them.

Sonia: Maybe you were learning how to love yourself, and looking at others with a little skepticism. The thought that keeps popping in my head is that you had certain expectations and values that had to be met, whether in a friend or a romantic relationship. You had to make sure they met your standard. You were starting to see what would make you a stronger woman, and understanding who you were. Who were you becoming?

Maria: Yes, that is true. I have been told to set up healthier boundaries for everyone. It is a very hard thing for me to do. I meet people and I instantly want to encourage them and bless them. I am becoming more careful with my heart though. My expectation is that God has someone just for me for the path that He has me on. And, that is why I said it is important for them to see my world. It really isn't for everyone. And, that is hard for me. I am relational. I want everyone to be a part of my world, but not everyone can be.

Sonia: What does "Being who God intended me to be" look like?

Maria: Earlier I had touched on CR and I think it is important to highlight. It was in those first few months of CR that I received a word from God. It was actually a dream while I was on the beach of Oahu. My best friend had gifted the trip post-divorce. While sunbathing, I had a vision of Jesus Christ. His heart was open, and He told me that I had a heart like His. A heart to love on people. He then gave me a mandate—a purpose: to love on his LOST people. Out of that dream birthed my ministry, Loving On Someone Today (LOST). He has always given me the ability to love on people. From the time I was a young girl until this day, I've had a heart of compassion, and I have an innate ability to feel what others are feeling. And no matter where I am, I can feel a person who needs to be loved on. It may be a person who's homeless. It may be a woman in the store with babies or an elderly man needing someone to talk to. I believe God has called me to love on people, no matter where they are and no matter the situation.

Sonia: I love that it's true love in action. God is giving you a keen vision for people who need to be loved on. Why does this break my heart at such a core level? I want you to expand on this area because I feel like it's your big "why." Let's break it down. Let's say you're at the grocery store and you see someone who's ready to cry. What do you do for that person?

Maria: It is my "why." I believe because I walked through an identity crisis—being physically, verbally, and mentally abused—having a drug addiction, and being abandoned by marriage vows and a father, I have more compassion for people. I can speak to that pain, that hurt, that betrayal, that addiction. I have been there.

In CR, there is a saying that I love. It states, "God never wastes a hurt" and He has not wasted any of my hurts. God always puts me with a person who's been through one of the areas I've walked through.

Regardless of where I go, I am a willing and able vessel. So if I am in a grocery store, driving my car, at work, seeing a client, on the phone, wherever, and if I feel that someone needs a hug, a call, prayer, a text, or something else, I will do it. I have been in the presence of people who I have never met before and I have felt their pain. Sometimes people just need to know that someone hears them, sees them, and cares for them. And, a hug goes a long way.

I do have a special place in my heart for the homeless and the elderly. I think it has to do with the fact that they're unwanted; they have no voice. No one wants to talk to them, see them, or really help them. There are times that they don't want to help themselves, but they just need to be loved on. I'm not saying I'm their savior, just that they matter. We all want to feel like we matter, don't we?

Sonia: Most people's purpose comes from pain. I also have a heart for women who don't have an identity or haven't found their purpose, because I've been there, too. But as long as I've known you, you've been compassionate with a big, huge heart, and funny with a spark like you're a little firecracker. That's who you are, which is what God put inside of you. Don't change it for anybody. You fit perfectly on this earth for a divine purpose. We need your spark. Now you're traveling to other countries and loving on people, and that is the most beautiful thing. You have a beautiful voice, a heartbeat of God.

What would you say to women who are crying and broken, and don't know what their next step should be? How do they get out of being stuck?

Maria: I'm thinking back to the times I was stuck, and what I told myself. I don't want to say the wrong thing, but I want to give women hope to know that there are others, like me, who've gone through the same thing.

I would say reach out to someone. Do not isolate and stay alone. I encourage them to take just one step. Not a giant leap like "Oh my God, I'm going to be drug-free and out of this situation right now." But one step.

Sonia: What do those little steps look like for them?

Maria: It could be something simple. For me, it was self-care, reading the Word or doing daily devotionals or listening to some anointed sermons on YouTube or being quiet in my space (renewing my mind). I didn't have a lot of money back then and so I read a lot. We hear so many voices on social media, and we need to get quiet and just "be" even if it's only for ten minutes. The longer the better. Take that step. It could be Celebrate Recovery or a program like that. Everything is so accessible that you can probably find a program without going too far. Find a Godly person, like a mentor. Someone who has walked through what you've gone through. Someone to speak light to you and tell you that you are an amazing woman. Because YOU ARE!

Find your space, practice self-care, seek help, and seek a mentor or a coach. My preference would be to not go to your girlfriends. They love you and they want the best for you, but they also know all your stories. And, sometimes, they'll speak to your story. They are great to cry with, to love on you in your time of need, and to be your support group—your tribe. What you also need in that moment is someone to objectively speak to your hurt and to give you the tools to move past that hurt.

Sonia: That makes sense because we need someone with a different perspective to see the blind spots that we need to work on.

Maria: Exactly. It was hard for me to reach out for help because I was a wife, I was in a church, and all this beautiful stuff. So for me to pick up the phone and say I was struggling, I was thinking about suicide, and I was having these issues—people who knew me would say, "You depressed?" "We didn't see that coming" or "You could get kicked out of the church." That was hard for me to say I needed help. I wanted to save face, but I was tired of trying.

Sonia: It's hard to keep up with a false identity. But you had the courage to go deeper within and discover who you were, and take simple steps to become who you were supposed to be.

Maria: Yes. I knew I had to do the work to get there. I knew all my work would collapse if I reverted to old behavior. I gave myself grace to do the work, even if it took me ten days, a year, or ten years. Now I can be myself. I will go into a space and be happy, and I've had people tell me, "Oh Maria, you're so loud!" And I say, "Aw baby, thank you!"

Sonia: It's an authenticity. You're now you, and the real Maria shows up. When you become yourself, you shine, and it's so beautiful.

Maria: It's so much easier to be yourself! It's not always easy, because there are still moments every day when the old Maria wants to say, "Yes or sure." But the new Maria says, "No, that's not going to work." I have to take the risk that people may walk away, or situations might affect my life or my business. But I'd rather be true to myself at any cost.

I'm not tied to labels or stuff. I got rid of practically everything so I could travel more. I've learned to live with very little because my ultimate hope is to be able to get up and go. When God says go, I go. When He says to talk to a lady over there because she needs to know that I love her, I do it. When he says go to another country and talk to someone, I go. To do that, it takes a lot of work because I always wanted to have roots. But I've come to realize that I don't need things. I know who I am in Christ. I know what He's given me. I want to do the opposite of most people. I feel like I have finally become like the young girl I saw praising God in church that day. I am living my life more with no walls, no rules, and all-out full abandonment. A "wild child."

Sonia: It sounds like your inner voice is now congruent with your actions. That's why God has opened up opportunities for you and blessed you financially, because now you are literally fulfilling your calling in the universe, and you're right where you're supposed to be. You're no longer like a lost child in the desert. You're in a place of wholeness and you see the broken people in the world, and you are a vessel that can pour out God's blessings on them.

Maria: That's it!

Sonia: I see you as an elegant woman, beautiful and spicy. You're just adorable. I also see the side of you that's feeding the homeless. You can show up in front of people in need, and show up in front of influential people. And either way, you can still be you. There are so many women out there who need to be in that space for themselves. I still have work to do on myself every day. I totally screwed up yesterday, but today is a new day, and I ask myself again, "Who do I want to be? What is my desire today?"

Maria: There's a saying that you move in the direction of your most dominant thought. If I wake up in the morning and dwell on feeling sad, my whole day could be sad. Or if I wake up and say, "I don't deserve to be happy," then I don't, and I won't. There's no covering on my windows, so when the sun comes in, BAM! The sunshine energizes me. I start my day in prayer and devotion, and thank God for waking me up, putting me on the right path, and bringing people who need to be loved on. My real estate business broke barriers this past year. Why? Because I'm not chasing business. I said, "Lord, bring people to me who need my service." The old me was broke and needed money and needed business. I was in that mental space of need. A broke mentality. I fired the old me!

Sonia: It's a mindset. You must be in a place of abundance for abundance to be attracted to you. I love your story. Life is not always perfect, but you are satisfied, you're fulfilled, you're in a place of gratitude every morning. You say, "The sun is shining on me, now let me go shine it on other people." Tell me what you do to bring out your passionate creativity. What are your personal desires? What music do you like? What do you do to feed your soul? Do you get out and dance and hug on everybody? Tell us about the exuberance of Maria.

Maria: My big love is travel, both locally and out of the country. I have served on several international mission trips: Cuba twice, Ecuador, Guatemala, Romania, Mexico for the last nine years and the Dominican Republic. Sometimes I'll get in my car and go along the river and just sit and be in love with nature. I love hiking even though I've never been an outdoorsy girl. But it goes back to being in God's presence and a quiet space. I also still love wine. It's funny, not funny, because I'm part of a church and sometimes people get weird about wine. But I even take trips to wineries with the purpose, again, of just being. When my dog, Rocky, was alive, I'd put him in the car, pack a blanket, and we'd go somewhere and sit, and I'd have some wine and he'd try to lick it, and we would just enjoy being at the winery.

I also love to salsa dance. I love street fairs, festivals, and music in the streets. I love all things about the theater, from musicals to ballet to the symphony. I often go alone, and I love every minute of it. I'm also a big foodie. I love to exercise by walking—it's a perfect time to spend with God. My new favorites are Hot Pilates, Hot Sculpt and Hot Move and Groove (all exercises done in rooms of 105–110-degree heat). One of my all-time favorite things to do is have a spa day (alone or with friends). I start the year by putting a full-on spa day in my calendar EVERY quarter and, depending on finances, I will do a massage a month.

I don't eat meat anymore, so sometimes I'll create videos on places to find good vegan or vegetarian options. For me, it's trying to create an environment where I can enjoy good food, from Soul food to Thai food to Spanish food to Mexican food. I find that a lot of things that

I love to do are in-the-moment things that don't cost a lot—except for the food part.

And, my tribe … I love LOVE gathering with friends who are near and dear to me and creating moments, and just being in their presence. I have a group of friends that during the summer we head to the local winery for free music Fridays. It is what I look forward to the most during the summer.

My family—love them so much. My sister and brothers are a few hours away and I do my best to see them as much as I can. Connecting to my roots.

My Son, Matias, is a well-rounded, grounded, adult who lives on his own. As much as we can, we travel and hang out. He has taught me so much about the cool places to go to in Sacramento and is always suggesting something that he thinks I should try or a place I should go. Although he doesn't know it—he saved my life when he was a baby. I was contemplating suicide because I was in such a bad place. I really didn't want to live anymore. It was because I didn't want him to live with the burden of my death that I decided to live. I decided to remove myself from a situation that was not healthy. So, to me, when I say he is my angel, he is.

My intention and my focus begin at the beginning of every year. I choose a new word for every year, and my word in 2018 was "Transformation." It's still about making those daily decisions, and sometimes I don't meet them. They become weekly and monthly decisions, and I think, "I'm wasting time; let's get on the ball here." But as soon as I started letting go of some things, the world opened up to me. I'm going all-in with Christ. My word for 2019 is actually a statement "Overflow of Abundance." I believe this year is a year continuing to be Transformed and Abundance will Overflow.

Sonia: You're refining your calling, and it's a beautiful thing. I love that you're in a place of wholeness, gratitude, and centeredness. You can love people with a God kind of love that comes from your heart. What else do you want to share with other women about transformation?

Maria: You may be a woman who is going through something right now, walking through a situation where you feel like you can't do it, or you're having an identity crisis. So many things and people are pulling at you. Just know that you have the courage to walk through it, and it's not going to last forever. You're born with a certain identity and purpose, and it's not the world's choice or anyone else's choice to tell you who you are. Instinctively, spiritually, and mentally you may know who you are, but you get it twisted when you allow others to tell you who you are.

Gather your courage and take the time to spend with yourself. Spend time in self-care and quietness to find out who you are. You can't give to others from a place of scarcity. Fill yourself up first.

Some women also give to their husbands and kids, and there's nothing wrong with that, of course, because we women were created to be nurturers and givers. But we have to start with ourselves. For example, I'm a bubble bath girl on Sundays and Wednesdays. I will take a half-hour bubble bath that may include a glass of wine. I started it when my son was a baby, and now he's thirty. That's my time to love on me, and I need to do this before I can love on others. If we love ourselves and listen to our own voices, it will give us discernment to sort out the voices of others, which may be caring and loving, but may be hurtful or manipulative.

Sonia: I love the Bible verse that says to love your neighbor as yourself. In other words, we cannot love others if we don't love ourselves first. Any final thoughts?

Maria: I began this chapter with a question of "Who Am I?" and I want to answer that question. I am an On-Fire Christian who loves Jesus. I want to do His will and I love with reckless abandonment. I talk loud, I am loud, and I sing off-key (and sometimes on-key) wherever I want. I love my family and all of our different shades of skin (from red hair and freckles to black skin and kinky hair). I am excited that I get to do these latter years the way God had intended me to, even though I had to pick up a few lessons along the way. I believe it has made me stronger and my heart bigger to those who need to be loved on. My assignment is clear: to LOVE on God's People. Plain and simple. I will go under freeways, highways, and along the byways to show the love of Christ.

I call myself the CLO—the Chief Loving Officer of LOST and, even in my real estate business, my tagline is "I am a Realtor on a Mission." I get to do this life intersecting all of the moving pieces into one purpose and one mandate: LOVE.

Sonia: Thank you for sharing your powerful story. I know it will bless so many women. Keep shining, keep being that butterfly undergoing a transformation, keep looking at the sun every morning and shining it on others. You are truly a Woman of Destiny.

Sonia Hassey

ABOUT MARIA DOMINGUEZ

Maria Dominguez is the Chief Loving Officer in her ministry and life with a successful career as a motivational speaker, community activist, missionary, Realtor*, and soon-to-be credentialed Pastor.

While serving her community, she is often referred to as Pastor Perky for her high-spirited energy and the love that she shares with those around her. She is the founder and creator of the L.O.S.T. (Loving On Someone Today) ministry. She is also an Assistant Trip Leader for Praying Pelican Missions in the San Francisco Bay Area, and co-leads a monthly outreach, Church on the Streets (COTS), where they feed, clothe and build relationships with the homeless community along the Sacramento River. She has also traveled around the world as a missionary where she has led groups to share the love of Christ to the people of the Bateys in the Dominican Republic, the children of the Gypsy communities in Romania, the families in El Cañón de Los Carretas (the garbage dumps outside of Tijuana, Mexico), Guatemala, Ecuador and Cuba.

Maria lives in Elk Grove, California, where she enjoys spending time visiting wineries and relaxing at the spa with her Women Warrior Tribe, sharing foodie and craft cocktail moments with her son, Matias, listening to live music and dancing to salsa.

To contact:

Direct: 916-627-8970
Email: MariaMDominguez2010@yahoo.com
Website: www.MariaMDominguez.com

Social Media:
Facebook: https://www.facebook.com/mariamdominguez
Instagram: https://www.instagram.com/mariamdominguez

CHAPTER 11

The Comfort Zone

Jenny Chamberlain

Sonia: I am here with Jenny Chamberlain, who is not only a wonderful friend but an incredible leader in her community. She has a wonderful story of leadership transformation. Jenny, just start your story from the beginning so everyone can fully understand your transformation.

Jenny: Last night I got out of my comfort zone and stepped into one of the most challenging roles of my life. I was asked to give a speech and share about what I do in the community to help the women's movement. In Spanish.

Although I have made hundreds of speeches and presentations, and I am Latina, I am not fluent in the language. I am what some consider a "Pocha." The Mexican side of my heritage goes back about five generations, and unfortunately, yes, the language gets lost in translation sometimes.

I tried numerous times to get out of the situation. When I first agreed to speak, I thought it was for the English version of the show and saw it as an opportunity for me. It was about two weeks before the performance before I realized it was for the Spanish version, by then it was too late to find a replacement, and no one was available. When I tried to sidestep the situation, I was reminded time and time again by a few friends and event organizers that my purpose for the night was to help women "Rise Up" and encourage them to get involved in the community, to become leaders and to be fierce role models for others to follow.

In order for me to do this, I knew what I must do. I had to make myself vulnerable, go out on a limb, and give something a shot that was foreign and unknown to me, knowing that I wasn't going to be one-hundred-percent perfect or feel comfortable in my own skin in doing so. But I had to be the example and show them that even someone who is known in the community for civic engagement and speaking in front of both large and small crowds does get nervous sometimes. I took a chance, putting myself out there to be an example.

As I was waiting in the back of the room for the first performance to get started, I ran into my friend's husband and shared my doubts of how I could actually be effective. "I don't know why they asked me to do this, they couldn't have picked the biggest "Pocha" in the world to do this speech in Spanish!" I said, laughing. He looked at me, waving his hands in an encouraging manner and said, "Jenny, you get up there and BE the best Pocha you can BE!"

Wow. What a profound statement that has changed my outlook on certain aspects of my life, especially how I see "me." He reminded me of who I am and where I come from, even during a moment in time when I thought I was going to let my weakness shine, when in truth, it was my strength that sparkled.

I was going to be the last one on stage, "the closer," and my goal, my mission, was to give a "call to action" to inspire the women in the room. Instead, I saw being the last one as an opportunity to hide in the dark shadows in the back. Yes, hide. I said it. This extrovert, social bee hid in the back of the room, drowned out the world, and found a little diversion to help me forget that I was eventually going to be required to go on stage. I even flipped through Facebook a couple of times and made two posts. Nervous? Na, not me (right).

I sat there in awe of how beautiful some of these women spoke both English and Spanish. I can't say that I was jealous of them, because when you are in awe and admire people, there is no place for jealousy, but I wished I was more like them and thought how lucky they were to know both languages so well, so eloquently.

It was intimidating, I'm not going to lie, it was. I kept hearing the words over and over in my head, "Jenny, be the best Pocha you can be!" My nerves were in action, and I was feeling a bit embarrassed and ashamed that I was about to make a speech in a language that I should know well. I mean, I took Spanish in high school and college, so why wasn't I fluent at this point? Finally, it was my turn to go on stage, and

I mustered up my courage as I walked the dark pathway from the back to the front of the room at the foot of the stage.

My friend Alegria introduced me. She has always been someone who I have had a lot of admiration for, an attorney who has advocated and helped countless numbers of people. Her heart is made of gold and I had the honor of her introducing me. She shared the work we did together during the Sonoma County Wildfires in October of 2017. My eyes got a little misty as she spoke, and I thought, "Is that me she is talking about? Yes, I did do all those things…" It never hit me how much I have done in the name of love for others, and I had to fight back the tears because I was about to go on stage.

As I walked up the stairs, I said to myself, "Okay, it's time," and I found my spot on the stage in front of the middle mic as I had rehearsed the night before in a fully lighted room. This time I looked into the darkened audience with two small standing spotlights shining upon me. Silence filled the room as I took a few deep breaths before I began to speak. Thoughts raced through my mind as I attempted to read my carefully prepared and practiced speech. "How did I get here? How did this happen? How in the world did I even get involved in community work? Why do people consider me a leader? And why in the world did I agree to do this in Spanish again? Ay! The things I get myself into!"

"Light please, I need a little bit more light," I asked as I struggled to see the words I typed in a big, huge font so that it would be easier for me to read. I didn't want to have to worry about wearing my reading glasses, but yet, it was still a challenge. The size sixteen font that I printed my speech on blended into the white paper and everything became a blur.

"Can someone turn on one of the main lights please?" I pleaded "It's a bit hard for me to see my words because it's so dark in here," I said after trying to read the first paragraph. I heard this voice in the background that said, "No, we can't turn on the lights in the main room."

"Shoot," I thought to myself, "I don't know if I can even finish my speech. What do I do?" I was trying to stay calm and not lose face. My friend Alegria who along with another performer where still on stage, they switched spots with me so that I could be closer to the spotlight in order for me to read my words better.

"Ah, nice," my mind thought, as I was able to see a bit clearer, which made the flow I practiced many times before to get closer to how I rehearsed it. "Why am I not nervous? Why aren't my hands sweaty? I am struggling here, but I feel okay, calm about it all …" I wondered. I had prepared my audience early on during my opening statements in order for them not to set high expectations of me to blurt out this amazing, beautiful speech in Spanish. I let them know that this was new for me and basically my Spanish was crappy. What I didn't embrace was that me being there was part of my story and I was using my efforts that night as an example for us to get outside of our box, in order to make a difference in the lives of others.

I looked into the audience one more time before I proceeded and paused … it was like I was about to veer into the looking glass.

"For I know the plans I have for you..." "I knew you before you were born..." those words of scripture that my mom and both of my grandmothers ingrained in me rang through my head. They reminded me to put all my fears aside, including the desire to be accepted as a Pocha and focus on my purpose that night, which I believe gave me the strength and courage to complete the challenge that was set before me.

As the words gradually and reluctantly left my lips, I began to think back on my life. It was like I took a seat backstage and was watching this girl, this woman, perform. I wondered what details and incidents led her there, on the stage that night, causing her to step out of her comfort zone, baring her soul, her insecurities, her true self, yet sharing her confidence, courage, and grace to the world.

Sonia: What did lead you there, to that place and time in your life? Tell us about your family background.

Jenny: I always say that I come from a strong line of women. I learned perseverance, hope, encouragement, and support from the women in my family. Those attributes and strengths were taught and handed down from generation to generation, from my grandmothers and those before them. They both grew up in Texas during a time where equality was something hoped and strived for despite having been born in a place where the odds were against you.

But that didn't stop them, they were adventurers, explorers in their own right, taking up all of their possessions and moving with their husbands and families from Texas to California in the late 1950s for better opportunities to start a new life. These pioneering women who came from cotton-picking families, left their home bases to venture into a new world with hopes and dreams, most of all to have their children pursue their dreams, of which I am a result.

Sonia: Tell us about your father.

Jenny: My dad is a middle child out of thirteen children. His family came from the Texan border cities of Brownsville and Harlingen. Fun fact: his third great-grandfather, Hiram Chamberlain, established the first Presbyterian church in Brownsville, Texas, in the late 1800s. Hiram's father and grandfather both were Revolutionary War patriots. Interesting, right? I am always asked how I got my last name, Chamberlain, since I am predominantly Mexican. It goes back that many generations. Hiram Chamberlain had a son named Peter Bland who married a woman named Filipa whose family was from Texas when it was still Mexico. His son Albert married a woman named Gabriela, and they had my grandfather Pedro, who married my grandmother Martina, who together had my dad George, who married my mom Rosalinda Lopez, who had four children, me and my three younger brothers Mike, Gabe, and Nathan. There you go!

My father was seven when his family first moved to Central California to pick strawberries and cucumbers. They eventually moved to Sonoma County where other Hispanic families from Texas migrated to during that same time period to pick grapes, pears, apples, and prunes. They said Sonoma County was the land of opportunity and the climate provided better working conditions to work in, and most importantly, farmworker housing was available to people with families, which was a plus for them.

I remember my dad sharing stories of him growing up, which were pretty hard times for his family back then. Stories of how he worked the fields at that age in order to make his contribution to the family. Mind you, this was a time when children were on a school break, they were allowed to work in the fields. He told us of a time when one of his teachers got the community together to find clothing donations for him and his siblings because they needed them. He ended up with a pair of old tap shoes that he had to take the metal "tap" part out, and wore a shirt with the name "Danny" on it, although his name was George. His hard work ethic was something he always has been proud of, which, for those who know me and my siblings as well, has been passed down to us. Having a high work ethic is a value that my parents instilled in us, of which I am thankful.

I was born toward the end of the Vietnam War, it was in December 1969, a few days after my dad's nineteenth birthday when he received his draft notice. In May of 1970, they stationed him at the Fort Ord Army Base in Monterey, California, for basic training. Months later, in December 1970, he received his infantry orders to fight on the front line in Vietnam, he had just turned twenty years old two days before. He was literally on the plane that would take him from D.C. to Vietnam when they pulled him off. The Army received notice that he had two older brothers already stationed there, and they would send him to Korea instead. I was born a week later in January 1971, I just barely missed meeting my dad, we didn't get to meet in person until I was two. My mother moved in with his family to help her take care of me while he was away. The last four girls of the Chamberlain family were still living at the house, so as my Tia Linda tells it, "You were so loved as a baby, whenever you would cry, there was always someone carrying you in their arms." My tias remind me all the time of how my Grandma Chamberlain would get up in the middle of the night and cradle me until I stopped crying so that my mom could sleep to go to work the next day. My grandpa Pedro was the first male figure in my life, and most of my first baby pictures taken had me in his arms, in his garden that he was so proud of. I will forever be grateful for his presence in my life. The bond that we formed during those early years only grew stronger as time passed.

Sonia: How was your relationship with your dad's family?

Jenny: My Grandma Chamberlain was like me. She was the eldest out of all boys. I always identified with her, and growing up she seemed like she understood me. There was no other love like I felt with my Grandma Chamberlain.

Her mother died when she was young. They always said it was from a headache, but nowadays, we all think it was either a brain tumor or hemorrhage that might have occurred that took her life so early on. Her mother's passing happened so unexpectedly and left her dad, who was a pastor, as a single father raising up a daughter and four boys. Being the eldest, she was left with having to tend to the family's needs.

I remember as a little girl, she came to live with us. She and I shared a room and before we went to sleep, she would tell me stories which I vaguely remember about her childhood. I could always tell that there was a little emptiness that lived within her as she missed her mom. Perhaps, she thought had her mother lived, life may have been a little bit different, perhaps she would have made better decisions. Maybe she wished that her mother could have met her children and seen all the things she taught them that she learned from her. I will never know for sure if those were her thoughts, she passed away when I was about seventeen and I was too young back then to even think about asking these sorts of questions. One thing I know for sure, her mother would have been proud of her. That is a fact, because I am.

There were times when she said that she would dream about mother and she would visit her in her dreams as if it were like yesterday that they had last seen each other. As a nine-year-old, I was bewildered of how that could be, but now as a woman who misses her every day of my life, I understand it. For me, it's been over thirty years since I have heard her voice, and I can still hear her sing to me so clearly as if it was moments ago. My eyes still tear up and I can imagine it's the same way she missed her mother. Now it's my turn to look forward to seeing her in my dreams.

When she didn't live with us or I with her, her house was around the corner from mine for most of my life. My brothers and I would walk over there every day for the yummy treats she would have waiting for us. She could always make something out of nothing and like magic, you would have the most delicious meal you have ever tasted! My brothers and I spent a lot of time with her in the kitchen learning how to cook. I still miss the smell of her tortillas and how she would take a hot fresh tortilla right off the comal, spread butter on it and hand it over to our waiting hands. Oh, my grandmother could love like no other; she loved all her grandchildren, more than twenty-four of us, equally yet different, loving us in our own unique way. My grandmother loved to sing, and she had this favorite old yellow 1970s-looking cushioned rocking chair that she sat on. I would sit on her lap and she would bring out this old hymnal and sing to me, "This Little Light of Mine," "Closer Walk With Thee," and many more.

I still know these hymns by heart. It is those hymns and her love that have gotten me through some of my darkest nights and brought me joy during some of my greatest victories. Her love reminds me of who I am, my purpose and my desire to make her proud of me. She believed in me and loved without condition. My grandmother was not a rich woman through material means, but her love and kindness made her wealthy and she was happy.

Why do I do what I do for the community? To honor her, to pass on her legacy, because it doesn't deserve to just stay with me, but to be shared, just like the way she loved. She shared her love and always, without fail, made the very best out of every situation.

Sonia: You said both of your parents were from Texas, tell me about your mother's family.

Jenny: When my mom was about six years old, her father, an aspiring entertainer, moved the family to Los Angeles, California, with five kids in tow, leaving one of my mother's brothers to be raised by my grandma's parents in Texas. Eleven kids later, his love for women and showbusiness surpassed his love for my grandmother, and they divorced, leaving her a single mom of eleven, raising her children in downtown L.A. with not one single family member around to give her any kind of support.

My "Grandma Calie" herself came from a family of twelve, three girls and nine brothers, they picked cotton in Texas. One thing I know for sure, she came from a home that supported and stood by each other's side, no matter what. That is how the Arismendez family did it and a value she installed into her children and us grandchildren.

Her brothers were always very protective of her, but being the independent woman my grandmother was, they gave her space and respect when making her own decisions when it came to her life.

When she divorced my grandfather in the mid-sixties, one of her brothers and uncle lived in the small, remote farming region of northern Sonoma County, California. They felt that the projects of Los Angeles were not a good place for a single mom to raise her kids. They made the eight-hour drive in a pick-up truck to Southern California to get her and her eleven children, taking them back to Sonoma County because they believed that her children would have a better chance at success there. Shortly after the move, her brother died of leukemia and eventually her uncle passed away, but this time she had cousins who she had as support, and community members who she had established strong relationships and ties with. By this time, she was married for a second time, and had kid number twelve. That marriage soon ended in divorce, and once again she was a single mother, now with twelve children. But this time was different, because of the friendships she established that became her extended family for the rest of her life.

I always wondered what went through her mind and what she felt like under her new circumstances, when she first became a single mother. When they first moved to Los Angeles eight years prior, she was a young, vibrant twenty-six-year-old leaving her family and everything she knew behind in Texas with hopes and dreams for herself and her six children. Now, here she was in her early thirties with eleven kids, alone with no family around that she could lean on, and trying to make ends meet. My grandfather was off to his new conquest and had little contact with my mom and siblings thereafter.

I can't tell you what I would have done, but I do know for sure her strength lives within me. How did she survive? How did she do it alone with all those kids? How many nights did she cry herself to sleep only to wake up in the morning knowing that she MUST BE victorious?

My grandmother never talked negatively about her life; that's something I remember about her. She was a woman of great faith, prayer, and a provider. She always provided, and somehow, she would manage with the tiny checks she would receive; she always found a way to get her children and her grandkids birthday and Christmas presents. That was very important to her. She had acute asthma, always in and out of the hospital, and never one time did I hear her complain. Wait, one time she did. My mom bought her a granny nightgown to wear in the hospital about a year before she died, and she called me over to visit her so that I could take it back to my mom. She said "Jenny, Mija! I don't know what your mom is thinking! She is trying to dress me like an old lady! I am young! I feel young! Tell her I like nice sexy things, not this!" I still crack up until this day.

Sonia: How was your relationship with your mom's family?

Jenny: I was very close to my mom's family too, my aunts and uncles on her side were very close in age to me and were like older brothers and sisters. I have an uncle who is a year older than me and we played and bumped heads together like siblings, till this day I have a hard time calling him uncle, it's too awkward. When I turned nineteen, I would later live with my aunt Darlene and her husband Alfred in Southern California who encouraged me to pursue my goals and till this day offering me wisdom and a rock to lean on.

You know, even though my Grandma Calie's two marriages didn't work out, she never gave up on love. She met the love of her life, Dwayne, in her mid-seventies, and he was a younger man by eight years, I believe!

I guess that is the reason why I have always been bewildered when people are so concerned about me being single in my late forties. Sometimes I get the sense they are depressed and extremely worried for me. But I never have been. I don't look back at relationships, both bad and good, and dwell on what went wrong or what didn't, or why I made a bad decision to stay in one. I think about my Grandma Calie and always say to myself, "Love can happen at any time, there is no sense to rush it. I am willing to wait for that right person at that right time. Heck, my grandma was in her mid-seventies and was head over heels in love like a high school girl with Dwayne. Love is worth the wait." Therefore, I am happy and free knowing that everything and anything I do, I MUST be victorious, at least for her.

Sonia: Tell us about your mom and what has she taught you?

Jenny: Although both families are from Texas, my parents met in Healdsburg, California, in high school. My mom was a junior and my dad a senior when they married in 1968, a day after my dad's eighteenth birthday. They actually eloped, and my Grandma Calie gave my mom consent to marry my dad. They found a pastor who had a tiny church off Fulton Rd which at that time was located in the rural part of Santa Rosa. She said they woke up the pastor in the early hours of a rainy morning, and the pastor married them in his living room of the church's parsonage in his pajamas and slippers. Ha! I always asked her why they married so young, and she said coming from large families it was easier for them financially to be married, and I am guessing it gave them more privacy too.

My mother always had this determination in her to go against the odds to make things happen. When she was a senior in high school, she didn't find out that she was pregnant with me until after my dad was stationed in Fort Ord. She always tells me that I was in her tummy when she walked on stage to get her high school diploma and that I walked with her. It is something that she has always been pretty proud of because she said that school officials and others had discouraged her from finishing regular high school and wanted her to finish through continuation school. It was 1970 and God forbid that they have a married senior on campus who was pregnant, right? What kind of example would that be for others to follow?

Well, an example she became! She graduated, went on to Santa Rosa Jr. College, got her degree in fashion, has been married to the same man for fifty years, and raised a beautiful family. In her own words, "I showed them!" She was eighteen when I was born. Although

I was born a few days after the New Year, I was the New Year's baby for the City of Healdsburg in 1971, and the community came around to support the Army Soldier's wife and showered her with gifts in celebration of the new arrival.

Anyone who knows my mom, knows her as a funny woman full of laughter, and a self-proclaimed goofy person. She always did her best to make our childhood fun, not just for me and my brothers, but my cousins as well. There was a time when she would babysit most of my cousins at our house, she would play the organ and have us dress up, march in a circle while she played songs like "When The Saints Go Marching In," if it wasn't that it was the Beatles. She would have us dress up, do lip-sync contests, plays and much more. I think I learned a lot of creativity and imagination from those days for sure.

I remember growing up, she would tell us these bedtime stories of these two naughty boys who outsmarted everyone while growing up in the streets of L.A. "The Adventures of Chorizo and Horquillas," she called it. My brothers and I would look forward to going to bed every night in anticipation to hear about their new adventures. She would make them sound so exciting and colorful! There was the story of when Chorizo and Horquillas went to the store to buy some milk and outsmarted the bullies who would come by to take their food by giving them fake boxes of cereal. There was a time they went shoe shining to make some money, and hid their money in the bottom of their socks so the bullies won't steal it, and gave them pennies instead—again, outsmarting those thugs! They had an uncle named Panzón who fell asleep on the couch one day and they got a broomstick and started tickling his ears and he thought it was flies bothering him. Chorizo and Horquillas outsmarted the Horse Lady at the foster home. The Horse Lady had no chance against them! My mom would laugh so hard telling us these stories and we wanted more as they were our own version of Nancy Drew and the Hardy Boys.

I was talking to her the other night and she shared something with me that she has shared in the past. I was too young to fully comprehend the impact and how it affected her life and as a result, how it has impacted mine as one of the major life-changing choices I am about to make.

She shared that a lot of these stories were based on childhood experiences of her brothers and herself. Chorizo and Horquillas were two of her younger brothers, and Uncle Panzón was her grandpa who would come from Texas to visit them in Los Angeles. She said that through her storytelling, she would change things up a bit and make them into an adventure. Instead of making them sad, she would turn the stories around to turn them into comedy and laughter.

When my uncle Roy died over fifteen years ago, they found $300 inside the socks he wore. Funny how we learn these habits when we are young and carry them with us for the rest of our lives.

One of those adventures that I never realized that has stood with me for all my life was when Chorizo and Horquillas went into the foster home. My mom, as long as I can remember, told me about the time my Grandma Calie was in the hospital for an extended period of time due to her asthma. CPS came by and took her and her brothers. There was only four of them in the house at that time, and they were still living in Texas. I have no idea what my grandpa was doing or where he was at the time, but they were taken away. My mom always shared with us this story since I can remember, and how terrible it was. As the oldest, she was taking care of her siblings, they were being naughty and playing the music loud. The lady next door called CPS and they came knocking on the door to take them away. She said the social worker lady was wearing a black dress and the men were in black suits and ties. They came inside the house and took her three brothers. She said she hid and locked the door, and when they realized that there was one more inside, they came knocking and demanded that she come with them. She refused, they shouted, and she still didn't budge. The only reason why she finally opened the door was because she saw through the window one of her younger brothers crying, and it broke her heart. As the big sister, she could not let them be alone. She must have not been older than six years old at this point.

She didn't have a pleasant experience at the home where they were placed. Mrs. Gladys, who they named "The Horse Lady" for unknown reasons, was not nice and they were fed oatmeal with no sugar. They were all put in one small room and couldn't leave. She said she often looked outside the window at the stars and the moon, and wondered if life was going to be different. It eventually did change, as my grandma's family, her parents, brothers, and sisters, got together and got her a good lawyer, and she got her kids back. My mom said my grandmother's greatest asset was her children, and she did everything she could to protect them.

Sonia: What part of your mother's story has made you want to make a life-changing decision?

Jenny: Ever since I can remember, I always wanted to adopt or be a foster parent. I didn't realize it until just now, hearing myself talk about my mother's experience with foster care, maybe that seed was planted in me years ago as a child and never left. Now that I am forty-eight years old, I feel that I am ready. To love a child that you did not give birth to is one of the greatest gifts I believe we can have live within us. But, maybe deep down inside of me, living that experience with my mom through her storytelling gave me the desire to provide a child who has gone through the same experience that my mother had a safe and loving home. That is all I have ever wanted to do, whether it be mentoring young people, taking them under my wing, or just showing them that someone loves, cares, and believes in them.

My mother is a resilient woman, yet calm under the most trying circumstances. People often mistake calmness as a weakness vs. those are more expressive with their emotions. I believe that is the opposite, as it takes more strength to keep your composure instead of letting it go. I learned from my mother to smile during my most trying times, always making time for laughter, and never forgetting to be silly sometimes by finding that child within you. I have been taught to hope and have faith that tomorrow will be a brighter day, and that rainy days are a blessing because without it, we do not have the opportunity to grow. This I know my mother learned from my grandmothers as they both equally influenced her life. She learned these qualities from their storytelling, sharing with her that even in the face of what might seem like defeat there is a window to the unknown. One that is to be opened, so that we can see a life full of many different possibilities waiting for us to grab hold of and write our own story, to be shared with others. Now, it is my turn, as the third generation to share "ours".

Sonia: Beautiful stories of transformation. What a blessing that you have had that opportunity to be around family and strong women, because a lot of women don't get to. How do you feel that their influence prepared you for your speech? Can you take us back to that night?

Jenny: As I ended my speech, there was more I wanted to express, but felt so constrained and restricted to the translation. There have been many times when I have sat on a panel as an "advisor" to women who were practicing their speeches for one reason or another. Many of them whose first language is Spanish and rehearsing for their first time a translated speech in English. Tears started flowing down my eyes as I thought of these brave women who have gone before me and stepped out of their comfort zone so that they can become changemakers and make a difference. Now the roles were flipped and I wanted to share these women's stories with the audience by sharing mine. I just didn't understand or admire their courage, this time I felt it. That took everything to a whole new level and at that moment, I experienced transformation with my eyes wide open, breathing in every moment of it, versus realizing it a later time through reflection. It hit me all at once, and I had to share this newfound revelation with those whose attention I had before me. It was a profound moment for me.

I looked into the crowd, this time, although it was still dark, I could see their faces, many of them who resembled the women in my life. By this time, the tears were rolling down my eyes as I shared my story of transformation with them. At that moment, it turned full circle for me, I knew that I could not have been there, mustering up the courage and confidence had it not been from the women in my life and everything they taught me. One of the most important things I learned is having a village whether it be family or friends that you can lean on. When the lights finally went back on, people came up to me and thanked me for being honest and open, they said I had them in tears and encouraged them to step out of their comfort zone. I was effective, I did make a difference and when I was in doubt, it was my village who reminded me I could.

Sonia: I know there has been challenging events that occurred in your life where you had to rise up and overcome. Why did you choose this most recent journey versus experiences from your past that are a part of your transformation story?

Jenny: There were a lot of things that came to mind to share with you about my journey and struggles. I didn't want it to be a story of all the details of my life that I created for myself that led me to the stage that night. I wanted it to be about all the amazing women in my life who led me there, by sharing their stories, their life with me.

I also wanted to give you something in "real time" vs. a series of reflections of past experiences, because the struggle is real. Many times, as women, we can look at each other's success and say to ourselves, "Oh, she hit all her goals, she overcame her hardships. It should be smooth sailing for her," or "Oh, she is such a good speaker, I am sure that she never gets nervous." Nope. Not true.

No matter how successful we are at something, we are always going to have to face some challenges and overcome insecurities in order for us to continue to grow and have grace and compassion upon others. I wanted to be in the "present moment" but also share with you the reason why I took the challenge and eventually overcame what I thought were my shortcomings.

Sonia: You mentioned earlier how you were taught to be part of a village. Can you elaborate more on what a village means to you and why it is important?

Jenny: It is about your village and the relationships that you establish, that are so important to your life. That is a legacy that my grandmothers and mother have shared with me. No matter how independent you are, it's important to understand the role that others play in your life. But we first must admit that we need to be loved, encouraged, and supported. It gives us the opportunity to be vulnerable, which is a beautiful thing.

Throughout this most recent experience, my village held me up when I thought I would fall. They opened my eyes and let me know that I was already victorious when I thought I was defeated. I tried numerous times to find someone else to do the speech who spoke better Spanish than me. Those I reached out to take my place, believed in me and encouraged me to be brave and do it. How was I supposed to write a speech in Spanish? Using a translating app wasn't going to help that much. But I had friends who stepped up to the plate on my behalf, took the time out of their personal lives to help me. They all wanted to make sure I was a success, because at that time, they had more faith in me than I did for myself.

Sonia: How did they help you?

Jenny: My friend Daniel did the first round of translation, he rearranged one of his appointments the same day I asked so that he could take some time out to translate for me. Later that night, I sent an email to my friend Linda to read my speech and asked her if my message made sense, she read it at ten p.m. knowing that I would have done the same for her. My friend Alma who while talking together on a business call, offered to go over my speech the day before the performance to translate my changes. There was a point where I wanted to add a sentence in at the very last minute. I showed up at this mixer with about sixty people, spotted my friend Ana in the middle of the crowd and asked her to make a quick translation, she texted to me on the spot. Alegria my friend and colleague who was to introduce me on stage took the time after our last rehearsal to record my speech in Spanish. I listened to that recording all the way home, before I went to bed at night and when I woke in the morning. She did this so that I could make a pause where it needed to be in order for me to emphasize emotion and pronunciation to help get my message across. It helped me feel secure when there was an inner battle with my confidence vs. my insecurities. My village believed me, and my confidence won.

I would have never thought about entertaining this idea if the values instilled within me from my family didn't exist. I was taught that humbleness and letting your guard down to accept help is one of the greatest lessons to be learned on the road to success. Like the women who raised me, I need my village, there is no other way I know how to live. We need to surround ourselves with a village that values us, and in turn, we value them.

Sonia: You have such a passion to serve and help people, how would you encourage others to get involved in community work?

Jenny: You first need to identify and build your village, it stems from what is inside you. Your village might be family based, centered around a specific cause or hobbies.

When people ask me how they can be involved in the community, I ask them these questions: What your biggest passion? What are the desires of your heart? What inspires you to grow? What causes you to take up a challenge? What drives you? What makes you want to stand up, rise up, and fight for what you believe in? Most of all, are you ready to get out of your comfort zone and grow into the person you were meant to be?

Asking yourself these questions is the first step to getting out of your comfort zone. Sometimes it requires us to dig deep to really find out what ignites us. Then the doubts start to fade away, and instead of asking yourself questions like, "Am I good enough?" or "Can I do this?" something inside of us becomes ignited, we move forward and through our actions we become active participants in our community.

This is when digging into the very core of who we are causes us to work out of passion, out of heart. Then, we become contagious. We start movements and others follow. We make a difference. Why? Because there is love and heart behind it and as a result, we encourage others to do the same. It goes from our bloodstream and infuses itself onto others.

Sonia: What is some advice that you would give to someone who is ready to step out of their comfort zone?

Jenny: One of the greatest contributors of fear is the unknown because making yourself vulnerable to either failure or success is a risk. But, to be true changemakers, we must step into the "unknown," into that little grey area that sometimes might seem like this big, dark black glob that is waiting to suck you in. The legacy that I have been left with is learning to be okay with the unknown, because therein lies the greatest adventure of our lives. It takes a lot of faith to do so, but growing our faith is also one of the greatest rewards. When we see it that way, there are no failures, only lessons learned and experiences we grow from.

Sonia: Destiny is already laid out, and it's up to us to choose that right path. And how do we get in that path? We fail forward. We learn from our mistakes, and we allow peace to guide the way. It goes back to destiny. Your destiny is not going to look like mine. Mine's not going to look like yours, but once we're in our own, it's going to be phenomenal. Thank you so much for sharing the vulnerable part, the heart part, because this is what has brought you to where you're at today. The strong woman. We need more women like you.

Jenny: When we allow ourselves to be vulnerable and share our story, baring our true selves we then are able to encourage others to "Rise UP" and live out their fullest potential and become changemakers.

Sonia: That was so beautiful. Thank you so much.

Sonia Hassey

ABOUT JENNY CHAMBERLAIN

Jenny has made it her lifelong passion to serve her community and encourage people to go beyond their expectations setting the path forward for others to follow. She is the Chief of Staff to Sonoma County 4th District Supervisor James Gore, Past President of the Hispanic Chamber of Commerce Sonoma County and currently serves on the Executive Board of the California Hispanic Chambers of Commerce. Jenny also writes two lifestyle blogs www.writeyourstory707.com, a motivational blog, and www.singlefabulousfostering.com , sharing her journey of becoming a single foster parent.

CHAPTER 12

Near Death to Awakened Soul

Jen Crowe

Sonia: I am here with Jen Crowe. Jen, please tell us about you, your story, and how you came about doing what you love.

Jen: I am the founder of Grow with Crowe, LLC, and now partnering to bring wellness, life purpose breakthroughs, and business mastery through the power of human connection both in Northern Ca and at the Hawaiian Sanctuary on the Big Island! I work with women, men, groups, and leaders all over.

What I'm doing now, as a Breakthrough Facilitator and "Next Level" Coach, is showing people how to achieve their life's purpose, renew their self-love, and I work with groups and leaders in a retreat with a classroom setting to show them how to grow in life or business through an awakened and newfound approach, including human connection. Teaching, influencing, and inspiring is a collaboration of what I've done in my career over the past twenty-five years. I had to go through a massive life transformation, however, to finally get to this point in my life where I'm now standing on top of my story, which is a little bit intense and long, and I'll get into that for you.

So, now I'm thriving in my life, influencing as many people as I can. I'm trying to reach eleven million women in eleven months and show them that transformation, owning yourself, harnessing your potential, and living a life that you love instead of a life you're settling for is wholly possible. If I can do it, you can do it. The only difference is that hopefully you won't be told that you have twenty-four hours to live.

I don't want anyone to look back on their lives and experience pain because they realize they didn't even begin to unleash their potential or they let their past determine their future. They didn't even begin to live with passion and love for themselves and everything and everyone around them. So that's what I do. I want to inspire people to start living the life that they're meant to live before they reach the point that I did.

Sonia: I know you didn't reach this fulfillment in one day, so share with us where it all began for you.

Jen: Absolutely. It actually took me thirty-nine years, one month, and twenty-eight days to get to this point. I like to take people and do that within ninety days through a virtual coaching program, or in less time through one of my retreats.

I grew up in Sonoma Valley, Northern California, in wine country. Looking in from the outside, people saw me as a little blonde white girl running around, playing sports, and having friends, and it was great. My parents were there, and I had my grandparents and my family. So, it looked like your everyday, wonderful childhood.

What happened with me was that behind closed doors, my life was very different than what people would have ever expected. I've just started unleashing my own story and telling my truth, and standing on top of my story rather than in it for the first time ever. It's the perceptions, right? I can remember when things started to shift and transform for me. I remember having a great childhood and everything was wonderful until I was about five years old. It's a funny story because the first time I ever started to understand what abuse was, was when I was about five, and I'll never forget that day I came home from school, and I walked in the door and I was repeating what I had heard at school. I was walking around the house singing "bucket, fuck it, bucket, fuck it, bucket, fuck it, bucket, fuck it, bucket, fuck it." I didn't know what it meant, I was just like, "lulu lulu." Just total innocence. I remember my dad coming around the corner asking, "What did you just say?" I went, "Bucket fuck it," and that was it. That was when it started to change. That's when my dad went through his own transformation. I had never felt a belt across my back or my backside in my life, but it started on that day.

It was an eye-opening moment. Here I was at five, with no idea what was happening to me or why. It was just the beginning of what would end up being the next fifteen, almost twenty years of complete trauma in my life, that didn't stop until I finally stopped it. So yes, abuse at five years old transformed into six and seven and continued. The interesting part of it is that my father had a history that I'm sure so many people can relate to. He was abused as a child. He went through crazy abuse. He was a Vietnam vet and I actually intend to write a book to tell the story of the children of the Vietnam vets. They don't often talk about what happens to the children in the home. He came back, went through massive depression, had falling outs with his father, and since I was the female child in the family, I became a target. That's how it started. For me, back then, it was fear. It was constant fear. Every single day I lived in fear.

Sonia: What did your day look like?

Jen: When I was six, my parents, my brother, and I ended up moving into my grandparents' house because they had moved out. My parents took it over. My mom was a nurse and she worked a lot of hours, just a fabulous and caring woman. My dad at that time was running his father's business with his father, which was not a good thing. And so, in my average day at six and seven years old, my brother and I had to get up on our own. My parents were both out the door by that time. I often had to make our lunches, and make our breakfast, and I made sure that we got out the door on time. We would have to run to the bus stop. We'd have to go sit at the bus stop, sometimes in the rain, and it didn't matter. If we were late, we'd have to haul ass, and pray to God that we didn't miss the bus because we knew we were going to be getting the wrath. We'd take the bus to school.

In my elementary years, I went through phases of craving and wanting attention and wanting something friendly, especially since I lived in an abusive home. So I acted out. I'd be hyper or I'd be super introvert and quiet, and people would pick on me or bully me throughout my school years. I went from abuse at home to being picked on while on the bus or at school, and then my brother would get picked on. So, the bus ride turned into a living hell for us, but it was something we had to do. You do it and you go to school.

At school, there was bullying because we would act out, or we would be too quiet, or we were different, or whatever it was, but we were never allowed to talk about what happened at home. That was just not an option. Nobody knew for years and years what was happening to us in our home. We would go and just do the daily. That was our average day. Go to school, get it done, we had lunch, we got picked on by bullies. We'd have good days and fun days in between, but it was the bus ride home, every single day for as long as I can remember, I would just dread, because once we got to the house, we did not know what would be on the other side of that door when we walked in. Very rarely, there were niceties. It was always my dad home first before my mom, and so it was either immediate screaming and yelling, pulling us into a corner, holding me by the neck, and just screaming about nonsense for hours. Or we would have to jump right into chores, and then without fail, the inevitable yelling and holding us hostage in my father's fits of rage, until who knows when.

Sonia: What was happening in your mind and emotions when you were on the bus ride home?

Jen: It was always extremely traumatic. A full spectrum swing of emotions, right? Even if the bullying on the bus was going on, everything was fine while I was on the bus. I would try to enjoy that moment for all twenty-three minutes of that bus ride home, and just savor it, because the second I got off, I knew that I was literally going to be walking into hell, and I didn't know what kind of hell it would be. So, that bus ride home for myself, and I won't speak for my brother, that's his own thing, but for me, it was to enjoy the moment, just sit here and be in the moment as long as you can. That went on throughout most of our school, and so it was about getting off the bus, and walking down the bus steps, not knowing what we were walking into. It was a long walk home. We didn't run home like some kids did. We would try to go slowly. There are just some images that you can never ever get out of your head, and for me, it was touching the doorknob, and turning the doorknob, and just barely opening the front door. Was he right there? Was he going to be waiting in the back of the house? Was he going to be grabbing me by the arm? It was crazy turmoil for sure.

Sonia: I can't even imagine. Being six years old, you had so much innocence. What was your mom's role with everything that was happening?

Jen: My mom was an extremely outgoing, strong, vibrant, full-of-life woman, and she would tell you today that in the beginning of her marriage with my dad, things were great, and then things started to turn, and she lost her strength. She succumbed to the torment as well. It became progressively worse over the years. Looking back on it, I found ways to save myself and survive. I became a survivor. I had techniques and tools to survive. My mom was never shown those tools. My dad was never shown those tools. They did what they did based on what they had at the time. For years, I resented my mother for not saving us. Only now can I look back and tell this story in a way that is not full of resentment, anger, pain, and suffering, because I can see it in such a different light.

Now that's not to say that I didn't have tools and I figured it out. So, everyone is capable of figuring it out, and reaching out for help when you know something's not right. I could never imagine watching my children be abused by anybody without wanting to absolutely kill the person. For me to be able to look at that from any parents' point of view as an abused wife or husband even, or to watch your children being abused, only very recently could I even begin to comprehend it. It's not easy to comprehend how somebody can be almost mentally erased and brainwashed to a point where they don't take action.

So that was my childhood up until I was fifteen. Every night from the time that we got home from school, it was always torture. His drinking would intensify between five and seven p.m., and when the drinking intensified, so did the verbal, emotional, and physical abuse. I can't tell you how many nights we would just be made to sit on the couch and let him just unleash a load on us for hours and hours and hours.

Sonia: You and your brother and your mom?

Jen: Not my mom. She was usually not there, or she was outside of the house, or would find ways to numb her pain. My dad always targeted me, and then sometimes my brother. It was like he was holding us hostage for hours and we weren't allowed to do our homework. We weren't allowed to do anything, and then we'd get yelled at, because our homework wasn't done, but we weren't allowed to get off the couch or we'd be smacked back down on the couch.

Sonia: What was going through your head as you were sitting there on that couch?

Jen: What went through my head changed tremendously as I got older. I remember one very vivid memory from when I was seven. The reason it's so vivid is that my dad used to love to preach the Bible and God to us, and so if you can imagine, while he's choking you or just calling you every nasty name in the book, and then saying, "God is this," and going into religious talk, for me as a child it was very confusing. Where is my God who's supposed to be this great and loving being? How is God letting this happen? But I was seven, and he would make me sit there and tell me that seven is the age of reason, and he unleashed this whole preaching on me. I didn't use bad words back then, but if I could have, I would have been like, "What the hell is he talking about? Just get me out of here. Just airlift me, transport me anywhere else but here. I would be in fear because I could never understand or even begin to comprehend why I was going through this. Things often became so horrible I tried to take my own life twice. Once when I was about eight, and the second time when I was eleven.

Many of my friends had happy home lives and lived what I believed to be a harmonious and loving life. I could not understand what I did to deserve what was happening to me. I was always a straight-A student. I never got in trouble. I was scared to death to do anything wrong. I was called a goody-goody in school for years. Yeah, it was complete torment and torture. As I got older, we knew better than to ever, ever, ever talk back. That was not an option. I didn't even ask why. My father would just accuse me of something and punish me, and I just took it because it would be so much worse if I resisted, and that was part of the survival to just take what was coming. Some nights he would have complete and utter mental breakdowns. He would go into these paranoid delusional states like he was in Vietnam, and start screaming about killing people. I can remember nights when he would grab a shotgun and make us load it, and point it at him. It was truly horrifying and awful. He would make us do it. He would sit there, and he would shove the guns into our hands and say, "This is what we had to deal with. This is what I had to go through, I sent people in to kill people." There are truly no words to describe what vets with PTSD live with, the trauma is real.

Night after night I just didn't know. I didn't know what traumatized side of my dad would appear. Would it be the sad, abused victim child that he was, or the tormented PTSD version of severe post-traumatic stress from the Vietnam War? Or the man who had no idea who he was, or at times a mix of it all coming out at once. My childhood went on that way every single day, every single night. If we wanted to go play with our friends on the weekend, we had to do an abundance of chores from cleaning the house (and I mean spotless) or shoveling mounds of gravel and wheelbarrow gravel, or doing loads of yard work, just to name a few. It may sound simple, but when you're young, we had to clean the whole house and it was just hours upon hours. I'm grateful for it now, but then I was like, "I want to go play. Let me get to the creek and build forts, I just want to get away, just let me go."

Sonia: As a child, that's the most natural thing to do.

Jen: It's not to say that we didn't do normal things. We had friends around the block, we had a creek behind the house that we played in and built forts. When I was young, we went on family vacations. We had a childhood. It's just, unfortunately, that the majority of it was not pleasant. And so it continued until I started to find my voice. **Sonia:** How old were you when you started finding your voice, and what brought you to that?

Jen: I had gotten to a point where my learned behavior was to stay quiet, but I realized that was not my natural desire or nature. As I got older and the more I started to realize what was happening to me, I knew it was wrong. It was not okay. I didn't do anything to deserve these things. I think I was around ten or eleven when I realized that, "No, I don't want to do that," or "That's not okay," or "Don't touch me." But it came down four times as hard as it would have if I had just stayed quiet, which made me scream and cry. I can't tell you how many times I'd be hysterically crying, and he would just look at me and go,

"Oh, so you want to be an actress today? Oh, you're a great actress. Real nice. Real nice," and he called me an actress for years. I tried not to cry and then I'd start to hyperventilate, and then it just made it worse. This went on until I was probably about twelve or thirteen. I was in middle school when I really decided, "You know what, this is bullshit. I'm pissed. I can't do this anymore. Enough is enough. No one is protecting me, so I have to try and protect myself."

My brother and I would go at it, viciously, because my dad somehow managed to pin us against each other, and that was so brutal. At twelve or thirteen, I finally just started standing up for myself, and I'd scream at my mom at that time and say, "Why aren't you doing anything? Help us. What's going on?" She would just cry, and she couldn't do anything. She was totally stripped of who she was, and she also felt so much fear and angst. The torment continued until I was about fifteen. My dad had terrible recurring bouts of paranoia. The more he drank, he'd get weird, paranoid delusions. More often than not, it was of myself or my brother "listening in on his conversations."

I will never forget that night when I was in the back room with my brother, we had a second brother at that time, and we were playing Nintendo Super Mario Brothers and getting into it. I walked from their room to my bedroom at the front of the house, next to the kitchen where he and my mom were fighting, to grab a game out of my room. When I was walking back, my dad just happened to come around the corner and he decided that I had actually been standing around the corner listening to their conversation. He thought I was eavesdropping and that I couldn't be trusted. I was fifteen. He just flipped his lid and grabbed me by the hair, and said, "Get out of my house. We can't have you here. I can't trust you. Think you're sneaky?!" and called me every name in the book. He threw me out, literally threw me out of my house with nothing, and I was hysterical, and I had to walk myself up to the corner store, which was a couple of blocks up, and called a friend to come pick me up. That was the last time I lived at my house. So I had just turned fifteen, and through high school, I ended up couch-hopping through six or seven different friends' homes and trying to maintain my grades and keep that up, and keep it together. I did pretty well, considering, I think. But you talk about an emotional roller coaster from feeling a type of newfound freedom, to feeling abandonment, to fear and not belonging. Feeling grateful to people that let me into their homes and treated me like one of theirs, to wonderful people allowing me to stay short-term, while at the same time, feeling like a burden or misfit.

Sonia: Were your parents looking for you?

Jen: No. My mom knew where I was, and so finally when I would stay at one house for more than a week or two, I think she would give them some money or something to help with food, but never tried to get me to come back, never kicked my dad out, and that was something that I was tormented with for a long time. I went through my own internal transitions, and one of them was, "Holy shit, I'm free." Another was, "I'm totally abandoned." I felt totally abandoned by everyone, judged, and very alone. My grandma didn't come after me at the time, I believe to avoid conflict or making things worse … what was she supposed to do? My family didn't come after me. Nobody did. I had to continually find places to go. I had to go to people I barely knew and ask if I could stay at their house. People can't imagine what that feels like to be completely dependent on people you don't know. That was most of high school.

Sonia: I only felt like that for one day, just for one day, and I was older. I believe I was in high school, and it was such despair. I cannot even begin to explain to you the feeling of not feeling wanted. Just seeing you now, what a powerful woman you are, but it didn't come without a cost.

Jen: I remember thinking that I had these survival tactics that kept me from dying. I even had thoughts of suicide at eight or nine years old, and actually tried around eleven years old because I wanted out so bad. I went from that survival technique to being on my own. I had to earn my own money. I had to buy everything and figure it all out, and so it turned into a completely different set of survival techniques. In the meantime, I also went a little wild and crazy, because I didn't know how to be free without constant fear, other than where I was going to sleep. I ended up just wanting to go out with friends or new people and doing things. In the midst of that, I didn't know how to show my love and gratitude for the people who were taking care of me at the time. This was a huge regret that I think a lot of people can relate to. All of a sudden, I was in between all these different emotions. I learned it's never too late to go back and say, "Thank you. I'm so grateful for you," but at the time it was part of the transition and the struggle for me.

During this time, I also met my best friend, Melissa, who became a rock and a most incredible friend. She and her family were there for me in ways, well, so many ways that this chapter would become a novel if I tried to share them all. But I will say, that when you find your person, or surround yourself with people that love, support, and challenge you, it can be the lifesaver you never knew existed. We are still best friends today, twenty-plus years later.

When I was about seventeen, things all started to happen for me at the same time. Big things, like I lost my virginity. I had my first drink. I ended up meeting the man who would become my daughter's father, which was a complete coincidence. In between all this time, once in a blue moon, I'd have to go back to my parents' house or we'd do Christmas or dinner, and there was never not a huge blowout with my dad.

At seventeen, it was the last time I went there. I remember I had borrowed my mom's car, and Melissa and I went to San Francisco to hang out and have a good time. We went to Treasure Island and hung out with the "navy boys." On the way back, I got a nail in the tire on the Bay Bridge, and it was the middle of the night, so we had to pull off of the Bay Bridge, and we ended up in the smack ghetto of Oakland at one o'clock in the morning, and we were there in our little tiny mini-skirts. We were in a red Dodge Daytona Turbo Z, a little red sports car. We got out and we were not meant to be where we were. I'll never forget this guy coming up to us with a crowbar at our door and saying, "What the hell are you two doing here?" I said, "We have a flat tire and we're waiting for the tow truck." This guy made me pay him twenty bucks to protect us, and no joke, he had to scare off three or four people away from our car while we sat there. So, then we get the car back to my parents' house the next morning and didn't divulge the entire story other than the nail and fixing the flat. My dad lost his mind because a nail had gotten in the tire, and he went to grab me around the neck again. His favorite thing in the past was to grab my neck and try and pull me off my feet. I don't know where it came from, but all I remember is that my right hand went back and I just swung, and he immediately ran out of the room, went to the phone, and called the cops. He called 911. And told them I was trying to beat him. I'll never forget that night.

Sonia: You're kidding.

Jen: Nope, he said that I was beating him up and he was scared for his life. It actually reminds me of another time in high school where people in authority positions of leadership are supposed to be there to protect us, but I was failed three separate times by counselors in high school who didn't turn in my father when I came to school, and they knew that something had happened. This time in particular, the night he called the police, I'll never forget that the police showed up and it was an older police officer and a newer, younger officer, and I was sitting there, I was hysterical, of course, and so, the police separated my dad and me, and they were both coming in and I was just screaming, right? I was just going back and trying to tell them what happened and why I did what I did, and the older officer looks at me and goes, "You shut your mouth. You respect your elders. He'll talk first." And I'll never forget it in my life. I couldn't believe it, and so at this time I just completely lost respect for authority. That was the second or third time that had happened to me where they totally let me down, and because of it, horrible things transpired. But the younger gentleman, he took me by the arm, and he took me outside and he said, "If you can go up to the store, go call a ride. You need to not be here right now."

That was not the first night the police had been called, and my father should have been taken to Oak Crest and again for the second time, he wasn't. The cops had been called to our house several times because neighbors could hear what was happening, and he was never taken in. I always wonder what our life would be like if anyone had done what they were supposed to do. Would my dad have gotten the help and support he needed? Would I have found a different path? We never know, but I do know that things have a way of happening exactly as they are supposed to. I definitely would not have been able to tell you that then, however. That memorable night I left that house and I ended up going off with my best friend, and that was the same night, ironically, that I ended up meeting my daughter's father, and he turned out to be just like my dad.

The story continues. I met him when I had just turned eighteen. He was extremely verbally and emotionally abusive as well. He'd hold me in a car for hours and just scream at me, and it was like déjà vu. I found out that I was pregnant, and at that same time, my brother was very, very sick (this is an incredible miracle story in itself). I have so many regrets about not being there more for my brother at that time, but I also realize I just didn't have the capacity or ability at that time to know what to do, for who, or how. I was spinning, again.

I ended up getting two jobs. I was trying to go to school, trying to get things done on my own, and I had a baby coming. I didn't want to go into the system. I refused to be a statistic. I was dealing with the craziness of my dad, and the insanity of my baby's daddy, another total alcoholic. My brother was dying of cancer. I had all these things happening, and I just went through the motions. Numbness, anxiety, fear, sorrow, alone, anger, hate, you name it.

My daughter and I are exactly nineteen years and a month apart. She just turned twenty-one, and I just turned forty this year.

Back at that time, my baby's daddy kept liquidating our bank accounts and taking all of our money, and spending hours at the bars. I didn't have enough money to pay rent and I could barely feed my daughter. I was working two jobs. When my daughter was four months old, I finally found the courage to say to her father, "Look, either get it together or get out." He didn't. I ended up kicking him out, and that's when everything transitioned for me again.

So there I was, a single mom, and much of my family was upset initially that I had her because they said I should have had an abortion. It was difficult for them, I believe, to understand how I could raise a child at eighteen years old. I dropped out of Jr. College, and that's when a friend of mine said, "I know you're going through a hard time. There's a dealership in Novato that's hiring. Would you ever consider selling cars?" I was in school to be a pediatrician, and I said, "Hell no. I would not be a car salesman. What are you talking about?" And then the next month went by and I couldn't make the rent, and I said, "I don't care what it is, I'll do anything." So, that's how I ended up transitioning into this world of crazy, male domination in the auto industry. It would never have been on my radar whatsoever.

I went for interviews and I got hired in sales. I was this nineteen-year-old girl with heels and tiny little skirts running around, getting in and out of cars, doing all this stuff and learning. At the same time, that was when I met someone that also introduced me to the likes of Tony Robbins, and motivational books that opened new doors of self-development for me. That was in 1997, and dealerships lived up to the crazy rumors. I was vulnerable. I didn't know any better. I didn't know what it was. All I knew at that time was that I had to feed my daughter. I had to keep a roof over her head. There were so many men who worked there who were the creepy crawly men, scuzzy car guys, discrimination, harassment, all the hype, right? And then there were the decent guys in between, but at the end of the day, it was a hellish place to be and learn to cope. So, I learned really quick. Either I was going to cry every single day and every single night, or I was going to figure out how to get in the game.

As a female with integrity in that industry, I started learning how to build relationships with customers, not try to sell customers. I became the top salesperson within five months, and then I decided I didn't want to do sales. I didn't like this whole running around in my heels in the rain, competing against shady characters, driving cars all over, and being a doormat.

I watched the finance lady, and I kept saying, "Well, she's sitting at a desk doing paperwork and I know she's making a lot of money each month. I can totally do what she's doing." They weren't going to teach me because you had to earn your rank and you had to become a veteran. I started staying after and teaching myself, observing, shadowing. At this point, I was now working eighty-plus-plus hours a week. I was raising my daughter as a single mother, with the incredible support of my best friend, Melissa, who ended up being my part-time nanny along with other sitters, and daycares. On an average day, I would get up, get out the door by six or seven in the morning, and often not get home until two o'clock in the morning. I lived in Sonoma, I drove to Novato, so that's a nice little forty- to sixty-minute trek each way.

I got into the finance office and then became a director by the time I was twenty-two, and had a finance team underneath me. By twenty-four, I was in a position where I was developing or creating new lending departments in dealerships. In September of 2011, I moved to and transferred to San Diego. The day I moved to San Diego was September 11, 2001. I woke up into my new life, turned on the TV, and saw the twin towers falling.

We lived in San Diego for a couple of years and I worked on the lending side of the automotive industry after starting a sub-prime lending department for a dealership. I met some great people, and there was one great guy in my life at that time. I would say he was the first person I was ever actually in love with. That's another story, for another time.

Within the lending circuit of the auto industry, it was brutal as a female at that time. I was abused and sexually harassed every single day. I was told that I was not worthy, that I was a piece of shit, and I was a bitch, and God forbid if I outsold one of the guys. And then there were all these different things going on behind my back like people saying, "Well, she didn't actually do that, I did," and it was just cutthroat and disgusting and horrible. I learned to go through the motions. I just kept rising up and rising up until I took over a dealership as management and I was running it. I learned quickly how to take all my survival skills and turn them into something productive.

I learned how to have thick skin. I learned how to develop myself and others. I learned how to redevelop a "known way" of doing business into something of integrity and success.

Sonia: Did you ever have moments of quitting because parts of it were like a repeat from earlier in your life? Was the financial part what kept you there?

Jen: Such good questions. Every day, I hated getting up in the morning. I hated going to work. I didn't love anything about what I did. I did it because I felt like, number one, everyone told me I couldn't have a daughter on my own and I couldn't make it happen. And two, I had to show them that hell yeah, I can. I wanted to quit every day because the abuse and the torment and the bullshit were so thick. I would find out that I was putting up numbers and doing more than the guys on the team. I was selling more. I was killing it. I was often on the leaderboard, and I was getting paid significantly, and I mean significantly less than what they were making. And it never stopped. I was putting in eighty to ninety hours a week. I had a babysitter and nanny and a daycare, paid rent, had the bills, and I didn't have a choice. I had to earn the money. I started to get really good at what I did, and see that there was a lot more that I could actually do as an innovator and a female in that industry. So I stuck with it and learned to grow with it, and create it versus just going along for the ride, if that makes sense?

There's a big difference between just existing and actually doing something about it. The money was difficult. I was in my early twenties making sixty to ninety grand a year. The only problem was that I didn't know what to do with it. I spent all this time working, and then I'd have guilt because I wasn't with my daughter, but then I would still want to somehow try to be a twenty-year-old, and I was constantly torn in every direction, still trying to figure it all out, and I had no idea who I was yet. I was just trying to raise a daughter and do it as best as I could, with the tools I had at the time.

I cried myself to sleep all the time. I'd feel guilty, like I wasn't there for her first steps because I had to work. I missed so much, and then I had all this money that I was making, which went to the daycare, my apartment, and loans. I was trapped because I couldn't see that there was another option for getting out of that and going into something fun, like to me it would be real estate.

I wish I would have had a mentor to say to me, "Girl, buy some property right now." I don't even think about that anymore because it would be too depressing, but I just did what I could until finally I didn't want to take it anymore. I couldn't see the other side of what was available to me, and I didn't have anyone to show me.

Sonia: You were in a pattern of survival. A lot was going against you. I see a pattern of grit with you, but from a lack of coaching or mentorship, you didn't see what else was out there.

Jen: Right. I didn't get that from school counselors. I didn't get that from family. I didn't get that from friends. I didn't get it at all. So, everything I came across was from self-discovery. The owner of the dealership I started at in 1997 was the first person who I actually began to have any respect for, and he was a double-edged personality. He was the person people were scared of, but he was also the person who brought a lot of respect. He opened my eyes to resources like Tony

Robbins, and books like, "Who Moved My Cheese?" He was hard core, but he had such belief in personal growth that I was open to begin to receive.

If he hadn't done that, I wouldn't have started reaching out on my own for resources. He was there at an incredibly transitional point in my life, and he didn't realize what he was doing, but he opened doors and brought my awareness forward for things I didn't know were out there. The next thing I know, I've got this stack of CDs and I'm trying to listen to every single one of them every day on my ride. I was in constant survival mode, and that went on for eighteen or nineteen years. I took a little hiatus in the middle of it when my daughter was getting into high school, and I could start to see the writing on the wall that she was dealing with stuff at school. I could see there were mentality shifts going on with her. At that point I decided, "I'm done with this eighty-hour-a-week thing, I'm done. I'm so burned out. It's been years." I got out.

I decided to do something fun, so I taught myself how to bartend, how to fill out a resume, how to get it done, and then I transitioned into what happened to me last fall, which has pulled everything back around.

Sonia: When did you start discovering your purpose?

Jen: My purpose began to come when I started managing people and leading people, and I started to see what was missing for others and what needs to be there, both from experience and having watched what training looked like for so many years. I watched people's style of training or mentoring or managing, which was so far from what people needed to survive and succeed. In 2014, I finally realized I wanted to work for myself and start my own company. An insurance company had been after me to open up an agency, and so I decided to. My purpose is to help people, and I want to help people in a way that I can show them how to do something that is meaningful. Insurance clicked for me. Insurance is something people hate to have, they hate to spend money on it, but they have to have it, and they're happy they have it when they need it. But they can also be taken advantage of and robbed blind, and it can be terrible, criminal. Well, as we are seeing now with all the fires, and now what I'm seeing in Hawaii with the Lava victims, it's absolutely disgusting, as I've come to learn.

Through a series of events, I declined the insurance opportunity in 2014 and I ended up going back into the dealership world for a little while. I worked in business development, hiring, and recruiting for a nine-dealership group and I created and implemented training programs for salespeople, internet sales and sales management. I did that for a year and a half, and I thought, "Okay, this is the transitional point." And then I hit a ceiling. I was told straight up that, "You want to be director of ops. Yes, you're totally qualified. You're the best person for the job, but you need to get the other male managers to vote you in." No shit. This was in 2016. I thought, "You know what, I'm over this fucking shit. Fuck you, and fuck you and fuck you … I choose me." Like "Nah." I went back to the insurance company and took a huge leap and started my own insurance agency. It took nine months of training and investing and learning how to invest in myself and my company. I knew how to recruit and hire an amazing team, so that was easy. I got that team in line and I started what's called a scratch agency, which means starting from zero. Most agents start with a book of business and you get to take it over, but I didn't have that option.

So, I started from ground zero and built up a pretty darn amazing agency within a year and a half. At this point, I had just gotten married. My ex-husband and I had been together for eight years. Ultimately, I had ended up with someone that couldn't honor and love me because ultimately, as I now know, I didn't do that for myself. He, too, became someone I was trying to fix, and we were unhappy. It was eight years of living with a lonely life, yet again. I didn't feel loved, I didn't feel like I was respected or adored, I had settled once again.

Meanwhile, I had created this agency and that was going great, but it was four months of not sleeping, staring at my ceiling, and going, "There's got to be something more for me. How the hell am I here? Why am I not happy? Why do I feel like I'm living life doing things because they're expected of me again?" And in September of 2017, I said, "That's it. I'm done." I left my husband. I had to sell the first home I bought, a four-bedroom house. I had to sell it, pack it, move it, and figure it out. Then I had three days to close down my insurance agency, and so, in thirty days, my daughter left home so I had an empty nest, I was separated and on my way to divorce, I sold a home, and closed my business.

Sonia: You lost everything.

Jen: Literally, everything was gone, and I did not have a single ounce of energy or life left in my body after that thirty days. I will never forget sitting there. I locked my door for my agency on October 1, and I left, and I went home and laid on the floor. I couldn't move. I was lifeless. Everything was drained out of me. You know how you see those little blurbs pop up on your computer that say, "Hey, fly to Hawaii for blah blah blah special!" And I don't know what it was, but with the tiny amount of energy I had in my entire body, when I heard that little ding and I looked over, I just clicked it and bought a ticket to Hawaii.

Sonia: How cool is that!

Jen: I said to myself, "Screw this noise. I'm out." I got a round-trip flight to Maui. I'd never traveled by myself. I didn't have a car. I didn't have a hotel. I didn't know where I was staying. I just knew that I was going on this plane with no plan. It was the most freeing experience I could ever have had. It was the best thing I could have done for myself. For the first time in my life, I started to feel like I was headed on the right track. I still get goosebumps just thinking about the feeling that I had when I was on that plane, because it felt like I was heading in the right direction. I remember landing in Maui and walking around. I found a rental car, a bright orange convertible Mustang, and I was out of there. I jumped in and started driving, and the only rule I made for myself was that whatever town I ended up in at eight p.m. is where I'd find a place to stay. I stayed in amazing hotels. I stayed with amazing people. I stayed in a hostel one night, on the beach in a glass house in a bunk bed. It was amazing.

Sonia: What an incredible experience.

Jen: The first few days were just outstanding, and I have just a firm belief that people cross your path or you cross their paths for a reason. I knew that anywhere I stopped just by accident or to get gas, I was meant to meet the people. It was crazy. I would meet a bartender and we'd be talking in a totally random bar, off the road because I got lost, and I ended up at a beach park. The Monday before, I was at home, and the Monday after, I was talking with a bartender in Hawaii who knew the guy I had played golf with just a week before! So much more to my Hawaii story, but for now I will just say that the universe is incredible, and no one crosses your path without a reason. Stay open, my friends.

It couldn't have been any better or more exciting. Then about four days into my trip, all of a sudden, I started feeling horrible, horrible side pain. I thought it was just because I had put my body and my mind literally through hell. I thought I was just having a fallout. So I pushed through, but the next day, I had a hard time breathing, and I was in a lot of pain. It was not going away, and it was progressively getting worse.

A girlfriend of mine flew in unexpectedly. I didn't know she was coming. I didn't want to tell her what was going on because she had just arrived, but the first night she was there, we went to dinner, and I was in cold sweats. I could barely see straight or walk or stand up. She finally said, "Are you drinking?" I said, "No, something's wrong." I went through another two days. We were staying at a hotel, and I was walking down to the front of the hotel to have them call me an ambulance because I knew something was really, really, really wrong. The pain had literally become that bad.

The second I started on my way down, my phone started blowing up because the fires had started in California. That was the night the fire started in Santa Rosa and Sonoma. Neighbors were calling saying, "The fire's approaching your parents' backyard." Nobody could find my parents. Nobody could find my daughter. I was up all night watching the news. It was insane trying to find out what was going on. Finally, after a very long and panicked night, I found out they were evacuated.

The next day, we went to dinner, and I collapsed. I was rushed to the emergency department in Hawaii, and the doctor looked at me and said, "You shouldn't be alive. You have been a dead woman walking." He went on to say I may have twenty-four hours to live, they have me on blood thinners, and they were able to connect with my mom, while she and my daughter were literally in the middle of being evacuated, to tell her I may have twenty-four hours to live, and to be on standby to catch a flight to Hawaii.

The thought of my parents and my daughter in the middle of being evacuated, and being told that I was probably going to die in twenty-four hours, and that they had to be on standby to get on a flight, is something I cannot explain. It is beyond devastating. There are no words to truly explain what that felt like.

Turns out I had a bilateral pulmonary embolism, so both my lungs had filled up with blood clots, and they were around my heart. It was not the pain that was killing me. It was literally looking back on my entire life and realizing I had never lived it for me. I never lived my potential. I didn't even know what happy was. I had no idea, and to think that I was going to die alone without my daughter, or without being able to show my daughter how to live a true life, that was the most harrowing feeling.

Sonia: You were in survival mode out of love. You were surviving for her as well.

Jen: One hundred percent. I fought through. I wasn't allowed to leave the island. I mean, if there's a positive lining, thank God it was Hawaii and not somewhere else! I was stuck in Hawaii for thirty days to recover and recoup. I fought through and came out on the other side, and in that moment, everything became so clear. I said, "I'm never going to allow another woman, anybody, to get to the point that I did, to have to look back and realize that they had everything it took to live exactly the life they wanted, but they didn't. I realized that it is already in each person to live exactly the life you want to live. You're born with it, you have full potential, and now it's time to unlock and unleash it.

That' my driving purpose.

Sonia: I love your story because you had your biggest high and your biggest low all in one week.

Jen: In seventy-two hours.

Sonia: You chose yourself for the first time.

Jen: Yes, the first time in forty years, because I was told that I may not live. It was part of my journey. Since I've been back, I've reconnected with the amazing people in my life. I've learned how to eliminate energy leaks in my life.

Sonia: What does that look like when you say energy leaks?

Jen: While this transformation was awakening, I became very aware of spirituality. Part of that is understanding, number one, who you are, what's your why, what's your purpose? Then understanding what the circle of influence looks like. Who's around you? Are they adding positive energy and challenging and supporting you and pushing you to want to become the best version of yourself that you possibly can? Or are they sucking energy from you, and taking from you, and making you feel down, or incapable, or not worthy, or all these things? Those are what I call your energy leaks.

So, anything in your life that's pulling out of you rather than pushing good and propelling you, are energy leaks. There's nothing like being told you may be dead and so everything else doesn't matter anymore, to be able to say, "You know what? Everything else doesn't matter anymore. The only thing now that matters is becoming the best version of myself that I can be because now I have a mission." I want to show other people how to do this too, and I can't emphasize it enough, you can't see it until either you go through something detrimental, or somebody just smacks you in the face with it. "You cannot become the best version of yourself if you are not willing to eliminate garbage around you. Garbage in, garbage out." That includes people, and sometimes it's the hardest thing to do, but you have to. It's part of the transformation. It's part of the process, and those people are on their own journeys. So, you're not eliminating people as in, "Go away. You're terrible." You're just saying, "You're in a part of your journey that's not benefiting or propelling me, and I'm on a mission for myself." So, then you have to also bring people to you. You know who's doing what you want to do? Who's showing you how to be the right person? Who's giving you that light that makes you want to just shine? I did a lot of eliminating. A lot of energy work.

I met incredible people, and you know what's so funny, is when you take that leap, it's almost like there's a door that was just waiting for you to finally open it. It's amazing how many things you attract. You're like a magnet all of a sudden for amazing abundance and people.

Sonia: I believe it's because you are meant to walk in your divine purpose. If there are roadblocks, you'll have to eliminate them to continue on.

Jen: You have to decide that you want a better life. You have to decide that you want to become the best version of yourself. When I'm speaking to women, especially women with daughters, I say, "How are you going to teach them not to follow in your footsteps?"

Sonia: Your story is very deep, but the transformation, I believe, is just the beginning for you. You're walking into it. It's all about timing now.

Jen: Timing and putting myself out there so that when people need me, I'm visible.

Sonia: I believe that your purpose came from pain. That's where we get our compassion for people, especially for women. You realized this is what you are supposed to be doing, and that's the most fulfilling thing ever. So, I'm hearing your story and I'm wondering what happened to your parents? Is there still abuse, and is your mom still quiet?

Jen: My parents are actually still together. For me, learning how to forgive and move past it, and I cannot tell you how difficult that is, but I also cannot even begin to describe the freedom of mind, heart, body, and soul that comes along with it, and just acknowledging that they didn't have the tools and they just couldn't, and that's not my fault, and I didn't do anything to deserve it, and I love my parents. The crazy thing—and this is the part when people say, "What?"—is that I'm grateful for my past. I'm grateful for everything that happened to me because it's part of the journey and it's the lesson. It's hard to look back and see until you forgive and forget and let it go.

My dad almost died a few years ago. My mom finally tried to leave, and he spiraled and ended up in a coma for some time. He, too, should not be here. He miraculously came through this whole thing. My mom went on her own journey of having to go to rock bottom to be lifted back up, and they both ended up getting help on their own, and both of them are completely clean and sober and redesigning their lives. We all get along now, and we all get together.

Sonia: Did your dad ever come to you and say, "Jen, I'm sorry?"

Jen: Yes, he did. He went through a massive life journey and transformation, and although I may not necessarily agree with everything that he believes, it's not my journey. It's his. Everything I needed to mend my relationship, I was able to do, it feels complete for me. There is no rule book. It's not supposed to look a certain way. You're not supposed to feel a certain way. All you need to know is that if you're open and you are willing to do the work for yourself, and you can come to realize people are as good as the tools they have, and there are things you may actually be grateful to them for, you begin to forgive. And then you begin to grow. Now I can be in a room with him and I don't want to throw up. I enjoy seeing my dad, we have great conversations, and there's a relationship for the first time that wasn't there before. That's progress. I may never know that feeling of being a daughter with a daddy, or having that loving father figure growing up, which I resented most of my life. I won't have those memories, but I have become content with my life, just the way it was.

Sonia: What amazing growth and transformation. I can see why you have a heart for doing deep work with women, and with people in general. Your journey was a rough one, but you are a rock today. It built the grit on the inside of you because now you can share your story with other women who are surviving.

Jen: Exactly. I look at things so much differently now. For example, when I think about all those men who were cruel in the car business, which was hell, I can look at them now and see who they were. I can now see and understand men, inside and out, from so many angles and I'm actually grateful for that. To see a person within, rather than just what they project or portray, is truly unique. Everyone's on a journey and it's what we choose to accept or tolerate, and what we choose to deny, what we choose to discover or embrace, that create the life we are experiencing.

Sonia: What would you say to those women who are still broken now but they have dreams?

Jen: The number-one thing, I believe, is this: If you can dream it, you can achieve it. It is completely possible. Everything any woman needs to become the woman that she idolizes or wishes she was, she already has within. The fact of the matter is that to dream of a life that you don't have, to actually see what it looks like, to actually experience or imagine what it feels like to love, to want to be loved, to be able to give love genuinely, to live your authentic truth, to be who you are, means it is already in you on a cellular level ... and when you are ready to learn how to love yourself, uncover your potential and purpose, you can. You already have what it takes. It's already in you.

I cannot tell you how incredibly transformative my life has become and continues to be. Once I put my own words into action, guess what ... things have been manifesting in ways that are just unbelievable! I'll be writing the blog or story as I go, but I ended up back in Hawaii, manifesting, creating, and I met the man of my dreams, someone who totally enhances me. I'm doing what I love every day, and I am bringing love and new life to others, and I'm just getting started! Oh my lord, miraculous.

It's truly a matter of deciding that you want it. You find a driving why, and your purpose is your own. Nobody can tell you what it looks like. Nobody can tell you what it means, and it takes that leap of faith. When you decide you want to take a leap, reach out to the person who you idolize. Reach out to a woman who's loud and in charge and say, "I want to. I'm ready. I want to transform." Find a coach, find a boot camp, find a whatever. Make the decision to go. There are resources. If you're scared, if you're financially scared, if you're scared of abuse, there are people and resources for every fear that you could possibly have to help you out of it. You just have to decide that you're ready.

The blueprint for how to get from where you are into a thriving life that you love is a lot simpler than people can even begin to realize, once you make the choice.

Sonia: Absolutely! Thank you so much for sharing. You're one powerful, beautiful woman who's going to change the world.

Jen: I so appreciate your kind words, Sonia. I'm on a mission. If there's one statement that I would tell people it's: "Quit riding bitch in your own life, it's time to take the wheel and DRIVE." Do You. Choose You. Love You. Let's Do this!"

Sonia: I love it. Thank you so much, Jen.

ABOUT JEN CROWE

Jen Crowe is a Breakthrough Facilitator and Next Level Coach. As an Empath and Strong Intuitive, Jen utilizes her vast experience and triumphs to show others how to Breakthrough their barriers and challenges to discover the answers to life's most personally "stumping" questions.

Jen would tell you, "It takes one, to know one. YOUR success is my success. I have learned over and over how to FAIL through life's most difficult situations, repeat destructive patterns, do everything the hard way, and then … HOW TO SUCCEED despite whatever life can throw at me. Don't settle for your status quo life, the life you're meant to LIVE is waiting for you, don't wait until it's your last twenty-four hours like I did. If you can DREAM it, you CAN ACHIEVE it.

CHAPTER 13

If You Can't Go Through It, Go Around It

Mary Rocha

Sonia: Hello, I am here with Mary Rocha, and I'm excited that she is going to share her powerful story of grit, transformation, success, community, and leadership. So Mary, start from the beginning and share your story.

Mary: I was a Latina born in a culture with strong family ties, and a time when a woman takes care of her man, stays at home, and takes care of her children. But I had a mother who was not in her own time, because she believed in women taking leadership, even though she didn't portray it.

When I was three, I went to live with my grandma, and I was in the Latino culture. When I was seven, I went back to live with my mother, and I was more in the American culture. I saw my parents following their parents' culture. I saw a mother who worked hard, took care of her family, and wasn't very social. She was a homebody. I saw the women in the family working and making sure they took care of their families. They were the strongholds in the family. But my whole life, my mother was telling me to assimilate into American life and to speak English, to make good and go to school. She wanted me to go to college.

The women in my family went to work in the canneries. My sister had gotten married at a young age, and I was the youngest in the family. All of my uncles and cousins were grown. They all wanted me to be the generation that succeeded. No one had graduated in my family, and they wanted me to be the one to graduate and go to college.

I was interested in nursing, which my mother said was good because things like nursing or teaching were important and they would get paid well. For her, the value was money, but for me, my value was being involved and part of a community. Even at a young age, I dreamed of being in the Girl Scouts, but my mother wasn't that type who would be part of the scout system.

We lived in a low-income area and I thought I was very poor because the area around me was poor. My sister had gotten married at a young age, and I was left alone as a twelve-year-old.

Sonia: What grounded you the most that has stayed with you all this time? Were family members a key part of your life?

Mary: When I lived with my grandma, it was a transitional time in her life. She had a son in the Marines, and he was in the South Pacific. I became her close ally or her close love, and she took care of me. I had a wonderful time with her. We would go to the Mexican movies and see all those wonderful old actors. I loved her love and attention toward me.

When I was seven, I went to live with my mom, and that's when things changed for me. In my mother's house, I was divided, and I had to be more Americanized because she didn't even allow me to speak to my father in Spanish, only English. He would speak to me in Spanish, but I had to respond in English. I lost my language and didn't regain it until I went to see my grandmother in Mexico when I was around twelve. When I got there, I found out that my dad, who I thought was named Jesus, was not his name. My dad's name was Emilio, and my uncle was Jesus. And my dad's last name was different also. So then I was really confused, but I found out that he came to the United States under an assumed name with a different family.

My life has been a little different and mixed. It was like I was walking on a tightrope, and on one side was Latino culture, and on the other side was the American way. I didn't know where I fit in.

But during that visit to Mexico, I got my language back because of my cousins, and I traveled around with them in Mexico for three weeks. Language is like a bicycle. If you don't ride it for a while, it comes back with practice. So that trip was a turning point for me because I realized that I was two people in one. I struggled with it when I went back in junior high. It seemed like I was involved with activities that were American, such as being a feature editor and the president of the Girls Athletic Association. I was also in the Honor Society, and doing well in school.

I didn't realize that it wasn't a trend for us Latinos. Mama wasn't the type who wanted to be part of the Girl Scouts or even come to my banquet for the Girls Athletic Association. She was a private person, very quiet. My dad was the one who loved to be in the public eye. It was him who wanted to do fiestas through his organization every weekend. My sister's boyfriend was a Marine and always brought his Marine Friends for parties at our house. My sister ended up marrying a Marine.

A young lady came to live with us when I was eleven, and took the space of my sister, and it was through this young lady that I learned how to Folklorico dance and I performed in my community with this group. She helped to develop my personality because also wanted a higher education. I was trying to stay involved in activities, but it was hard to keep up. It took me a year to bring up my grades. I graduated with good grades and decided to go on to junior college.

During this time in high school, I met Dolores Huerta, because I was running for the 16th September Queen. She was well-known as Cesar Chavez's right-hand person. Dolores took a liking to me and wanted me to go with her to these meetings, and I didn't know what the meetings were about. I went to one or two and I saw these two big, tall men who looked like German men, and they were helping people organize to get their benefits and get their empowerment. I didn't know it was the beginning of organizing the Union. Dolores was in the middle of it. She kept encouraging me to come, but at that time I met my future husband.

So here's what I always tell my family: who knows, I might have gone with Dolores and you guys would never have been born because I could have stayed with her but instead, I split off to get married. And so my life started on a whole different path again.

Sonia: How old were you when you got married?

Mary: I was seventeen and my mother had to sign for me.

It was interesting because when I was a child, I had seen all the things my mother did. At age three or four, you've already learned where you fit and what you're supposed to do, and what your culture is about. In my Latino culture, the man came first, and the woman took care of him. The woman might be a hard worker behind the man, but she made sure his clothing, his food, his everything was in place. If you had children, you had to make sure they were taken care of, but the man was the priority. That's the way I was raised and that's the way my family was.

But what a switch in those days, because it was the fifties when things were changing. Women were looking at issues, the music was changing, and Elvis Presley was big. But I ended up catering to my husband, and then he went into the service and was in Korea for a couple of years. When he came back, we moved to Oakland. My children were born in Oakland, two boys, they were thirteen months apart.

So I was a young mom with two babies, and my life was concentrated on the family. It became the sixties, and if you remember, there was a whole revolution going on, with the whole segregation issue, everything being questioned, and women saying, "Who are we?" Living in Stockton I felt oppressed like I couldn't do anything beyond what I was supposed to do.

I wasn't supposed to go to college, even though my mother was still pushing me. We moved to Oakland, and I loved it. It offered a kind of freedom, and I didn't have the pressures of what I could or couldn't do. My mother always looked perfect when she went out the door. I used to hate that because I didn't care how I looked. I was fighting her style, you know. I wanted to be me and just wear whatever I wanted, put my hair up or not, and do what I wanted to do.

We lived in Oakland for about five years, then Concord for another five more years. Then we moved to Antioch, into a neighborhood with five hundred houses in a new area, and nobody knew anybody. The problem that occurred was that there was only one Elementary school to serve all these children. We had to wait until seven o'clock one morning to sign them up, or they would be shipped to different schools. I couldn't figure out why, and they said, "People here won't pass the bond issue." I thought, "Well, we need a school," so I got involved and before I knew it, my husband and I were the PTA presidents.

I couldn't believe it. It was almost like it happened by accident. I wanted to be a PTA member because it's a good connection. In my culture, the connections were either with school or church. I wanted to get involved, and I came up with an idea. This is the only thing I can tell you: my husband and I have been married for sixty-one years, and I have always had to find a way to go around him. I learned that strategy which has helped me in my political career because if you learn how to go around and get your idea across, you can't be stopped, if you know what I mean.

Sonia: It does make sense. You turned something that could have stopped you in your tracks into something where you found a way to leverage getting involved in the community and making a difference.

Mary: Yes. Concord was a white community and my next-door neighbor was the PTA president she wanted me to go to the meetings, and my husband said no, I couldn't go. So I decided that I would be the cupcake lady so I could get involved. I would pick up cupcakes, set up my table, and sell my cupcakes to the kids. By four o'clock, I was home, I had cleaned up the car, and I was ready to be the housewife. But that was the way I had to do it. Also, I would make lunch for the teachers at the end of the school year, and that lunch was good because I learned it from my mother-in-law. My Enchiladas were the best because I made them from flour tortillas. So that was how I eventually got involved with the PTA.

So back to enrolling the kids in school and signing up for the PTA. I found out that they were looking for a PTA president husband-and-wife team, because the previous one had just left. It was just before school started, and they called me because they knew I had a history of working in Concord. I said I'd love to, but didn't know about my husband. I said I would ask him.

Then I thought, he's going to get out of the shower and ask what that conversation was about, and I'll have to tell him we're the president of the PTA of our elementary school. He didn't say no. So I told him he could do the president's part and call the meetings and all that, and I would do the work. He said, "Okay, okay."

So that was the way we did it. We got it started, and I came up with all kinds of activities. And what happened? I went around and got everybody to sign up to pass the bond issue. I got to meet a lot of people. We also did a neighborhood watch and had women putting signs in their front windows, so I had captains on every street. When the election came, they delivered the materials before the election to make sure people voted, and we won the election. So a grassroots type of working is how I learned. So to me, everything in my life was by accident because I didn't have the knowledge. Opportunities came to me.

Sonia: It seems to me that you were always a woman of intention. You set your intention and saw a crack of opportunity, and took it. You grabbed opportunities, and that is so important for everyone to understand. When we see an opportunity, we take it.

Mary: I was still taking care of my position and I did it because I needed that school for my kids. But here is where the politics start. I was at home in the kitchen one day, and I had on an apron and making tortillas, I was cooking food for my kids and my husband, because he was going to come home from work. And I get a knock on the door at about 3:30, and who's there but the superintendent of schools. I didn't know him, but I knew who he was. He was a powerful man, and he started talking to me through the screen door. He told me he wanted me to run for school board, but I said I didn't know anything about that.

He said, "Oh, you've got the knowledge, you know how to run a campaign." I kept saying, "No, my husband would never allow that," etc. And then he said something, and before I knew it, my head must have been as big as a balloon and I signed the paper. When I signed the paper, he took off to the county and put it in the election process, and I had nothing to do with it. I had signed the paper, though. I thought, "Oh my God, what am I going to tell my husband? I'm in trouble now!"

I went to a lady who was a mentor for me. She was a prominent person in my city. I was crying and telling her to get me off of this election ballot. I had signed a paper and I didn't want to do it anymore. She started talking to me, calming me down, and had tea with me. After I talked with her, she told me the most important thing I've ever heard. She said, "Mary, I'm going to vote for you because I know that you'll be a good candidate!" Once she said that, something hit me. "I'm okay, I can do it, she likes me, she wants me to run, she believes in me! I can do it." I didn't know I had a part of me that wants to win, a drive that says I'm going to go and do it.

Then I had to talk to my husband and tell him what I had done. The first thing he said was, "I don't care. You're not going to win anyway, so go ahead, do whatever you want to do, but just leave me out of it." So my girlfriends got together with me and we used a little mimeograph paper, a half sheet of paper, and put my name, who I was, and PTA.

In those days before Prop 13, the people on the school board wanted to make sure the money was being spent well. People on the board were from a high society industry community at that time, so these were people with positions, and I was a nobody. According to the paper, I was just a mother. So what happened is that I did my own little movement. I was working at one side of town, and the principal sent out a message to say I was a good candidate and that side was taken care of. The side of town that I was in had five hundred houses, and I figured there were two voters per house, and they all knew me, so I had that side. Then there was the downtown area, so I walked that area and talked to the lady who was my big supporter, and everybody knew her. She was on the phone telling everybody that I was the right candidate.

So with eight people, I came in as number three, and everybody else on that list had some title, they were this or that or professors, and I was at the bottom of the totem pole with Mary Rocha, the mother. That's it. Not even a BA. That's all I was, and I won the election.

I remember that day, it was our anniversary, and we went to a pizza place with another couple. I said to my husband, "I wonder maybe if I should call and find out if I have won or not?" And he said, "You're not going to win. What the heck?" So I called and found out I came in third, and I went back to the table and said, "Guess what? I won." Everybody was shocked, especially me. Now I had to go through the process, the transition in my brain, about how I was going to go about with this new journey. I was only thirty-five or less at that time, and I only had the one lady mentor, and the superintendent who wanted me to run for the reason that he wanted to save his job. He needed three votes and he only had two votes on the board, so he figured if I got elected, I would give him his third vote and he could succeed as the superintendent of the school district.

What he didn't know is that I admired the lady who was on the board with me. I followed her and did everything she said to do, and she voted against him and I voted against him, so he lost his job. That's the end of that little story.

So that's my learning. Now right off the bat, I went to the school board associations conference, because that's what you do if you're elected. I had never been on an airplane, never been in a hotel, never been to a big restaurant. My family didn't have that opportunity when I was young. We used to go to a family restaurant maybe once a year, and that was it. I had to go through a whole change in my life, learning all this that was new to me. I was like a sponge. I watched people and took in information to help me, and realized later in life that that was my personality. I watch and watch until I knew how to act. So that made a difference, and it was the beginning of my journey as a school board member.

My city was almost ninety-percent Caucasian. How did I win? The Latinos in my community weren't united. I think it helped that my last name was Rocha. It's a Portuguese name. My husband is not Portuguese, but back in his life somewhere there's a Portuguese.

The families in my town had a higher percentage of Portuguese, and there was a well-known lady named Mary Rocha. So between the new people that moved there and the fact that they thought I was involved with Portuguese, is what got me elected. I also learned something else: You don't wave your flag. I was a Latina and I believed in my country of Mexico.

Earlier on, I worked on child care issues, for a nonprofit organization, and I became labeled as a child care advocate. To this day, there is a child care center in my name.

After I got elected, I used to say, "If nothing else, they can't talk about us in a closed session," or "They can't say anything about us because I'm here." I joined up with a group of Latino School board members. They were movers and shakers, and I was one of the only females at that time. I already had my daughter who was about three years old. My husband had to recognize the change that was taking place for both of us and I was still trying to take care of both. This Latino group was able to make a change in the School Board Association which then recognized Latinos, African Americans, and Asians as directors.

We decided we were going to have a piece of the action and create a Latino school board association. In those days we called ourselves the Hispanic

School Board. We kept meeting on a regular basis at conferences, and it became a big thing. We were standing on the issue of bilingual education.

We went on to start a National Latino School Board Association, and I was part of it. We talked about things that happened in our

Schools. I made friends with a lady who wanted to run for the National School Board Association. She didn't make National President the first time, but she did the second time. She was putting me in all of the committees that paid for the person to go, and before I knew it, I was flying around the country and going to all these different events.

I was seeing more of the country than I ever thought I would, and learning to fly on my own. It was a whole growing experience for me. She picked me out of the group because I was a Latina. The people always questioned it at the national level and said, "Wait a minute, she's not even the president of the School Board Association of California, so how come she's in this position?" It was because the president wanted it that way. That was my level of connection.

Sonia: You were leveraging the current opportunity.

Mary: Yes, it was good for me because I got to see a whole lot of the country. My school never had to put a penny out there, never had to question what I did because it wasn't coming out of their pockets, so that was my other big achievement.

But I haven't talked about the change in my own personality—remember back when I told you I'd had a child? It was interesting because I said to my friend after I got elected that I wanted to have one more child. She said, "What the heck?" I wanted a little girl and I knew I was going to have her, isn't it interesting? I was getting to that age and so I got myself pregnant, and the way I did it, this is funny, my husband said, "No more kids." He was one of eight children, and we already had two children, and he didn't want our children to suffer and so he said no more.

They were thirteen months apart, so by the time they were six and seven, and then seven and eight, I kept insisting that we needed to have a girl, and he kept saying no. So I took him to the Mexico border and got him drunk and got pregnant. That was my way of getting what I wanted, and again, again, I had to go around the corner to get what I wanted. I dropped the pill, and I got pregnant like that, and I had my little girl and that was remarkable! Everyone questioned me, why I would run again, but it was already starting to be something I enjoyed. I was thinking I had to get a college education, so I went to Los Medanos Junior College, which is the nearest college to us, and I put my daughter in an after-school program so I could attend.

I went to a speech class, a woman who was beyond her time, a very pro-woman. On the first day of class we were supposed to talk about ourselves for three minutes, and I said, "Oh, I just got elected and I have to go to two meetings and blah, blah, blah." What I didn't hear was what she said that I had said, which was, "I go to meetings if my husband lets me."

I didn't realize that I said that. So she stopped me after class and said she wanted to talk to me. I didn't know what it was about. She said, "Mary, did you realize what you said?" I said, "No." She said, "You said you can't go out at night unless your husband lets you." And I said to myself, "Holy heck, what's the matter with me, what?" At a time when change was coming up and women were rising up in the sixties. And bra-burning era, if you remember. Although I know you wouldn't, but it was a time when women were getting up in rank. And I was like, "Oh. My God, how would I say that?" Her message resonated with me, and it changed me!

Sonia: That is empowerment.

Mary: I was doing all these things and empowering myself without knowing it, and then when it hit me in the face, I realized that "Oh my God, he can't control me. I'm a person and I have a life of my own. I've proved that I can get elected. I've proved that I can be somebody. I have a life, too." That was the beginning and I just kept going. I've been on the school board from 1970 to 1986, and then I decided to run for the City Council. During that time I had become so involved in special education that the state of California appointed me the commissioner for four years. When I started attending these meetings, I met people who were educated in special education, and I started to learn their language and what they were doing. Soon I was on panels within my school board, talking about special education.

In 1986 I decided to run for City Council, knowing it would take me several terms to get in because I was not a part of the old boys' system, or a planning commissioner. To my surprise, I won my election the first time around.

The school board and city council are two different worlds. In the city, there were cars on the street that shouldn't be there, holes in the street, dogs barking. You learn that you have to maneuver this one differently than the other. I stayed on the city council, and for the first term, I lost an election. I had not lost an election all that time until then.

And I know why, because I wasn't paying attention to the business and the city was growing, but I had grandchildren and I was the grandma who had to take care of them so my son could continue his education. So I would come home from my work, run over there and take care of them. I wasn't paying attention to the election part. So in 1992, my son said, "Mom, do you want to go back?" And I said I did. He said he'd help me. I won again and I got back on. And then the city council mayor's position was coming up and I thought maybe I should try it just for the heck of it, because at that time women were becoming stronger. I ran for the mayor's position in 1996 and I won. I was a mayor for four years.

I decided to run for County Supervisor and lost. Now comes a new journey of going to my community and working with families.

I became a director of a Child Development Center working with Spanish speaking families. We were dealing with child development from birth to age five, and it was free education for families. I was well-known for getting involved, but after eight years it was time to run again. In the meantime, it bought me time to pay attention to my parents and be a grandmother.

After Obama won the presidency, I decided to run for city council again, and I won. So I went back on the city council for two terms, and then two years ago at the end of a term, I lost, and I know why. It's because I was still in the old-fashioned way of doing things like, knocking on doors and mailing fliers. Social media had come into the picture and the old way wasn't working anymore.

Sonia: You never hired anybody?

Mary: I never hired anybody in all of my past campaigns. I didn't believe in hiring anybody because that's extra money. My friends and I were always the ones in charge of my campaign and our strategy was more signs and fliers and people you talk to, so that was a new learning experience for me, and I realized I had to change my ways if I ever wanted to come back. So the opportunity came, but now our city is in districts and I decided I wanted to go back to the school board and administrations because it's a warm feeling and you're dealing with children's lives, you're dealing with education, you're dealing with a different world and not the city life, which is the garbage, the dogs, and the politics.

One time a man called me when I was a mayor. He said, "I just moved here, and these planes are going over my house. Would you please tell those planes to go someplace else?" And I thought to myself, "Sure, I'm going to tell the planes they can't fly." They expect that a mayor can do anything.

I was enriched by everything I did, and now I'm the new school board member and starting a new journey.

Sonia: This is very exciting. A whole new journey for you. But how was this last experience different?

Mary: First of all, this election was with a committee. I had never done it with a committee before. I was coming up with the strategy. An issue happened that led me to get involved. We had a charter school issue in our district. The one we had for about twenty years was a good charter that expanded and had two sections from K to eighth grade. We had a good relationship with it, and then comes in one from San Jose with big money. The three board members that should have kept them out gave in and gave them the three votes. They were able to come in and set up their building. What people don't realize is that when a charter comes in, the money you allocate to your children now goes to this other charter, so if you take so many children away from your school district, then you're reducing the resources over here, and you have to give money to this charter school because it's within the school system.

The state sends the money to the school system, the charter school gets a percentage, so it does affect the schools. If you approve it in your school district, then you have to put the administrator on top of the whole process. After that charter came in, then another one wanted to come in, and the same three board members accepted the other one. That did it, and I was so upset about the whole thing. I had been going to meetings and objecting to it, so when the time came when we had them in our system, I said it was ridiculous. It caused me to run for office because I got mad. I got upset because I wanted money to go back to the regular school system.

Sonia: Righteous anger.

Mary: Yes. I said, "I'm going to run." Everybody wanted me to run because they trusted me. They felt I would be at least neutral, and knowingly I would protect the school system. That's what happened. The committee had a public relations person who was an excellent writer and happens to be a Latina. We had to reach the young people and we knew it was going to be a big election, so we had to use social media. It was my worry because now the theme was "kick out the old people and bring in the new people." I was thinking, "Wait a minute. I'm the old person. I don't know if they're going to elect me, so how are we going to change this attitude about my age?" Believe it or not, it was the first time in my life that I had a billboard on the highway with my name on it.

We got a logo, and my logo was an apple, but it turned out to be a heart. They made it into a heart and so now, Mary cares. The logo and my signs were everywhere, with Mary Rocha and a heart. You know Mary cares, and that was it. A short slogan, and I'm telling you, I had a big sign and even buttons. It was amazing, and then the flier was so well done. It was an interesting election because it was not the way I was used to doing things. I used to pay someone to do my flier and it would be like $10,000, a good chunk of money, and every election I would go out and walk the streets and every one of those fliers was gone. After this election, I still had two or three boxes left that I didn't even touch. Why? Because I didn't do that much walking. So I took a chance and changed the pattern of how we do elections. And videos also became a big thing.

Sonia: The video is a big thing for many people.

Mary: Oh my God, we had three or four different people each speaking on my behalf about how wonderful I was and all that stuff. And then a couple of videos on me, short and long. And then they put it on Facebook and YouTube. I had to pay an outside person to get that through because I was having trouble with my own Facebook. So I did it and then when the election came, I was shocked. I had the highest votes, 10,000 votes. It was unbelievable. It was a landslide!

Sonia: Wow. That's incredible. Something to be very proud of. I love your story of courage and how you kept just moving forward. You're a way-maker.

Mary: When they say to me that I've made a difference in people's lives, I still have not gotten hold of it. I know that I have done things, but I don't look back to see what's happened. People have said, "You have opened the doors," and I was at the beginning of the wave of women rising up. I was motivated to do the right thing, at the right places, and it just happened.

Sonia: I love that you said that. What would you say to all those women who aspire to have the confidence, who aspire to go after that dream, to go and be a part of something big? What would you say to those women?

Mary: The idea to be out in public is that you're fearless and you need to connect with people in organizations so that they know who you are, and then you learn the skills of running campaigns or doing programs or being a chair of something. That gives you the knowledge, and when it's complete, you'll understand that you can do it.

Learn something from everybody when you speak with them. The other day I learned something from a lady who never gave up on her dream. She wanted to go work in other countries, but she got lost in the process. She got married and had children and now she's in her sixties, and an opportunity came through and she decided to go to a country and help out. And she did. She gave a speech and showed pictures of what she did, and what I got out of it is that she never lost her dream. No matter where you are, if you have a dream, there's always a chance you can pick up on that dream again and go forward. The opportunities are here for women much more than in the past.

Sonia: And once we step out in faith, it shows up, but we have to be ready for it.

Mary: Yes. I've been married to a man for sixty-one years, who I thought I would have lost him a long time ago because I was busy, and that's not the way our culture said that women were to be. My family and friends said, "Oh my God, Mary, you're going to lose your husband. You can't be in politics. You've got to take care of him." To tell you the truth, he has been my strongest supporter. He's the one who ended up making my first signs for my first election. He painted four signs. He's always been there with me. He did everything for me. When he met me, he probably thought I was a woman he was going to control, and then he found out it didn't happen that way, and he didn't know it at the time. That's how two started, and we're still together to this day.

And then I said before that culture can tend to hold you back. In my time, it did, but I don't know that it does now. Those of us who were born or raised here have a different way of thinking and feeling about ourselves. You see the entrepreneurship of women is amazing, and how many women go forward and start their businesses. I'm thinking, "Wow, that is something. I'm sure they face their fears and they face a lot of things, but they haven't lost their dreams. They know they have a dream. I didn't know I had a dream. I didn't know it was in me. I fell into these positions.

Sonia: You took action.

Mary: I took action, and that's how I ended up doing what I wanted to do.

Sonia: Because we can dream all day long and be at home and then we're just dreamers, but if we have a dream and we take action on it, we can realize our dreams.

Mary: It's taking chances and you don't know where those chances are going to take you, but if you believe that you have a reason to be here in this world, then it's going to come out okay. I still feel like I must be alright because I'm going to be eighty and I'm still around. So God must have wanted me to do more. I'm enjoying every minute of it.

Sonia: You're living a life of purpose, and every part of your journey has been purposeful. You always just kept going. It's about perspective and moving forward.

Mary: And finding a way to go around it. You can't go through it, but you can go around it. That's been the best part for me. I got it done.

Sonia: Thank you so much, Mary Rocha, your story is incredible. You're making me want to feel like I want to go after it, no matter what. So many women are going to be inspired by your story.

Mary: Thank you.

ABOUT MARY ROCHA

Mary Rocha has been a force for good in the Antioch community for more than 40 years. She started her work with the PTA and quickly moved her way to the Antioch Unified School District, where she made strides for many during her time as a trustee. Later, Mary took her can-do attitude to the Antioch City Council and eventually became the first Latina to be elected Mayor. Additionally, a child center was named for her, she was AUSD Personnel Commissioner, an admired child advocate and named Contra Costa County Commission Woman of the Year. Today, Mary has come full circle and is back on the AUSD school board helping students and their families reach their potential.

CHAPTER 14

The Girl from El Paso and Her Dream

Genoveva Calloway

Sonia: I am here with Genoveva Garcia Calloway, mayor of San Pablo. Genoveva, please share your story with us, and tell us how it all began for you to become a woman in leadership who serves her community.

Genoveva: When I first started my journey in writing this chapter for *Destiny Talks*, I was Mayor in San Pablo, California. In December of 2018, I retired from my elected office as Council member and Mayor, after sixteen years in office. I am very proud of being considered a woman in leadership and am proud and honored to be included in this book.

I was born and raised in El Paso, Texas, and upon high school graduation, I left town to pursue my dream I had had since I was a child in elementary school. My dream was to attend college.

My story began with my parents in Mexico. In 1945, my mother was sixteen, and she was kidnapped by my father. When they returned to town the next day, their parents arranged for them to get married immediately. In her town, once a young woman was kidnapped by a man, they were obligated to marry since no other single man would want to marry her. The reason being that the young woman would no longer be a virgin. My parents had their first child, my sister, and after that, my dad left to go to Texas by himself to find a better life. He left my mom in Mexico, which was common, and happens to a lot of women. The men come here to work and leave the wife and kids behind with extended family. My mother was left with her in-laws. My grandfather, my dad's dad, told my mother that if she stayed in Mexico, my dad would just come back once a year, impregnate her and leave again. He asked her, "Is that what you want? Or can I take you to him in El Paso, Texas?"

My mom accepted (likely knowing that in Mexico, she had no family resources). I think it was a brave decision on her part to cross the Rio Grande River into the USA. My mother experienced the same migration phenomenon that is happening now on the national level: economic survival. My mom did not know how to swim, and she was scared of water. At age seventeen and with a child, she was determined to have a better life, knowing that she was carrying her second child. While crossing the Rio Grande River, as my mom describes, my dad was hanging onto her on one side, and my grandpa was on the other side. My sister was on my dad's shoulders, and her feet were dangling in the water. To me, her little feet dangling in the water must have meant the river was very deep and how scared my mom must've have been. They settled in El Paso and ended up having a total of fourteen children. I am the third oldest of fourteen children.

I learned from a young age the meaning of being a union member and its benefits. My dad worked for American Smelter Refinery and he was a loyal union member. When my dad was on strike, he would never cross a picket line; the entire family would go to a friend's farm to pick cotton to help make ends meet. My mom could never work as she was always pregnant. We walked to elementary school and back. My mom could never help us with homework because she did not know how to read or write. She had never gone to school. But somehow, we made it, with my parents' goal for us to graduate from high school.

As a young student, I listened closely to my teachers and had some influence from television. I started dreaming that I wanted to go to college. In my high school years, that dream became even more powerful since I did not want to be like my older sisters, who chose to get married instead as their only means to leave home. I saw how my dad, as the sole breadwinner, was in charge of the household. What he said was the law in our home! He was very strict with us girls. We couldn't play outside, stay after school, or visit a girlfriend's house. We had to return straight back home after school. Our only source of entertainment was TV. I would go to the library to escape, and thus became an avid reader and read about the world outside of El Paso.

While growing up in El Paso, I remember two historical events that happened. The first one was in 1963, when John F. Kennedy, thirty-fifth President of the US, was assassinated in Dallas, Texas. I was thirteen years old then. I recall being in school and some students and teachers crying over the news. From TV news and newspaper articles, I knew him as a "great President," so I, too, was sad and got glued to the TV news to learn the details of the assassination.

The second historical event was known as The Chamizal dispute. It was a border conflict over six hundred acres on the Mexico-United States border between El Paso, Texas, and Ciudad Juarez, Chihuahua. The dispute was caused by the Rio Grande shifting its course after a flood in 1864. The river continually shifted south between 1852 and 1868. Both the US and Mexico were claiming the six hundred acres. The dispute was formally settled on January 14, 1964. I had just turned fourteen years old at that time. I vividly remember the entire hoopla loop that occurred in town during that time. Of course, I was not at the celebratory event; I watched it on TV at home. The agreement consisted of building a man-made channel to prevent the Rio Grande from blurring the international boundary in the future. The channel was constructed, and the two governments shared the cost of the channel, along with the cost of three new bridges.

The United States established a museum known as the Chamizal National Memorial in 1974 to increase visitor awareness of cooperation, diplomacy, and cultural values as a basic means to conflict resolution. It is ironic, that with the current federal situation that our country is experiencing related to immigrants, how I would recall these incidents. How I wish that our current border issue could be addressed in a similar manner: cooperation, diplomacy, and respect for cultural values.

I realized at a young age that in order to realize my dream to attend college, I would have to leave my home and town.

Sonia: What made you feel that you wanted to get out of the house?

Genoveva: As my dream of attending college continued to flourish in my mind, I knew there were more things to learn out there, things to see or hear, but any opportunity required having my dad's permission. You know how girls will go to the mall or the movies, and that's how they meet other people? Since I couldn't go to those places, I went to the library because it was related to school, and I liked to read. My father allowed me to go to the library by myself on the bus when I was in the fifth or sixth grade. I went to the library to read. I learned about the world, and was kind of like, "Oh my God, there are other places." I decided that I had to go to college so that I wouldn't be stuck like my mother at home with so many kids and not having a say-so in the household she ran. Now, looking back and chatting with her, she was unable to make any other choices because she was isolated and uninformed. My ninety-one-year-old mom now tells me, "Who would have told me otherwise, I had no one to confide in or to guide me!" During that time, I developed the insight that information is power!

Sonia: Was your family situation just the Mexican culture?

Genoveva: My siblings and I grew up with a mother who was Catholic. My dad was Catholic too, but he did not practice the religious ceremonies, such as mass. We were raised primarily within the Mexican culture. To me, as I was growing up, I understood we were Mexican and Catholic. Catholic religion and Mexican culture both teach women to be submissive. I started kindergarten in Catholic school, but I told my mom to take me out because I didn't want to be kneeling every hour to pray. So, she moved me to the public school, and I learned to pray and understand religion when I wasn't forced. For me, religion became a process to show gratitude and to give thanks to God and particular Saints, especially the Virgin de Guadalupe. After many years of not quite understanding religion(s), I now believe in a Higher Power and that Power can be called whatever the person chooses to call it: God, Jesus, etc.

Every Sunday, my mom would send us to church. She hardly ever went except to baptize her current baby that needed to be baptized. We studied catechism and then made our first communion. Besides giving thanks, religion taught me that girls/women are either pure virgins, or you're a *whore*. As a female, those were my two choices. I think to this day, because of religion, some women continue seeking a middle ground because they may not be either one. And still many women choose marriage as their first option, or dream, because of religion. It still teaches women to be obedient and humble to the man who marries them.

But as you know, the world is no longer so contained; now we have all options of who we desire to marry, either a man or a woman (same sex), or to postpone marriage in order to pursue an education. I ironically did both at the same time. I was a student when I married my first time, because I was pregnant but continued to study right after my daughter was born. She was two weeks old and was at a babysitter in order for me to return to school. I waited eight years until I had my next child. An older gentleman who was very wise gave me the advice to finish school after having had my first child, but to wait until I completed my graduate studies and work two years in my chosen profession before having my second child. I listened to his advice and I feel now that I was a better parent to my second child.

In high school, I liked tennis, but I couldn't join the Tennis Club because it met after school, and I had to go straight home. During my junior year, the school had a program where you could go to school in the morning and work in the afternoon. I joined the program to have more opportunities to get out of the house. My first job was reception work at an ophthalmologist's office. My second job was at an ice cream parlor in a shopping center. I had more exposure to a diverse group of people. I was exposed to a variety of men and women within and outside my culture. El Paso is an Army town, and there were a lot of military personnel at the shopping mall where I worked.

A family friend of my parents moved to San Pablo, California, with her husband and children. During my junior year in high school, I decided that I was going to plan behind my parents' back. I planned to visit them, and this might be my opportunity to leave El Paso after I graduated. I figured my dad would allow me to go because they were close friends of the family. I had worked through the summer after graduation and saved money for my airfare. I told my dad that I would be back and that I had the money for airfare. He said, "Yeah, okay." That became my getaway plan. I flew from El Paso to San Francisco, knowing that my plan was never to return to live, only to visit. My godparents came to pick me up at the San Francisco Airport. The next day I went looking for a job.

Sonia: You had an intention. You told your dad you were going to visit, but you had a dream inside.

Genoveva: My intentions were to follow my dream. Yes, I knew I had to find a job and do my one-year residency so I would qualify for community college. In 1969, it was free in California. There were no fees. In El Paso, it wasn't free. They had community colleges, but one had to pay fees to attend. I knew my parents couldn't afford to send me to college. I arrived in California with the plan of going to college. I immediately looked for a job. I was bilingual and I could type—those were my two skills. I found a job as a part-time teacher's aide. I called my dad, and I don't remember if I said, "Can I stay?" or if I said, "I'm going to stay." But he said as long as I worked and I wasn't letting someone else take care of me, it was okay. I stayed with his blessing.

Sonia: Did you live with the family that you went to visit?

Genoveva: I lived with the family's friend in San Pablo for about a year. I was going to college part-time, and I was able to get a full-time job as a secretary of a nonprofit called United Council of Spanish-Speaking Organizations. This was during the 1970 civil rights movement during Johnson's presidency and the war on poverty. They gave a lot of money to nonprofits. I don't know about other states, but California received a lot of money. That's when I started understanding what was going on in the community, and what advocates were asking for. In other words, I started to understand politics and started getting politicized.

I started tagging along with the executive director of the organization, as his secretary, and I fell in love with him. I was nineteen at the time. A year later I got pregnant. This part of my story has to do with birth control, sex, and love. I can say now that I had been brainwashed into thinking that sex was synonymous with love, and that if you love someone, you're going to have sex and accept the consequences. I couldn't use birth control because it had been instilled in me that it was bad to use, especially if you were not married. And, if you took birth control, it meant you wanted to be wild and not get pregnant. So that's why I got pregnant, because *I believed* that sex was synonymous with love and that birth control was bad. But the day after having my daughter, my "love baby," I said, "Give me the birth control pills." There was a small human being who *I was now* responsible for, and I could not have another one and another one. My opinion changed about birth control, and I understood it in a different way. I think this is an issue for a lot of women in various cultures and religions. They all preach the same thing: Sex is for being in love and marriage, then God blesses you with children.

I knew I didn't want any more babies at that time. With my daughter, I qualified for welfare and food stamps. This allowed me to go to school full-time. At two weeks old, my daughter went to a babysitter and I returned to college. I knew I was choosing to postpone my time with my daughter and that I was sacrificing my time with her for my goal of completing college. By that time, I was very determined to finish college and knew that I would be able to provide a better life for her in the future.

Sonia: You had all that help because of the child, and you used it temporarily for the right reasons.

Genoveva: I used welfare and food stamps temporarily, and I never felt ashamed for using the help. I was in school for six years. Two years at junior college, two years at Mills College, and two years at UC Berkeley. After I started working as a Clinical Social Worker, I paid back the financial help and felt I needed to, so someone else in need could use it. During my college years, I developed my political viewpoints in terms of advocacy and making policy changes. I became part of the Chicano Student Union, and we advocated for a Chicano Studies Department, which we got. We then had classes that were relevant to us as Chicanos, for example, History of the Southwest, Chicano Psychology, Mexican Art and Dance, etc. This knowledge empowered us as Chicano students, and from a group of twenty students that formed the Chicano Student Union, we all pursued graduate studies. For me, it was very important to belong to a group of persons that all had one common goal: educate ourselves to better serve our families and community.

Sonia: How did you get interested in those areas?

Genoveva: I got interested in joining the Chicano Student Club because I had a desire to belong to a group that I could relate to. I also was far away from my family and sought to replace it with friendships that had goals and meaning. I found groups to join, and this Chicano student group appealed to me. We all came from different parts of

Mexico, and at one point, we went around saying how we considered ourselves. One person said, "I'm Mexican-American." Another said, "I'm Mexican." Another said, "I'm Chicana," which is what I called myself. Another woman said, "I'm Spanish," but by the end of the semester, she was saying, "I'm Chicana." The class transformed each one of us. What we had in common was that we all wanted to achieve a college education and do something in the community. We went to the high schools to recruit students to the college. When I finished my BA degree, doors were opened to me because I had been part of the recruiting committee. That's why I've always been committed to opening doors for others, too. Currently, I am appointed to the Equal Employment Opportunity Commission of Contra Costa College District, by College District Trustee John Marquez, who was one of the twenty students that I was part of at Contra Costa College. At the current time, the College District does not have enough college faculty to reflect the student population. So the struggle continues.

Sonia: We don't even hear the word "Chicano" nowadays.

Genoveva: Fifty years later, the situation is very different. In my opinion, terms change in order to become more inclusive and reflect the current environment. During the '70s, the majority of students were from Mexico or with Mexican descent. Presently the student population that is Latino are from a variety of Latin American countries. Thus the terms: Latinox (which includes gay and all other Latinos who are more comfortable having a different gender description), Hispanic, and Raza are more modern terms that are used in the college and university settings to be more inclusive. Latinox students continue to transform in those settings, especially where there may be Raza Studies or Latino Studies.

Because knowledge is power, I still believe all students go through a transformation as they pursue their university degrees and professions. My hope is that students become more aware of our capitalist system of government and how poor people in this type of government will be left behind, unless there are others who will continue opening doors for them. Because of budget cuts, sometimes it is more difficult to complete your university studies and/or get hired in key positions in your profession. So the struggles are the same. University students fight for social justice on their campuses and we on the outside support the struggle by sitting on boards or elected offices and advocating for social justice policies.

Many persons have admired me for my accomplishments. But a lot of people helped me along the way. I did not accomplish it by myself. I do not believe anyone does. My passion and dreams were guided by many persons on my journey. It started out with my parents who valued education, even if it was only a high school diploma. The family friends who had left El Paso and moved to California were very supportive of my dream to attend college. Looking back, I chose to associate myself with persons that had similar values to mine and who were supportive in their own manners of my attainment of a college degree.

Sonia: I give you a lot of credit because you were taking the initiative, moving forward, and building community along the way. You gravitated to the right people who guided you into your passion.

Genoveva: Yes. For example, after I had my "love baby," an older gentleman, who was on the board of directors of the nonprofit I worked for then, advised me to finish my university studies and do not have any more children until I completed my graduate degree and worked full time for two years. After that, he said, "You can have all the children you want, and you will be prepared to return to work in your desired field." I listened to his advice and waited eight years between my two children. I also believe I was able to stay away from negative influences (not all the time) because of my dad's strict upbringing. He instilled fear in me when he would tell us what not to do and that we knew better. So I grew up being afraid to do "bad" things until I left home and fell in love and had my "love baby" without being married. Fortunately for me, my partner was very supportive of me completing my college degree, and after having my daughter, my focus on completing my college degree became even more important. Now I had to continue preparing myself to provide a good life for my daughter.

During my graduate studies and upon finishing my master's in social work from U.C. Berkeley, I worked at La Clinica De La Raza. I first worked there as an intern, and then they hired me, and I worked there for five years. When my son was born, eight years later with my same partner, I quit working and planned on staying home for a year so I could breastfeed my son and spend time with him. During that same time, I was appointed to the Contra Costa County Mental Health Advisory Board. During those years, there was a service model of halfway houses for the mentally ill. Because of my networking on the Advisory Board, I was asked to set up and open a halfway house for Latino mentally ill individuals. I accepted the job, especially since I could bring my son with me to work. During that period of setting up the program, there were no clients in the house. My job was to set up guidelines and procedures for the program and to hire the first director to open the program so we could accept clients. Once we hired a permanent director, she took over and I had accomplished my goals.

The following year, while still on the Mental Health Commission as a board member, I met and worked with the medical director of the Contra Costa County Mental Health Division. He had been involved with the Black Panther movement. He valued my politics in advocating for social justice policies and connected me to the manager of mental health services for the region in the county that I represented. She, too, had been part of the Black Panthers. When I met her, I said, "Can I come and work for you?" She said she could bring me in on a temporary basis because she did not have an open permanent position. So, I worked for the county for three years with no benefits, just a salary. Then I took the civil service exam and passed it, and she hired me as a supervisor. She was a role model for me. She adjusted the program to fit who our clients were and so we sometimes had to break some rules, but no one was hurt in the process. It was all about providing services in a bilingual/bicultural manner. It was during that time that I decided I was going to work for the County until I retired. More to come on that later on.

Sonia: Can you explain a little about what the Black Panther movement was all about?

Genoveva: I mention that my two colleagues had been with the Black Panther Movement. It was a political organization founded by

Bobby Seale and Huey Newton in 1966 in Oakland, California. Their primary goal was to arm African American citizens into patrol units to monitor the behavior of officers of the Oakland Police Department. Chapters arose all over the country until 1982. It also had international chapters operating in the United Kingdom in the early 1970s and in Algeria from 1969 until 1972. I personally became aware of them in 1969 after my arrival in Richmond, California. During that time, there had been civil riots in downtown Richmond, where businesses were burned down, and it looked like a ghost town. I was working in downtown Richmond with the nonprofit I mentioned earlier. That is where I learned about racism and how blacks and Mexicans were being discriminated against, and police departments did not look favorably on them. That is why the Black Panther was organized to fight against all the racism and discrimination.

Even though the Black Panther Party was militant, they also believed in social programs. They instituted a variety of community social programs, most extensively the Free Breakfast for Children Programs and community health clinics to address issues like food injustice and medical care. They believed that if a child was fed, the child would learn better. Working for the nonprofit and learning about the Black Panther Party, I quickly learned what social justice was about and determined for myself that I, too, was going to advocate for social justice with everything I did. Later on in my Mills College days, I met Barbara Lee, now Congresswoman Barbara Lee. Then she was a student with the Black Student Movement and had been or was a Black Panther Party member too. I just knew her from her activist population within the Mills Community.

Sonia: Were you married at the time?

Genoveva: Because my partner and father of my two children was married, we did not get married until my daughter was eight years old. We then had a son and stayed married for five years. During that time, I decided I needed to divorce my husband. He had been twenty years my senior and we had grown apart. I initiated the divorce and became a single, divorced mother with two children. Our age finally caught up with us. I was in my thirties; he was in his fifties. I was beginning to blossom in my profession and making professional contacts. He started getting jealous of my male co-workers. I realized that it wasn't the kind of love/marriage I needed. I filed for divorce. We went through attorneys, and it was a difficult process. Fortunately for me, I had listened to a friend/colleague who said to postpone having more children; I had finished my graduate degree and was working for the county and could financially support myself and my children. I was not financially dependent on him and therefore did not have to hold back because of that. Unfortunately for some women, they stay in unhealthy relationships because of financial reasons.

Sonia: Where did you go from there?

Genoveva: After that, I was in my thirties and divorced with two kids. I had my tubes tied right after my son was born. I knew at thirty that I did not want any more children; even though I knew I might fall in love with someone else. I loved my job providing mental health services to the Latino community. When I started working with the county, the staff would say, "Do Latinos need mental health services? They do not call the clinic." I would tell them, how can they, when there have been no Spanish-speaking capabilities, starting with the clerical staff who don't speak Spanish?" With my involvement and feedback, we changed things. We hired bilingual clerks and bilingual therapists, and I was instrumental in those changes.

During that time, I met a wonderful man and we were married a year later. We were married for thirty-five years. Cal was the best husband a woman could ask for. He respected and supported my professional and personal goals and he helped me raise my son, who at that time was six years old. My daughter, who was a teenager at that time, got upset with me and went to live with her dad. During my marriage to him, I got interested in running for office in my City of San Pablo. Thanks to my best friend, Maria Alegria, the first Latina to get elected in the City of Pinole. Maria mentored me and became my campaign manager (unpaid) for all of my four terms that I got elected. Cal, too, was very supportive and walked precincts with me. He was honest with me, and he never quite understood why I would work so hard in campaigning and staying in office for so many years, but he supported me and never felt neglected. I believe that is what true love is about.

Marriage or intimate partnerships are about supporting each other and coming together to share our lives and dreams. Shortly after we married, we bought a property in Oroville, California. It was a seven-acre parcel with nothing on it. But it was on a hill and we both fell in love with the property and developed it through the years. We started by using the property to camp out under the oak trees, and both my husband and son riding their dirt motorcycles up and down the hills. It was out in the country with no fences separating the properties. We eventually brought in a double-wide, premanufactured home onto the property and had a water well drilled, had a septic tank installed, and a butane gas tank. The only utility that we had was electricity from PGE. Our plan was to retire to that property and continue sharing our lives. Sadly, we were unable to make that dream come true. He was diagnosed with prostate cancer and passed away four years ago. I am adjusting to missing him and starting a new life for myself.

I have been a widow and last year I felt I was ready to meet new men and begin dating. I decided to go online and sign up on a dating website. I was nervous but again was determined to try it, since no men were going to come knocking on my door to ask me out. My circle of friends and colleagues was limiting me in meeting new men. I paid for six months and intended not to pay for any longer if I was not successful in meeting men. I met eight men and there was no chemistry between us until I met number nine. On our first meetup date, sparkles were felt by both of us and we have continued to date each other exclusively. We are both the same age, sixty-nine. He is African American, raised in San Francisco. My deceased husband was too, and was born and raised in Arkansas. My first husband was Mexican American, born and raised in Richmond, California. Each one has been very different but at the same time has been very supportive of my wishes and dreams.

In my profession, I've always held positions where I could advocate for Latinos, poor community members, and the disenfranchised adult mentally ill individuals. Approximately twenty years ago, I was given the opportunity to run for office. I saw the opportunity as another manner where I could make bigger policy decisions that applied to more people. In my job as a manager, I could change policy in terms of hiring valuable staff. But as an elected official, the policies I would make could affect the whole city. I was ready for that.

Sonia: So it empowered you. You could totally take this to the next level.

Genoveva: Yes, and as I mentioned earlier, Maria Alegria mentored me and "pushed me out" when my first opportunity arose to run for City Clerk. There was an open position for city clerk, and a council member called me and asked, "Do you want to run for city clerk? If you do, we'll support you." So the established old guard supported me, I ran, and I won. I got asked because they did not like the other candidate that was going to run for that office. I felt they were using me, but I decided I would use the opportunity to run, and if elected, to serve my community. The position of City Clerk does not have a vote in the decisions, the clerk only records the meetings. I used those four years as elected City Clerk to learn city government and what it took to pursue a Council seat.

When the time came for me to run, the current Council members, who had supported me wholeheartedly, did not support me for my Council run. It became clear to me that I was good enough for them as City Clerk but not as a Council member. I decided to run for the City Council after I realized that it did not take any particular skills or credentials to qualify to run for Council. It only required the desire to serve the public. That I knew, since San Pablo was fifty-five percent Latino. I ran and was elected the first Latina to Council in all of its history. I also was the highest vote-getter among all the candidates. I had proven to the "established status quo Council" that it was time for a change in San Pablo.

Once sworn in to Council, I immediately realized that my community values were not supported by the rest of the Council members. In San Pablo, Council consists of five elected members. And in order to pass an ordinance or a resolution leading to a new policy, a majority vote is needed. At my first meeting, I motioned for the City's exceptional newsletter be published in English and Spanish. The vote came down to four against mine. With Council members stating that we live in the US and therefore all residents need to learn English. So rather than giving up, I asked myself, "What needs to happen?" What needed to happen was to elect more progressive thinkers on the Council. It took me and my allies six years to change the Council. Every two years the voters added more progressive Council members. Six years later, the Council had a majority of progressive Council members. On the evening that new Council members were sworn in, the City Manager instructed staff to publish the city's newsletter in Spanish too. By this time of my leadership development, there was no problem that I would not be able to provide the leadership and vision to make San Pablo a better and safer city for all residents, regardless of what language they spoke.

Sonia: What was your main purpose for wanting to change that part of the community?

Genoveva: A city's mission and goal is to provide services to all its residents. Since San Pablo by then was fifty-five percent, the city had the responsibility to provide services sensitive to their culture and language. Among many changes, one of the most important to me was having the opportunity to hire a new City Manager who understood the needs of the residents and thus was able to implement the vision of the Council. The City Manager hired the first Latina Police Chief, who intentionally started recruiting candidates of color and bilingual officers, and she also implemented several new programs in our schools and in the community: School Resource Officers, Cops on Bikes, Coffee with a Cop, High School Cadet Program, etc.

The policy change in our police department was changed to Community Policing. Another important policy change and direction was for the city to work/partner with our school district. In the past, Council did not support such a partnership. To me it was a "no brainer," the school district and city both serve the same students and families. For the past eight years, we have had a Schools in Community Program in most of our elementary schools, which currently the City contributes $650,000 toward that effort.

The Community In Schools Model is where needed agencies come into the schools to make them more accessible to our students and their families. Currently, the city spends about $600,000 of the city's budget in our schools toward Communities In Schools programming. I furthermore provided the leadership for Council to appoint a Task Force after we learned that San Pablo had the highest rate of childhood obesity. This task force had representatives from the schools, nonprofits, County Public Health and residents. The Task Force was instrumental in funding new pilot projects to address the epidemic. We have been unable to track or measure any specific data to show that we indeed lowered the rate. In the Task Force, all members became very knowledgeable about the addictive nature of sugar and how the obesity epidemic needed to address soda consumption and get kids to drink more water. To begin to address the epidemic in our schools, we provided funding for water stations and salad bar equipment. We still have a long way to go. At present, the Council has designated $350,000 toward ongoing funding for programming to continue addressing the prevention of childhood obesity. It also has formed an advisory committee to oversee this funding.

I learned a few years ago the literacy rate of our third-graders in our schools. It is very low and unacceptable. The prison industry decides how many prisons to build based on third-graders, because they can predict how many of those kids will end up in the prison system. In other words, if a child is not at grade level by the third grade, they're doomed not to succeed, and it's a pipeline to prison. On my last year on Council, I was successful at making early childhood literacy a priority in our work plan. A Task Force was formed. We met once with staff from nonprofits, school district administrators, school principals, and education advocates, and we all agreed the problem existed and committed to continue meeting about finding solutions.

It is a very complicated problem, and in my opinion, we need to stop pointing the fingers at parents and teachers. We all have a responsibility to teach our kids to be at a third-grade level, but we have to work together and not in silos. It begins at home when young parents or caretakers can instill the importance and value of reading to the children. But sometimes our parents are working two jobs and they don't have the time, or they are not able to read. Bottom line, all parents desire the best for their children. The City provided funding for a pilot in one school where we gave more services to the preschoolers by providing them with books and teaching parents how to support their child and their books at home. We may not have the answers, but we have the responsibility to attempt to do something about it.

Sonia: What's your greatest passion right now? You've gone the political route, you've definitely been a trailblazer, and you made a lot of things happen. You are absolutely incredible. I know you have grandkids now and that's a big part of your life, but you don't want to leave the community. How will you still make an impact in these important areas of your life?

Genoveva: I have accomplished my dreams and am proud of those accomplishments. My dream of getting a college degree, now retired from a very fulfilling social work profession in serving the adult mentally ill in our community, raising my two children with support from many persons, being married twice and both times being able to pursue my dreams, recently retired after sixteen years in public office, watching and helping my kids raise their children, being a great grandma, and I can go on and on.

Sonia: That's wonderful! Listening to your story makes me feel that your life is fulfilled. Is there anything that you really want that you haven't done yet, whether something personally or something that will bring more of an impact? Is there anything causing a hole in your heart?

Genoveva: I honestly do not feel I have a hole in my heart at this point of my life. I had the privilege and am very grateful to have been able to take care of my husband at his last stage of his life and allow him and my family to have him pass in our home. For that, I will be eternally grateful.

In gratitude, I am healthy and will continue to have an active life and continue being a "trailblazer," as I have been called. My family is my priority. Included in my family is my boyfriend, who I love dearly. I plan to spend as much time as I can with them. I plan to visit my ninety-one-year-old mother in El Paso as much as I can, and show her my gratitude for having given me birth and raising all of her children. She is my ultimate role model and HERO. I plan to continue eating in a healthier manner and attend my five a.m. Boot Camp class a minimum three times a week. I also plan to do more traveling. My bucket list includes many places to visit including visiting all of the National Parks in the US. I will share my romance chapter/story in our next book!

I plan to continue staying involved in my community. Currently I am:

- A board member of Weigh of Life, Inc., which provides exercise and nutrition information to its members.

- An elected Delegate to the Democratic Party in Contra Costa County.

- Now off the Council, have recently been appointed to two advisory committees for the City of San Pablo to continue my work on prevention of Childhood Obesity and Early Childhood Literacy.

- A volunteer at our local Richmond High School, where I co-lead a female student support group with a friend who is a retired school teacher and recently elected to the School Board. We provide mentoring, guidance, and discussions of important topics to them. Helping these young women also builds their confidence that their dreams can come true. We connect them with the right resources, and support them to get out there and ask questions!

- Will continue to work as a member of the Contra Costa College District's Equal Opportunity Commission, representing the community.

- Will continue on an advisory group with Travis Credit Union.

- Will continue being involved in spaces where I can share my knowledge and wisdom.

In my Golden Years, WHO AM I NOW? And what else do I want to do for ME, without feeling selfish?

My new challenge will be to learn to give myself time for myself. To figure out who I am besides a caretaker and taking care of others in the community. Wish me luck!

Sonia: It's your golden years! Do what you want to do. You've done a lot for your communities. If it wasn't for you, things wouldn't be where they are right now. What would you tell other women who have so many aspirations?

Genoveva: I advise other young women and all women, not to give up on their DREAMS! None of us can do it by ourselves, do not hesitate to ask for help and to keep learning about what it will require to make your DREAM(s) come to reality! Take baby steps but never lose sight of your DREAM! If you're not happy with something, find support and set a plan to make a change. Confidence comes from within, and no one's going to give it to you. Find it by going to a class, joining a support group, and reading self-help books. You have to learn what you need to learn and make yourself wiser. It's on us to keep learning and choosing to be around people who are going through a similar journey, and some may be more successful than others.

Sonia: What would you say to women who don't have the confidence to make big changes or commitments?

Genoveva: That's why women's support groups are so important, because we realize we're not the only ones who are struggling, and we can get support and give support. During each woman's journey, they will find their passion and purpose. That is so important to know as you pursue your goals. All dreams require passion and a purpose. Be fearful and nervous, but go out and find yours!

Sonia: What do you want your legacy to be?

Genoveva: I hope it will be the values my children, grandchildren, and great-grandchildren will practice in their lives that have to do with kindness, fairness, and respect. I feel I have led my life with those core values, and they have kept me humble and grateful. Those values are very important in all we do, including public service.

Sonia: That's wonderful!

Genoveva: I now end with gratitude for you, Sonia, who brought us all together and fulfilled our entire DREAM in being co-authors of this book. Thank you, Sonia!

Sonia: Thank you for sharing your story.

Sonia Hassey

ABOUT GENOVEVA GARCIA CALLOWAY

Personal background

Born and raised in El Paso, Texas. I am one of 14 children, and the *first* in my family to graduate from college. I am the proud parent of two adult children, four grandchildren and one great-granddaughter. **I happily retired from my profession as a Clinical Social Worker in 2015.**

Elected/Public Office Experience:

- Elected San Pablo City Clerk (1998 to 2002)
- San Pablo City Council (Elected November 2002, re-elected in 2006, 2010,
- and 2014 through November 2018)
- Served as Mayor four times
- **December 2018 Retired from Public Office**

Education:

1973 A.A. Liberal Arts, Contra Costa College in San Pablo, California

1976 B.A. Degree in Psychology, Mills College – Oakland, California

1978 Master's Degree in Social Work, University of California, Berkeley

Community Involvement:

1979 – Co-Founder of Familias Unidas, a non-profit community counseling and information center to serve families of West Contra Costa County.

2006 to 2017 – Co-Founder of Concilio Latino, a network of Service Providers of West Contra Costa County to promote intra agency collaboration.

2003–Present – Cofounder of Peace and Unity Cinco de Mayo Parade with City of San Pablo and City of Richmond, CA, a non-profit community initiative to promote youth & families.

COMMUNITY RECOGNITION:

2006 – **Distinguished Alumni Award** – *Outstanding Community Service, Leadership and Personal Achievement*, Contra Costa Community College

2009 – **Founder's Award** – Familias Unidas 30th Anniversary

2017 – **Partner of the Year** – *Outstanding Contribution to Public Education* by West Contra Costa Unified School District Board of Education

2018 – **Appreciation Award and Guest Speaker** – 21st TSC WOMEN'S EQUALITY DAY –Army Post in Kaiserslautern, Germany

CHAPTER 15

Being Latina with a Vision

Rose Mendoza

Sonia: Hello, I am here with Rose Mendoza and she is one incredible woman who is going to share her personal story of transformation and success. Rose, just share your story and your heart with us.

Rose: Thanks, Sonia. I am California native, raised in Orange County, not far from Disneyland in a barrio called "El Campo" also called "The Camp." A small community of farmworkers, in a town called La Habra. With the help of a social movement, empowering hermanas, I moved to San Jose to become a cultural activist and educated Latina.

After a successful career in Silicon Valley, I am now celebrating becoming an entrepreneur, owner of a travel company called Dulce

Vida Travel, LLC, specializing in travel to the Mexican Heritage Towns, following my passion to honor and celebrate my Mexican heritage. The company offers tours and celebrates Mexican culture experiences. I am proud to be a member of the Silicon Valley Hispanic Chamber based in San Jose.

I asked myself, where did this passion for celebrating Mexican culture come from, and why become a cultural activist? Growing in a barrio, with ten brothers and sisters, and basic needs being met, family and Mexican cultural traditions became my main assets. My father migrated from Guadalajara, Mexico to the United States when he was eighteen years old. He was a proud Mexican, a farmworker picking oranges in the fields in Orange County, across the street from Disneyland by day, and a celebrated Mexican Charro, (Mexican Cowboy) in his spare time. My mother was a homemaker, with an intense gift of gab and expert tortilla maker. My grandmother a dedicated, witty Catholic. I remember her most as an admirer of the Virgin de Guadalupe, and leader of her social club "Guadalupanas." She was a dominant influence in our lives, as my mother was raising ten kids, in the barrio, she did not always have much time to give us all the attention and guidance that we needed. As a member of a large, intense, and proud family, and the beginnings of a powerful social movement, all set the stage for my future.

One of the most distinct memories of my youth, I recall was news reports on television, of a man named Cesar Chavez, an advocate for farmworker rights. News stories reported he was leading a farm workers' movement to gain awareness that farmworkers deserved better housing, working conditions and wages. My father, being a farm worker, would yell at the television, "How does a Mexican man think he is going to impact change? Look at him, he is short, dark and speaks Spanish. Why would he even think he could help us farm workers?" With an angry face, he walked out of the room. I was a young adult at the time, and I believed my father.

I survived living in this small quiet town until high school. The Camp was my home and kept me safe, until I was seventeen, entering my senior in high school, there was a farm workers event in La Habra, curious and walking distance from our home I attended. A Chicano Theater group called "Teatro Espiritu de Aztlan" performed skits about the Farmworkers strike. The performers were students from Fullerton College, led by Cesar Flores. They invited me to attend a rally at Fullerton College, in which Cesar Chavez would be speaking. I became even more curious, recalling my father's attitude toward Cesar Chavez. I attended, also performed a skit with the "teatro." Cesar Chavez spoke to the thousands of supporters, who were there to listen to his message about farmworkers deserving better working conditions.

After the rally, Cesar Chavez walked straight up to me, I was surrounded by thousands of supporters, and he stuck his hand out and said, "Thank you for your support." It was such an impactful moment, I realized that it did not matter what you looked like, it did not matter the color of your skin. What matters is to have a vision and clear goals. It was that moment when I realized I wanted to support the rights of Latinos. Along with supporting farmworkers' rights, we were advocating for better access to education, housing, and job training.

These were all the issues in the late seventies/eighties that continue to be social issues for the Latino community.

Sonia: I want to go back to the moment you met him, and when he came up to you. What did that do to your physiology at that moment?

Rose: My best friend was standing next to me, and it was a surreal moment. With thousands of people, why did he choose me? He thanked lots of people, but I was one of many, and I was very young. It just made an impression. It was the very first time in my life that I actually met somebody that impactful, with a clear vision and goals, beyond survival mode!

Sonia: Wow. Would you say that was your moment in time when it took you to a new level in your life and your way of thinking?

Rose: It really was. I have had three of these moments, but this was so impactful because I was raised in a small town, forbidden to go to outside of our small town, especially, due to the LA riots and protest reported on the news. The only other social experience outside of church was a visit to Disneyland. I was never around people of influence or social status. I was a young Chicana, in this little town, going to school, being with my family, and that was it, with no expectations of getting an education or to be a successful entrepreneur. Be happy and survive.

Still living in The Camp, my mother was now a single mother, with eight children at the time. My friends who lived in Fullerton encouraged me, "Rose, why don't you come finish school in Fullerton and then we will help you get into college." During this time, my family lived in a two-bedroom apartment, hand-me-downs, food stamps, and welfare payments are how we survived. I could see my mother struggling. She had no time to nurture us, to encourage us, she had just enough energy to feed us and keep us safe. Though she did have the gift of gab and kept us constantly entertained with her funny outlook on life.

We just had the basics. I was never hungry, I was never cold, and I was never lonely. We had our grandmother to make sure that we understood values, morals, what it takes to be a good person.

But I decided to move out when of my mother's home, when I was seventeen years old with the thought that I was doing my mother a favor, one less mouth to feed. I made it as a high school senior, and that is when I moved out to live with my friend Eva, and roommates to finish high school and get help to begin college. I recall thinking, will my mother notice me gone? with all the chaos raising so many children!

Sonia: What happened once you left?

Rose: My best friend, Eva, who is still my best friend to this very day, took me under her wing. They were involved in the Chicano movement, going to the farm workers rallies. She just said, "Come along, you're going to join the movement." I got a part-time job, and I finished high school with honors. Upon graduating from high school, we got a job opportunity in San Jose. We got hired to work as activists with a political theater called "Teatro De La Gente" led by Adrian Vargas. Eva and I drove to San Jose, auditioned, and got hired. That is how I landed in San Jose.

Sonia: That is so incredible. I want to go back just a bit because you captured me with the mention of your grandmother, and I want to know how she affected your life on a daily basis. What did she do, or who was she, that brought so much impact into your life and the life of your family?

Rose: Yes, my grandmother was a devoted Catholic, she went to church every single day. Every Sunday we all visited our grandmother's house, she had close to thirty grandchildren. She would talk to us about the importance of having values, respect for elders, of being a good person, and working hard. She would have these conversations with the grandchildren, and with the adults in the room, to remind them as well. She would remind us of the repercussions of sin, in Catholic terms. She lectured on the value of good character, convictions, the importance to fight for basic human respect. She was my brother and sisters' moral compass, and although she is gone, her spirit remains within us. Though my grandmother was most influential in developing my character and values, it was my father that made me proud of being Mexican. That importance of my Mexican culture and heritage that would later define me.

I am proud of who I am. Any person who I meet and that spends more than an hour with me knows that I am Mexican, I make it very clear. As a second-generation Mexican-American, I was lucky to be born into a culture admired world-wide.

Sonia: Wow. That is incredible just for the reason that a lot of people are losing their heritage. I love that you are filling that gap. Would you say that between your dad, your grandmother and your mother, they built your character and it became a driving force for who you are today?

Rose: Yes, very much so. They prepared me to be the adult who I wanted to be. My favorite saying is, "The more prepared you are, the luckier you will feel." As I became a young adult, all the choices that I made shaped my life. I was from a family of eleven children and the only one who completed a college education. I completed my Associates Arts Program, entered the workforce, then returned to school as a working adult completed my B.A. and finally an MBA at the young age of forty. Though I am proud to say; all my siblings continue to have successful careers.

Sonia: What helped you to say that you were going to move forward with your education?

Rose: The Chicano movement at the time made me aware of the importance and value of an education. Then, of course, my friends who were college-educated encouraged me to pursue a college education.

Another important factor is to have a supportive family. I have been blessed to be married to my husband for more than thirty years, and my son and daughter are very successful creatives,

and I am proud of them. My husband embodies the low-rider culture, and he is also proud of his Mexican heritage. My sisters are also a major motivation in reaching my goals. Always supportive and willing to help me be successful. Gracias Hermanas!!!!

Another turning point in my life was when I completed my master's degree. Intel Corporation in Santa Clara offered me a Finance Manager position in their corporate office. I was the only Latina in the finance department at the time of my hiring. My timing of entering the corporate workforce was nicely aligned with Silicon Valley embracing and committing to a diverse workforce. My early efforts for advocating for Latinos having equal access to employment opportunities paid off. Intel Corporation, along with many other Silicon Valley companies, actively recruit and are committed to a diverse workforce.

Sonia: How did that make you feel?

Rose: I felt powerful, and accomplished, not only because I was the only Latina, within Intel's Corporate Finance group at the time, but the executives were willing to sponsor me, and champion my career to make sure I was successful at Intel, they let me know that I had potential. They also knew I would need someone to help me along the way. I joined the Intel Latino Network employee resource group and convinced Intel to fund the National Hispanic MBA Association scholarship grants. I used my position to help advance other Latinos in education.

I faced many challenges as well. My first years at Intel it was tough, as my peer group was very competitive. Intel practiced meritocracy, meaning they rewarded the highest performers. The more results you influence, the higher the compensation. I worked with men who often told me they were smarter than me, and I did not stand a chance of advancement, I really had to fight for my career, there were challenging moments. Colleagues from the National Society Hispanic

MBA shared an insight with me. They said, "Were you not raised in the barrio?" And, "Did you learn little about how to be street tough? That is why you will survive at Intel because you got that street tough and survival mentality." I needed to be tough, to deal with failure and taking risks, and focus on my own successes. I eventually was awarded two Finance Achievement Awards and was assigned to manage the intern program, and role model successful behaviors.

Sonia: What did you learn from that experience?

Rose: It was powerful, and I also understood the impact of my work. It was between 2000 and 2003 when Intel launched the first Wi-Fi-enabled mobile microchip. The infrastructure did not exist to support Wi-Fi, unlike it exist today. I was part of the engineering team that launched Wi-Fi technology globally worldwide. I did receive an award for my participation while working in the finance department. It was so powerful to see how I could contribute to something impacting the world and improve people's lives. It took teamwork, hard work, being around influencers and visionaries. It was a long road, from a young Latina/Chicana from La Habra, with no knowledge of the world, now traveling the world launching a technology known as Wi-Fi.

Sonia: I totally agree. We do have to be around people who will help us move forward. Talk with us about your passion for Dulce Travel and how it began at the incubator stage.

Rose: Upon completing my MBA, I now had the skills for how to become an entrepreneur. After twenty years in Silicon Valley, I change my focus and decided I was ready to start a small business.

Ready to be the CEO of my destiny. I had saved enough money to open a small business selling Mexican folk art, as my goal was to focus on promoting the Mexican culture and heritage. Developing the business required traveling to Mexico to purchase the folk art from the artist directly. I had become so familiar with the artisan towns, I later decided to also offer all-inclusive tours, the travel business was born!

Sonia: It is an incredible business model that is needed. I want to go and experience and touch the land and know the culture a bit more and fall in love with it again.

Rose: Before I opened my business, my first exposure to the beauty and wealth of the culture was cooking classes I attended in San Miguel de Allende MX with my sisters. San Miguel de Allende is a beautiful historic town, soon became my piece of heaven on earth. It was on that very trip that sparked my idea to establish a business model promoting Mexican art and culinary experiences.

Art and culture are necessary, but we still do not emphasize education. That is the part I still see every day and I'm trying to figure out how to tie culture and education to empower more Latinas to pursue their education. There are impactful Latina organizations that are doing that, and I support them. Trying to understand how we can use our culture and heritage to advance ourselves and to be educated. It doesn't have to be an advanced degree; any form of education will ensure we are represented as a heritage. I recently participated in a study published by Hispana Organization for political equality, citing that Latina micro business owners are too big to ignore. A barrier to growth was access to capital. Better financial literacy would improve Latina business owner to grow.

Sonia: Yes, no doubt education is important. And what do you think about self-development for every individual to understand their purpose so they can find their passion?

Rose: Self-development is critical to keep motivated. You can find a mentor, somebody who you aspire to be. I have three role models who I look up to and who have helped me stay on top of my game. I attend workshops, attend conferences, & webinars, anything from social media to yoga. I also want to understand what is happening in our political world, especially with Latinas and politics. I take the initiative to always stay involved and develop my understanding and skill set. Funny, I consider investing in self-development as rewarding myself, for a job well done.

Sonia: That is awesome. Self-confidence plays a big role in self-development and education, believing in yourself and in your abilities. How important do you think that is?

Rose: Self-confidence is a challenge when you start your own business. Along with major wins, you will have failures, when you think, "I am done, I am out of money, I am out of resources." You've got to have self-confidence to move forward and know you can build a business. Part of your self-confidence is establishing, a mission, and a vision statement. The biggest thing is knowing there will be failure along the way. I usually just sleep on it, and the next day figure out a solution.

Sonia: That is why self-confidence is crucial, because if we don't have it and we have a setback, then we want to quit, and a lot of people do actually.

Rose: Then, the other issue is imposter syndrome. After three years at Intel, I had serious imposter syndrome. I thought, "When are they going to figure me out? When are they going to know I am a girl from the barrio? Do they know that I did not go to an important college?" I later learned at a professional development conference, that imposter syndrome impacts many professionals. Then I had the self-confidence to say, "Okay, I got this, forget about imposter syndrome. I am going to move forward." That is something to be very aware of, it is very real, and can impact our self-confidence.

Sonia: This makes a lot of sense about the value of self-development, self-confidence, and working on understanding your abilities and having faith in your abilities. We fail forward. Do you agree with the concept of failing forward?

Rose: Yes. That is a good one. It is hard to be successful without failure, you will learn from your failures to move forward.

Sonia: Share an experience of either a family or a person who went on a tour with you to Mexico and had the experience that made you realize, "This is why I do what I do."

Rose: I shared about my experience in San Miguel de Allende. *Travel and Leisure* magazine published an article about a town in Mexico called San Miguel de Allende. The town was rated the number one travel destination in the world. That is when we decided to attend the cooking school, we spent a week with seven other women, we were taught Mexican traditional cooking. We realized that our heritage and our culture have so much to offer. It was a game-changer for me because it was not too long after that when I decided to leave Silicon Valley career and start my own business.

Another epiphany type moment was on a business trip to New York. I was strolling out of the marketing office on 5th Avenue, and came across a Lucky Clothing Brand storefront, they had ten-feet tall Loteria cards. They were associating the Lucky brand with the Mexican Culture. Loteria is a Mexican version of Bingo. The images on the cards reflect the Mexican culture. I stood in front of the Lucky Brand store for twenty minutes, just blown away. I had come to realize, not only was Mexican culture popular, it was cool. Lucky Brand is a premium brand, and they chose the Mexican culture to promote their lifestyle. My culture was being highlighted on Fifth Avenue and I realized promoting the Mexican culture can be profitable. I thought, I can capitalize on our culture!

Sonia: That is incredible. Tell me, what brings you the most passion right now?

Rose: What brings me the most passion is when I get to do cultural work. I love hosting women travelers on culinary & heritage tours to Mexico. I get to see them get them inspired and fall in love with the culture. I just published an eBook on kindle called *Frida's Passions: A Mexico City Travel Guide*. It was a big moment because I always wanted to be a published author, to share my knowledge with others. My amiga & mentor, Kathy Murillo AKA Crafty Chica gave me great advise "Just start on Kindle, Rose, Kindle's really easy." I wrote the guide and published, such an exciting time for me. It's funny, the book sells for two dollars and ninety-nine cents. I receive seventy percent of the sale. Kindle sent me an email a couple of weeks ago saying, "We sold one book. We owe you a dollar ninety-three."

Sonia: I love that.

Rose: But that dollar ninety-three felt like a million dollars to me! It felt like earned a million dollars because I had fulfilled one of my goals and one of my passions, I know I am not going to get wealthy selling this book, but the fact that I'm able to share my story about Frida Kahlo and what it is like to experience Mexico City was a true goal in my life. When does a dollar ninety-three equate to a million dollars? When you fulfill your passion and achieve your goals.

Sonia: There you go. That is incredible. What would you say is your favorite place to go? What are your favorite experiences personally?

Rose: My favorite experiences are definitely with my family. I have a beautiful, loving family. I have been able to fulfill my goals and have a strong family that supports me. They are patient with me, as I travel a lot, but I am also supportive of them. A proud moment of my life was when we were able to pay for my son's bachelor's degree. He earned a degree at the San Francisco Art's Institute. We were able to pay for his education, with no student loans. My son has a promising career as a graphic designer in the sports industry. I was able to break the cycle, by ensuring my son had access to a good education.

Sonia: What an accomplishment. What would you attribute that to?

Rose: The ability to have a successful career in Silicon Valley, good financial literary & establishing financial goals.

Sonia: I love that. What do you think about goal-setting?

Rose: I am very goal oriented! Believe it or not, I make a checklist every single day. I write goals every single month. I check them twice a week. That is how I live my life. Without it, I just feel completely lost. Goal-setting reminds me what my priorities are and how to balance out my life.

I've always had a five-year plan. I was about twenty-five, I started thinking about what my life was going to be like at thirty-five. That is how I was able to complete my college education in increments, because I was a working parent and I couldn't go full-time. I thought, "I am going to get my associate's, then my bachelor's, then my master's, and then I am going to get a bad-ass job. Check, Check and Check!

Sonia: Where do you see yourself five years from now?

Rose: Five years from now I want to be generating at least a million dollars in income. I want to have a staff. I want to author at least three more books. I want to be a speaker and influencer in the travel industry, promoting Mexican heritage travel and continuing to do community work while promoting the culture. I am one-tenth of the way to my dream. It is doable. I want to retire in fifteen years, so my five-year plans are getting very short. Eventually, travel to other parts of the world and bring the grandkids.

Sonia: I love the fact that not only are you setting goals, but you are very clear about your goals. Having clarity and knowing exactly what you want is how you are going to get there. If you have vague goals, you will get vague results, but if you have clear goals, you will get clear results. Right?

Rose: I agree with that. Also keep in mind to take a stand no matter how controversial it is. Take a stand on an issue and go fight for it because that will help shape who you are. The stand that I took at an early age is that Mexicans are being treated poorly and I am going to go fight for them. I took a strong stand. Then I said, "I need to be educated because now I do not want to be in constant survival mode." I took a stand and I went for it. Everybody has a passion. It could be animals, or helping elderly people, or homeless people. Take a stand, partner and collaborate with like-minded people. I always keep in mind a saying by Nelson Mandela "It always seems impossible, until it is done".

Sonia: Would you say it is about making that decision and sticking to it, and then being inspired to action?

Rose: Stick to it and take risks. Taking risks that aligned to your goals, is super scary, but all of a sudden you are going to be quite surprised what you were able to accomplish. You may remind yourself, I cannot believe I did that or there is was no way this person will call me back or that person to respond, or willing to hear my ideas. One of my mentors, Kathy Cano-Murillo, is a well-known Latina, and super successful creative. I wrote to her with some ideas, and I wondered if she would write back, well she did and responded, "Rose, let's work together."

Sonia: I love what you said. You never know. You just never know. But if we do not take the risk, then we know the answer.

Rose: Yes. When I was a board member with a local non-profit, I was coached to "just ask. They might say yes." Sometimes we do not ask because we already think we know the answer. Such as asking for a donation. I get so nervous to ask! We prejudge the response. I have learned just to make the ask.

Sonia: What about attitude?

Rose: I have always had a positive outlook in life. Many have commented that I have such a positive attitude and not much gets me down. They also say I appear to be naïve, as I see the positive in most situations, and willing to support. Having a positive attitude is what makes all the difference and it comes naturally for me. My daughter has a wonderful saying "We all may be a little broken, but we continue smiling and trying".

Sonia: Do you agree that a positive attitude plays a huge part in success?

Rose: Yes. It plays a big part. If your influencers, colleagues, and friends have positive attitudes, it will help you find solutions and get back on the right track. I have partnered with Latina colleagues, and some are even more positive than me. I naturally work with the Latinas who have the same attitude and similar work ethics.

Sonia: What would you say to the women who are thinking in their hearts that they have dreams, but do not even know how to begin to fulfill them?

Rose: If you have a goal of starting a business or entering into a new career field, research and understand what it takes to be successful in that field. The local chambers of commerce have a wealth of resources, coaches, and mentors to connect you with somebody who is already in that business and knows what it takes to be successful. Get training, certifications & join professional groups. A college degree may not be required, but it is never too late to start. Do not let your age & lack of startup funds stop you. Does require dedicated time to research and connect with people in that field who could mentor and champion your success. I have had many mentors, and I mentored many young professionals. My recent obsession is Dolores Huerta, co-founder of the Farmworkers Union, alongside Cesar Chavez, she is eighty-seven years old, and remains a strong advocate for basic human rights. Her signature saying "Power belongs to the People"

Sonia: It is never too late to live your passion. Not only to be future-focused, but also to be present-focused. Live in the present, but set your goals and live your dreams.

Rose: And remember to have fun along the way. We all work hard but remember to reward yourself. No one else is going to reward you. I signed up for a painting class. I am a terrible painter and I do not know how to paint. I thought it would be fun to learn something new. The classes were so much fun, and I even got a booking out of it, because I talked about the business.

Sonia: Rose, thank you so much. You are very inspiring, and I know that you are going to bless so many people. Your energy, love, and passion for what you do are incredible.

Rose: Thank you, Sonia. A final thought to consider: *"Every moment is an organizing opportunity, every person a potential activist, every minute a chance to change the world."* —Dolores Huerta Co-Founder of the Farmworkers Union

ABOUT ROSE MENDOZA

Rose Mendoza is a cultural activist, and believes culture matters.

She is a California native, 2nd generation Mexican, the daughter of a farmworker and famed Mexican *Charro* (Mexican Cowboy), and granddaughter of a *Guadalupana* (admirer of Virgen de Guadalupe). Mexican culture and religion were etched in her soul and consumed her identity. She maintains a master's degree, with an emphasis on Marketing and Branding, and has held senior level positions within high profile Silicon Valley companies.

Rose Mendoza established *Dulce Vida Travel LLC* to promote the beauty of the Mexican culture via travel concierge services, and hosted Mexican Heritage tours.

She has traveled extensively throughout Mexico, exploring Mexico's Magic Towns, and her family hometown of Guadalajara. Rose is also the author of Kindle e-book "Frida Kahlo's Passions, a Mexico City Travel Guide."

www.dulcevidatravel.com
info@dulcevidatravel.com
408.495.2411
@dulcevidatravel

CHAPTER 16

Because You Are Worth It

Carmen Gomez

Sonia: I am here with Carmen Gomez, who is going to share her story and what she's been through and where she is now.

Carmen: I am a woman who is happy to be part of this beautiful planet, a mother of two amazing teenagers, Michelle and Marcos. I love spending time with my family and with friends. I enjoy being an entrepreneur, enjoy traveling, and I love personal development work, leadership, and being involved in the community. I have owned an insurance business for the past twelve years, and I love educating and helping the community on their insurance needs, whether it is for personal insurance, business, life, health, or planning for retirement.

I was born in Mexico in the state of Sinaloa, and my mother and father had five children, two brothers and two sisters. Then years later, after my father's passing, my mother gave us one more brother. Which for me, it's my third brother. I don't see him as a step-brother. I was only three years old when my father passed away. He left my mother with five children to take care of and raise. That has been one of the most impactful experiences in my life. I didn't get to experience my father's company or love, and I also lost my mom in a way, because she was not really present with us since she had five children to care for and raise on her own. It was very tough. I think my mother saw life as difficult and unfair. She was not a very expressive parent. I admire my mom; she's a very strong woman with great values. My mom has always being a very integrated and responsible woman. Sometimes I ask myself where she found that strength to carry herself forward and provide the best she could for me and my siblings. I do want to acknowledge my dad's family who helped her financially, and my mom's family helped her more on the emotional aspect. But yet she was the one that kept moving forward to provide for us within the best of her abilities.

I came to the United States when I was thirteen and I didn't know a word in English. I was friendly, so I made friends right away. It was difficult to learn English, but I wanted to be really good at it. Coming from Mexico, and with my grandfather's job as a rancher, we didn't have many resources for education. Where I lived, they provided schooling up to the sixth grade. When I came here at thirteen, that's when I learned that education exists to the level that it does.

I completed junior high then my four years of high school, and then I started attending Woodland Community College. I was going for business administration classes, but while attending there, I fell in love with the father of my son and daughter. I got pregnant and gave birth to my daughter when I was twenty, and that's when I stopped going to college. My son was born two years after my daughter. The relationship didn't work out. Because of not knowing what we both wanted in the other person, or for being too young. I fell in love or what I thought love was, and we got together and lived together for ten years, but we never got married. What took me to this dark part of my life was my guilt for not "choosing correctly." I truly wanted what most women want: a good husband to love me, respect me, and to create a happy matrimony. In other words, a beautiful family. What I had was not what I wanted. My beautiful children, yes, but not the type of relationship that I wanted. It was the total opposite of what I wanted. I didn't feel loved or appreciated. During my ten years of being together with my children's father, I felt and it seemed like a was a single mom. I used to do pretty much everything by myself in the company of Michelle and Marc Anthony, my daughter and son. I remember feeling small, unwanted, and embarrassed for not having my children's father with us. I felt incomplete; I even thought that something was wrong with me. I remember comparing myself with other women and didn't have an answer as to why they had what I thought I should have: a good man by their side, taking care of them; a father to their children, which my son and daughter had but he wasn't around. I remember not only feeling bad for myself, but for my children too. It was then that I started feeling resentment toward my son and daughter's father. The love that I felt for him started to vanish.

Our disagreements started to grow as well as the arguments. The house environment became very unhealthy. It was not what I wanted for myself or for Michelle and Marcos. I felt trapped, very unfulfilled, and unhappy. My self-esteem went to the ground. I honestly thought that something was wrong with me.

Sonia: I'm sure there were moments of, "I need to work this out for the sake of the children." Tell me about your driving force to get through the hard times.

Carmen: My driving force was my desire for my son and daughter to grow in a family environment with mom and dad together. I wanted them to have what I didn't have, because I lost my father at the age of three. It was hard to leave my children's father because my grandmother, my mom, and everyone had this belief that if you were with a man, you had to stay with him no matter what. But, one day as I was changing the television channels, I saw a commercial by Anthony Robbins. He was promoting a personal growth and development package. I secretly ordered the package; I would listen to his CDs on my way to and from work. It was then that I started to discover that I wasn't the only one feeling trapped, with guilt and shame. I had so many other options. I was a powerful soul and had the choice to stay in the relationship or take a risk and pursue my happiness. I started to gain my power back. I started to ask for what I wanted. It worked for very short periods of time. That lasted five more years until one day we had an argument and he pushed me outside our house. He did it in front of Michelle and Marc Anthony, and for me, that was it. That's when I got the courage to tell him that I couldn't continue in that relationship anymore, that I wanted to separate, and we did.

The first three years of getting separated, I felt guilty, doubtful, and wondered if I did the right thing. I got depressed. I did not go to the doctor to get diagnosed with depression, but I had all the symptoms. I wasn't the woman I knew and experienced myself being. I just wanted to be alone, and I didn't want to go out or talk to friends. I wouldn't even answer the phone. The worst part was that I had my business at this point, and I was losing my passion for my business. I didn't know if I wanted to sell it or just quit. It got ugly. I was not in the best stage of my life.

As a business owner, I had to invest a lot of time in building my business, and I couldn't be in two places at the same time. I was a single parent and I did not have help, and sometimes I had to close my office for meetings, parent conferences, and doctor and dentist appointments for my children.

My driving force was the love for my children, but most importantly, the love for myself, SELF-LOVE. I have always known that I am worth it! Meaning, I'm entitled to live the type of life I want, even though it didn't seem like it while experiencing the life I was living. I did! I knew I deserved to live a different type of life than the one I was experiencing, and that it was within my power to provide a happier environment for my son and daughter.

Sonia: That must have been tough. What did you do in those moments of "I don't like this feeling"?

Carmen: Yes, it was very difficult and at the same time, sad. I used to work extra hours, go to church, and I would also go shopping. At church, I felt a beautiful peace. At work, I would buy extra time not to go home to an unhealthy environment. And at the mall, I would say I used to do some damage there. Leaving my children's father took a lot of courage and also self-love. I knew that my children and I deserved something better. Luckily, my family has always been there for me and I have the blessing of counting on great friends, and their support as well. A friend invited me to a Landmark personal development course, and that's when I got present with my greatness and my power, and most importantly, I got reconnected with myself. I had been forgetting who I was, what I wanted, my passion for life, and what's important to me. It truly changed my view toward life.

Now my life is filled with self-love, peace, adventure, courage, confidence, fulfillment, curiosity, and joy, and I experience myself being open to change and new opportunities. I discovered for myself that if you don't love yourself first, you cannot love anyone or anything fully. I had heard that before so many times, but hadn't experienced it until then. I got reconnected to my power within me. And I found the courage to take action, go after my goals, and accomplish everything that is important to me.

Sonia: Take us through that process, because it's not an overnight thing.

Carmen: For me, what did it was taking that personal development course. When you do any type of course, it doesn't end there. You have to continue to work on yourself day by day, which is what I have been doing. I have surrounded myself with positive people, especially with people that are a contribution to my community and society. I don't allow myself to think negative thoughts; I focus on the positive. I am present to my dreams and goals and what I want to accomplish for myself and for my family's future. I write my goals down and keep reminding myself of the intention behind every goal I have. I focus on things that make me happy, excited, and empowered. There are different venues to empower yourself, which will support you in achieving your goals: God, positive people, books, seminars, courses, mentors, friends, motivational podcasts, but, the most important individual is yourself—your thoughts, your commitments, and your actions to create the results that you are committed to having.

Sonia, tell me something, who is the most important person in your life?

Sonia: I would say "myself," so that I can impact and serve more people. If I become better, everything around me will become better.

Carmen: Yes! A lot of women are not fully aware of that. Some women don't know who they are, and don't know how to start a path to work on themselves to get to their full potential. They forget to cherish themselves, they don't do what makes them happy, some of them don't even know what makes them happy. They tend to ignore their dreams. What's worse is that a lot of women, including men, don't know where to obtain the help they require to move out of that dark place or where they experience themselves being stuck. The majority of women tend to be there for others and forget about themselves.

Sonia: When we don't take care of ourselves, we lack fulfillment and miss the very thing we were created for—purpose. All that's lost if we don't love ourselves or know ourselves.

Carmen: Exactly! In the majority of cases, when people don't love themselves or don't know their life's purpose, it's because it's hidden from their view. It's a blind spot. We don't see it. Other people see it, but we don't. How can someone have a life of purpose when that person doesn't even know him or herself? The first personal development course I took helped me see things that I was carrying from my past that wouldn't allow me to move forward. Even though I lost my dad when I was little, and my mom wasn't as present for me as I wished she would have been. My mother did get financial and emotional support for my siblings and me from both families, my dad's family as well as my mom's family.

I adored my maternal grandfather. His name was Roberto. He showed me the love that no one had shown me, not even my parents. Not the way he did. His love toward me was unconditional love. The unconditional love that people talk about, I received from him. I remember that when he would come to my mom's house, I would get so happy because I knew I was going to get cherished, tickled, hugged, and loved in a way only my grandfather Roberto knew how. For me, that meant the world; he was the only man to make me feel like a princess after my father's passing. He made me feel loved, important, like the most important girl in the universe. He used to refer to me as a piece of gold for him. He used to call me "Bola de Oro." He was very loving, affectionate, fun, and patient with me. I loved the energy he transmitted with his loving attentions toward me.

Sonia: That's so beautiful. Who have you become because of your experiences with your grandparents?

Carmen: I would say that because of what I saw with my maternal grandparents, I love being involved with a community, contributing to others, and being of service to people. My father's parents also helped my mom financially and helped her raise the five of us. I got my entrepreneur side from my dad's family. Now that I come to think about it, it was the perfect combination. Both families are beautiful, caring, and loving. I'm lucky to be part of them.

Sonia: Now that you're in a place of fulfillment, what is keeping you there on a day-to-day basis? And what is success to you as a whole?

Carmen: To me, the short version is "to be happy and to feel complete." I think that success is living the life that I was designed to live. Fulfilling what I say I want to accomplish. Success is also having a great relationship with my family; great communication, love and support; and having my finances in order. To experience feeling happy, fulfilled, blessed, and free. Success isn't only about me, either. Success is much better living a life with purpose and fulfilling what's important to me so that I can share it with others too.

Sonia: So now that you have found that "sacred place," how does that feel? You know what it's like to be in a place of lack and feeling lonely, but now you're here.

Carmen: I feel at a place of bliss; everything is exactly where it needs to be. I am a blessed woman. I am living the life that I am committed to living. Yes, its work, but every day I feel accomplished and fulfilled. I wake up feeling thankful to God, and just being present. I start my day being grateful and then I design the rest.

Sonia: I love your life because you've learned to embrace it after hard times. You experienced a hardship and you were broken, but you made the decision to take action. So now here you are, living on purpose. What would you say to other women who are entrepreneurs and who are hurting or broken, and not feeling fulfilled even if they're successful?

Carmen: What I would tell them is that they are not alone. There are a lot of people out there, feeling the same way as them. But, in case they are alone, listening to their mind and feeling depressed, confused, afraid, sad, or unhappy, I would tell them to invest in yourself and surround yourself with positive people. It's okay to ask for help or to share with someone that you're going through this and ask if they can help support you.

I want to tell women that there is always a person in your life who is going to invite you somewhere or tell you what you need to hear in that moment, so stay open. Invest in yourself because you are the most important person in your life. And this is important: You attract who you are. If you're always thinking negative thoughts, you're going to attract negative things into your life. But if you stay positive and you have a dream, a vision, and a purpose, then you will surround yourself with positive people who are going to help you fulfill your purpose.

Sonia: Earlier you said that when we focus only on ourselves, we need to get out of your own way and start focusing on our purpose. If you help someone else, it shifts something in your heart when you let go of self-centeredness. We work in the now, but where are we going? What legacy do we want to leave for our children and everyone that we serve?

Carmen: If you had asked me five years ago, "What legacy would you like to leave for your children?" my first thought would have been about money or assets. But now I think the best legacy that I can leave for my children is to expand their love to other people, regardless of what they can get in return, to serve others in need. I want to provide gifts to people of self-love, courage, peace of mind, happiness, joy, and passion.

I'm going to continue to grow financially and leave them that type of legacy as well. But for them to see acts of service and to grow in their spirituality—that's what will make them happy. The legacy that I can leave for my children is for them to become great humanitarians because that's where the real joy is found. When they acquire those qualities, then I will know I have done a fantastic job as a mother.

Sonia: Is there anything else that you want the women to walk away with?

Carmen: Because I am a spiritual person, I would say to seek God and have a great relationship with Him because He's the one who gives you the strength to move forward and to heal any pain. He gives you the courage to get out of a situation or a relationship if you're not happy, and He gives you the courage to become disciplined. Make God your best friend. No one is going to give you the peace or the love or the blessings like He does.

I heard once that is not about how much you have, but who you have in your life. Also, that it's the free things in life that give you the greatest memories. The best thing about that is that you get to create whatever you want of every situation. You get to decide if you want to make it a negative experience or a learning experience to lead to making a better choice for your future. Some people tell you to forgive and forget. We all know that we can't forget, but we can choose to forgive. And when you forgive, you allow room for freedom, and with freedom comes joy, peace, and happiness. We cannot change the things that happened in the past nor can we predict what will happen in the future. We certainly have the power to choose what we make of every situation in the present. We must be present in the NOW. Because it is your life that you are living. When you are focused in the past, you tend to be stressed; if you are thinking about the future, you tend to experience anxiety. Therefore, you should practice every day to be present to what's happening around you and with your loved ones.

I wouldn't change anything from my past because it has made me who I am today. If I could go back, I would make better choices, of course I would. I would have listened to advice from the people who loved me and who I knew wanted the best for me. I would like to share something that I believe will make a difference with young ladies and single women, and it is for them to be fully aware of which qualities they want in the man they would like for their husband. Choosing the right man will make a great difference in their life, marriage, future, and happiness. And the most important choice for you women out there: choose yourself every day of your life. Love yourself first. **Because you are worth it!**

Do everything with love, and surround yourself with positive and like-minded people. Commit to your goals and take the necessary actions and you will achieve great things.

Sonia: Absolutely, God gives us the peace that surpasses all understanding, and that's what guides us into true fulfillment, an abundant life, and joy. It's all there for us, but we have to choose it. Thank you so much for sharing. You are an inspiration as a mother and as an entrepreneur, because everything that you are doing brings meaning and purpose. You pour into yourself and that means that you love yourself enough to continue to pour into other people's lives too.

Carmen: I love the work that you do. I love that you love empowering women. A lot of women don't know who they are, and they don't know their worth. I appreciate what you do for women; you are inspiring and a contribution in this world. Love you.

Sonia: Thank you. My service to women grew because I lost myself and I needed to find my own purpose. Like you, now I know where I'm going, and I want to share it with as many women as possible.

Carmen: Thank you, Sonia. My wish is for everyone to experience true bliss in the world, because they are worth it! I think everyone should have everything they want for themselves and their lives. I would like to add that even though I am not married yet, I do, however, have a beautiful, supportive, loving, and amazing family.

ABOUT CARMEN GOMEZ

I am currently living and creating a life I love spending time with beautiful, loving people, such as my family, friends, customers and people that I surround myself with. If I ever feel weak, I get my strength and motivation when I think of Michelle and Marcos my wonderful daughter and son. I have always been a go getter, driven and committed in my moments in which I doubted myself they were the engine for me to keep moving forward. I am an entrepreneur with 20 years of experience in the insurance industry. I have owned my insurance agency for 12 years, and my mission is to help our insureds Save Now for a better tomorrow. I help our community with integrity, honesty and professionalism.

I also contribute with my precious time at personal development courses where I have learned and grown a lot. I am currently getting certified to become a life coach and possibly a business coach, so that I can share my knowledge and help individuals achieve their personal and business goals.

Another important chapter in my life that I would like to complete, is to get married. I believe in marriage and that's one unfulfilled goal for me to complete.

"For you reading this book and chapter no matter where you are in life or who you are with, remember that you are important, valuable, deserving, powerful person and definitely worth it."

Sonia Hassey

Contact Information
Super Savings Insurance Services Inc (Lic# 0H64718)
678 Cottonwood St
Woodland CA 95695
Te: (530) 662-2520
carmen@supersavingsins.com
www.supersavingsins.com

CHAPTER 17

Because of My Sister Gina

Isabel Carrasco

Sonia: I am here with Isabel Carrasco and her story of courage and success on her incredible journey. Isabel, let's start from the beginning. Tell us where you're from and just begin your story from there.

Isabel: I was born in Mexico but my parents immigrated to the United States when I was about a year old. My parents had five daughters of which I am the second eldest. Although they come from a humble background, they nevertheless accomplished a lot with what they had. When we first arrived in the United States, we lived in a one-bedroom house. At the time, seven people living in a small single-family house was very crowded, but what I remember most about those days wasn't the tight accommodations but how close we were as a family. My parents, despite their humble background, wanted the very best for us, and with their love and unconditional support, they raised five successful daughters. They taught us that family was more important than material possessions. I know that our finances were limited when I was growing up, but we never felt the lack because we had each other.

Sonia: And that set a foundation for you.

Isabel: Yes. My parents taught us that the love of family is very important, but they also taught us that in order to achieve one's goals it also takes hard work and discipline. As we were growing up, we were taught the importance of hard work. As far back as I remember, my sisters and I helped our parents financially by working in various jobs during our free time. Unlike today, things were very different and it wasn't uncommon for children to work to help with the household finances. This is something I appreciate more now than when I was growing up because it taught me to value what I have—when you have to earn every single dime to afford that extra something special, you appreciate it more because all the hard work that went into it. Nothing was given to us; we had to work for it. It's important for people to understand this point.

Sonia: Where did your family work?

Isabel: My parents were itinerant seasonal farm workers cultivating fields and harvesting fruit in orchards. This is very hard work. It's physically demanding under very adverse environmental conditions. Working as a farm laborer requires eight to twelve hours under a hot sun, sometimes carrying up to twenty pounds of fruit or being bent over with a short hoe in hand cultivating hard soil. Unless one has worked in the fields or in an orchard, as I have, it is very difficult for people to understand how physically exhausting and demanding it is in these conditions. You have to remember that farm work is seasonal and in order for a family of seven to survive financially from year to year, at that time, required that everyone in the family work. It never occurred to me or my sisters to question how we were brought up because we knew our parents loved us and wanted the best for us and so, as a family, we knew we had to work.

Sonia: So you worked with your parents?

Isabel: Yes. Throughout our childhood but especially as teenagers, my sisters and I helped out by working alongside them during our afternoons, weekends, holidays, and definitely summers. You have to remember that to feed, clothe, and house a family of seven on a minimum wage is not easy. Both my parents worked very hard and, of course, we did too. However, it wasn't just about working and making ends meet; they also taught us to enjoy ourselves and appreciate the finer things in life. We all worked hard so we could dress in nice clothes, afford vacations to places like Disneyland and Lake Tahoe, long vacations to Mexico, and eventually a nice larger home. I can never repay my parents for what they did, not only for the material things or places we visited, but also those family values that are very important to be a successful and happy adult. But there is another individual that made me the women I am today—my oldest sister Gina. She was everything to me. Her influence continues to shape the person I am and affects the decisions I make to this day. She was beautiful not only physically but spiritually. She had a great and loving heart. I always felt protected by her and felt that no harm could ever touch me and no one could ever bully me. She encouraged me to reach my full potential through study and excelling in my field. She strongly believed that anyone could transcend their humble origins through school and hard work.

Sonia: She almost seems like a second mom.

Isabel: Yes. She was a second mom to me, she was my hero, my mentor, my everything. She took care of all of us, including my parents. She was an outgoing and loving person who made people feel special in an effortless way. It never seemed forced or fake because it came naturally to her and she wanted the best for everyone she cared for, especially her family.

When I was in first grade, I didn't know how to speak English because I had not gone to kindergarten. I was very shy and introverted. I was not like my sister who was outgoing and outspoken. I remember one day at school, I went to the restroom and an older girl started bullying me. I remember being confused and wondering what I had done to this girl because I didn't understand what she was saying to me as she was speaking in English and I only spoke Spanish.

I didn't say anything when she pushed me against the wall. I remember being scared and not knowing what to do. During recess, I saw my sister and told her what had happened. Without missing a beat, my guardian angel, Gina, went up to the girl and confronted her and made it clear to this bully that she was never to touch or frighten me again. After that incident, the bully never bothered me again. How can you not love someone that is looking out for you and protecting you?

Sonia: Wow! How did that make you feel to know your sister had your back?

Isabel: It made me feel very special and this was one incident of many and set the pattern that my sister was to follow for the rest of her life. My trust in Gina was never misplaced because without any doubt I knew she had my back but, what sticks most in my mind is how brave she was.

Sonia: Tell us about your family life in the home.

Isabel: Our parents loved us unconditionally. In many ways, they were very strict and very traditional and perhaps I didn't like this when I was growing up, but as I grew older, I learned that it was for our own good. I know that I wouldn't be the person I am today without this upbringing. In our home, we never lacked for love and we always felt secure and protected. This is the type of gift that keeps on giving and I will always be grateful to my parents for this blessing; moreover, words cannot describe how lucky I was to have had an additional great role model, Gina. Sadly, she left us much too soon. When I think about her and all the things she gave me, I have to wonder what she could have accomplished for herself had circumstances been different. For one thing, after she graduated from high school, she was unable to attend college for various unavoidable reasons. Without a doubt she could have been a successful lawyer or politician because she was incredibly smart, had boundless energy, and had a very caring nature. People naturally were drawn to her. Perhaps because of this, she always encouraged me to further my education. After graduating from high school, I was not considering attending college, but she convinced me that a college degree would give me a higher standard of living and will open career paths for me. Even back then, Gina was acting as my mentor because she always had my best interest at heart.

To continue, I decided to go to college for fashion design because that's what I liked to do at the time. On many occasions, I would call my sister crying and say, "Gina, this is too much. I can't do this anymore, I'm just giving up." She would say, "No, you are not a quitter. You're going to continue. You can do this." I'm so glad I followed her advice and encouragement. She would always call me and ask how I was doing, and let me know that she was there to help. I had not been a straight-A student in high school, but I was in college. I focused so hard on my education and as a result of all my work, I won two fashion shows for the best designer in my class. Those were some of the best feelings I have ever experienced. I remember all the attendees in the fashion show were standing up and applauding me. I felt I was on top of the world. I love fashion design and everything about it and when you love what you do, you can't help but succeed.

Sonia: That is incredible. You said, "I'm going to do this. I'm going to believe in myself." But prior to that time, did you have issues with insecurity?

Isabel: Yes. Why? I think because my mom would put Gina on a pedestal, and I felt like I wanted to prove to my mother that I could do just as well as my sister. As a young girl, I was very timid and shy because it was my nature. My sister, on the other hand, was outgoing and sociable. I wrongly believed that I could never be like her. I couldn't compare myself to her, but I wanted to have the confidence that came so easily to her; and, above all, I wanted to make my mom proud. Eventually, I realized that Gina believed in me and that I had a lot to give; consequently, I also began to believe in myself.

Sonia: Okay, back to the fashion design award. What did that do for your self-image?

Isabel: My confidence increased exponentially. It was incredible. I felt like I could do anything I wanted. The award proved to myself that I could be successful in my chosen field and it also proved to others, especially my mother, that I had unique gifts and talents that were equally important. What I discovered was a revelation and I also learned my mother was proud of me. It was a feeling of success. I did it with a lot of hard work and sleepless nights, but I was able to succeed in something I believed in.

Sonia: What was your next step after graduating?

Isabel: After graduating from fashion design, I decided not to pursue a career in that field, and instead I applied for and was hired to a very good government job, an excellent career choice for me at the time. I remember that around three hundred people applied for the one position that I eventually was offered. I had to go through several obstacles and meet all these stringent requirements to land the position. I put myself in the mindset of, "Yes, I can do this." I believe that people can do anything if they set their mind to succeed. In order to move forward, individuals need faith in themselves and a belief in success. I firmly believe that a person needs to fix the desired goal in their mind and not give up until they achieve it.

Sonia: That's so true. We have to believe in ourselves. Because if we can't believe in ourselves, how do we expect anybody else to believe in us? At that point, you were hired for that job, and you were feeling great, right?

Isabel: Yes I was. I beat out many people to get that job. This was a great accomplishment. I liked working for the government, but what I didn't like was working behind a desk. I realized that I had become a people person and that I was no longer that shy and timid girl—success will do that for you. Furthermore, I discovered I liked helping people and had a natural ability for it. I loved that the job came with a good retirement plan, good benefits, and an excellent salary. The thing I didn't like about it was the commute—an hour and a half of pure traffic hell first to get to my job and then to get back to my home. Three hours out of my day was spent going and coming from work; time that I could have spent with my family. I stayed with this job for over twenty years because it was safe and I wasn't ready to make a change.

One day, someone introduced me to an opportunity in the life insurance industry. At first, I was skeptical but then I realized that it was not the typical type of life insurance most of us are used to. This new modern type of life insurance is the kind of life insurance that YOU DON'T HAVE TO DIE TO USE, because it offers a critical, chronic, and terminal rider, at no additional cost! These rider benefits not only change lives, but save lives, and it was incredible. This type of insurance helps people during one's lifetime: it has living benefits and replaces old traditional life insurance policies that only pay out after you die and only to your beneficiaries. This was a revelation to me, and I thought, "Wow, you know what? I can work in this industry." I felt intrigued.

Sonia: What inspired you to make a career change and get into life insurance?

Isabel: Well, let me go back a little. When I was working for the government, I received the devastating news that my sister Gina, my hero, my mentor, my everything, was diagnosed with stage III breast cancer. She would have been the ideal candidate for the type of life insurance that I work with, but unfortunately, I was not aware of these policies. It was the worst news I have ever received. I didn't want to accept it. I was in denial. But unfortunately, it was true. My beautiful and vibrant sister went through horribly debilitating and physically damaging radiation and chemotherapy. It was a devastating blow to the whole family.

Her various therapies made her lose her hair, but she never wanted us to see her bald. She always wore wigs or scarves. She had a lot of pride. She never wanted to show us that she was suffering or in pain. She would say, "Oh, I'm fine, I'm fine." But we knew she wasn't fine. She battled cancer for five years and was in remission for those five years. Unexpectedly and devastatingly she lost her battle against the disease on August 29 of 2003. It was the worst day of my life when she died. I felt like part of me died with her. I thought, "Nobody can fill her shoes and no one has."

I am who I am because of my sister. If she wouldn't have encouraged me to continue my education, I probably would have just been living a mediocre life. But she pushed me to believe in myself.

Now I'm living the life she wanted me to live and I feel grateful and fortunate for all the years she was a part of my life. Not one day goes by that I don't think about her and all the things I miss such as her wonderful smile, her beautiful heart, and her joy of life.

Sonia: What a treasure. What happened next in your family?

Isabel: Soon after my sister died, her eldest son had a terrible accident when he fell from a moving quad and broke his neck. He was paralyzed from the neck down on Thanksgiving 2011. He was only twenty-five—it was so devastating. He was so young and had his whole life ahead of him. He was an incredible athlete, smart like his mother, the life of the party, contagious laughter, and had his mother's smile. He died a year and a half after his accident. Again, a perfect candidate for the policies we offer. To lose two close family members under such conditions in such a short time was very difficult for all of us.

These two incidents impelled me to change careers. I liked helping people and so when I was recruited on behalf of Freedom Equity Group, I discovered I could help people going through similar tragic events. I found my true calling. Life insurance with living benefits means one has the ability to accelerate their death benefits while still alive when you need it most. It is so rewarding to help families keep from losing everything when one of their members is diagnosed with a terminal illness like cancer, stroke, heart attack, or an incapacitating injury. In these cases, seventy percent of people don't die, but they also can't work, resulting in devastating financial reversals. The bad news is that over fifty percent of the people who live will go bankrupt in the process.

I'm here to protect these types of families. A lot of people don't know that you can build wealth through life insurance and obtain living benefits with a tax-free retirement plan. When I learned about these things, I wanted to participate full time. I could not continue working in my government job because it would be a conflict of interest. I worked in Human Resources and we offered retirement plans and traditional life insurance. Because of what happened to my sister and my nephew, I felt like I needed to do something different and follow my passion and help people. On the plus side, I didn't have to commute anymore.

It was the best decision I've ever made. I was able to build a comfortable income as it's an incredible business opportunity. I am blessed to have found something like this and know that I'm also helping many families change their lives. During the course of my duties, I help people protect their most important asset—their income. People think their home is their most important asset, but we're protecting people's ability to earn an income. If they can't earn an income, how are they going to pay their bills? It's heartbreaking to see GoFundMe accounts because people don't have the resources to bury a loved one, pay for medical bills, or take them to the doctor. If they had a plan like this, they would have the funds when they need it the most.

I love what I do and I'm passionate about it. I can't tell you how incredible this opportunity has been for me.

Sonia: You feel so good because you give people hope and help them financially in a difficult situation.

Isabel: Exactly. As an example, a client bought a term policy for half a million dollars and had only paid into it for a couple of years before she was diagnosed with breast cancer. She was able to take out $400,000 of that life insurance, almost ninety percent of it. She survived, and she's not worrying about money right now. She was able to collect the money and pay off her mortgage. It's a win-win for everyone. Imagine delivering a check to a person who would be financially devastated if they wouldn't have had it. They can do whatever they want with the money. They don't even have to use it for their treatment; they can pay off their mortgage or go on vacation. It's their money. I'm passionate in what I do and want to share it with others. I'm building a team right now and I'm excited to offer a great opportunity for people to help others and earned an incredible income at the same time.

Sonia: Tell us more about how you overcame your insecurities and realized you could accomplish anything. What made you decide that you were going to go after this and succeed?

Isabel: Of course, I already mentioned my family's example of hard work, and my sister's influence with her confidence in me. I realized that I had to work hard to get what I wanted. I had to push myself and not be afraid of taking risks. I remember when my husband and I started investing in real estate. We started investing in homes, then we decided to invest in an apartment building. People began to talk us out of it stating that we didn't know what we're getting into and that it was too difficult and that we were in over our heads.

I looked at these naysayers who were telling me all these things, and I thought, "Is this coming from individuals who are successful and doing something positive for themselves?" We had to consider the source. I said, "We're going to go for it." And it has been an incredible return on our investment. Our apartment building has flourished incredibly. If we hadn't taken the risk, we never would have known that it would work. Real estate is one of the best investments out there if you can do it. Having experienced this and helped ourselves by taking these risks, we learned valuable lessons. Similarly, I help people through Freedom Equity Group. I learned not to listen to naysayers, and to surround myself with positive individuals.

As a mentor, I tell other women that they have to get out of their comfort zones and take risks. They have to get out there and just do it and not look back and always move forward. One will find challenges and barriers along the way, but they can be overcome with the proper mindset. Never quit. To be successful, one must overcome one's fears and take risks. Another piece of advice is to be around positive people who have the same mindset as you.

I encourage others to emulate people who are doing big things, talk to them and listen to them because they know what they are talking about and have gone through similar experiences.

Sonia: I love everything you just said. Not taking a risk is the greatest risk! You have to work hard now so you can enjoy a fulfilled life later. Also, we must be keen to that inner voice that says, "What are you doing?" and "Don't do it." We must switch it to a positive affirmation.

Isabel: It's also very important to build relationships with people. It's about integrity and trust.

Sonia: I see your love for people and your love for helping people. And people helped you get where you are, because no one succeeds alone.

Isabel: Of course, my sister helped me the most, but there have been others who believed in me and supported me. I thank God every day for them, and I am grateful for every opportunity. Since I was a little girl, nothing has ever been given to me for free, I learned about hard work and having gratitude for everything. I still appreciate everything now.

I tell my sons they have to work hard to get ahead. I don't make things easy for them, I want them to earn their success. I want them to have the same values that I have, so that they can teach their children how to work to succeed. It's a fact that we appreciate and value more of those things we work hard for.

Sonia: We're in the "now" generation; we want everything right now. But character doesn't work that way. Having a strong work ethic, and the sweat and tears that go along with it, builds character.

Isabel: Yes, and some people will say, "Oh, you're so lucky." No, I'm not lucky, I worked hard for what I have! I'm still the one who gets up in the middle of the night when something goes wrong in the apartment building. I have sleepless nights. I go through challenges. But I have to tell myself, "I'm going to continue on. I'm going to focus on what I need to do to overcome these challenges." Every single day is a new beginning and it starts with me.

I get up every day and do my exercises. I might listen to motivational speakers. We all need to have faith and belief in ourselves to succeed. I made a decision that I didn't want to live a mediocre life. I know I have to work hard now so I can enjoy my later years, and also provide for my family.

Sonia: That's beautiful. What would you say to women who want it so badly, but they're not quite at that level of success?

Isabel: You must focus and believe in yourself to succeed. Don't be afraid of rejection or failure. It's so important for people to get out of their comfort zones and take risks. Rejection is part of being successful. When you have faith in yourself and continue going forward, even through difficult points in your life. Later on, you can look back and think, "I overcame all that."

Sonia: It all goes back to the power of believing in yourself. Where do you see yourself five years from now?

Isabel: I see myself traveling! I will have created my wealth through real estate, My Freedom Equity Group business, and my pension from my previous job. I see myself enjoying life. We don't know how much longer we'll be here, so we have to enjoy ourselves and live a life of abundance today. It's very important to understand how to be present with a future focus. One has to have the mindset that life is good right now. It makes me happy to know that I've been able to change people's lives by protecting them from losing everything. The true reward is being able to touch the lives of others in a positive way.

Many people helped me in my early years, and now it's my turn to give back. It makes me appreciate life so much more because it's not about me; it's about the other person. I encourage others to think,

"How many people can I help? How many people can I build up today?"

Sonia: That's beautiful. That's fulfillment. You built your character and you honored into your meaning and purpose, and now you share this fulfillment with others.

Isabel: I feel very blessed I have worked hard all my life, but I feel that a lot has been given to me too. I want to thank God first for all the gifts he's given me including my wonderful sons and husband that give me so much joy. In addition, I want to thank my extended family and Freedom Equity Group (FEG) including the owners, leaders, and team for their support through my journey of discovery.

I would like to dedicate this chapter in loving memory of my sister Gina Martin and my nephew Leo Martin Jr.

To learn more about my business please visit: www.Isabel.freedomequitygroup.com

ABOUT ISABEL CARRASCO

Isabel Carrasco, NVP
Life Insurance Agent

Life insurance with living benefits–you don't have to die to use.
Tax-free retirement plans–retire with dignity.
A commitment to serve with integrity.

www.isabel.freedomequitygroup.com
email: Isabel.feg5008@gmail.com
Contact: 925-848-7107

CHAPTER 18

Rising Beyond My Limits

Columba Perez

Sonia: Hello, I am here with Columba Perez, and she has one of the most powerful testimonies I've ever heard. Columba, go ahead and share your story from the beginning.

Columba: I was born in Guadalajara, Mexico, and I have four sisters and two brothers. My dad came to the United States when he was thirty-five years old, but my mom stayed in Mexico to raise all of us kids. She's a strong woman, and that's why I'm the woman that I am. I know that she was always struggling to give us a good education. She's a positive person, she works hard, and she believes in God. She was always thinking about the family first, and then her kids, and then herself.

When I was ten years old, my mom decided to move to the United States with me, so we could be with my dad. My brothers were already here, but my four sisters stayed in Mexico because they were all married. It was hard. It was a big change for us.

We moved to Pittsburgh. When we got here, the only language that I knew was Spanish. I couldn't speak English at all, and it was a challenge in school, but I learned English so I could have a good life and provide a better life to help my mom and dad. I always worked hard and studied hard.

After I graduated from high school, I got a scholarship because of my good grades. I started going to college to study computer graphics, and I had a job during that time, too.

Sonia: You were determined! It sounds like life was going well for you. Then what happened?

Columba: When I was eighteen years old, I was driving to my job, and somebody hit the back of my car. I was on the freeway, and we were going fast, maybe seventy miles an hour, and I felt a car hit me. That car pushed me off the freeway and down a mountain. When my car was going down, I flew out of the window and landed a few feet away from my car.

I don't remember too much, but I do remember a guy saying, "Give me your mom's number." I gave him my mom's number. It was hard for the ambulance to get to me because more and more cars got hit and it was a big accident. I wasn't bleeding, so all the injuries were internal. A helicopter took me to the hospital.

At the hospital, I was told that my spinal bones were broken and that I wasn't going to be able to walk again. They said, "You need to have surgery right away, and we'll see what's going to happen." And I said, "Okay, do whatever you need to do, but I have to go back to school because I have this project that I have to turn in." And they said, "Do you know what's going on?"

I had surgery on my back for eight hours, and I was like a baby. For ten days I couldn't move. So right now, I have metal and screws in my back.

Sonia: What went through your mind, what were you feeling, what were you thinking? Because your whole life was before you and you had no idea where you were going to be even a month from then.

Columba: Well, I was on the bed lying down, and the bed was turning sideways. And at one point it was like an angel came into my room. This was unusual because nobody could come into the room except the nurse or my mom. And this lady came in and she held my hand and she said, "Don't worry, you're going to be fine. Everything's going to be fine."

At that moment, I was like, "Oh my God." I felt this energy, this new me. I thought, "Everything is going to be fine, this is just something that I'm going to deal with, and it's going to be nothing for me."

Sonia: Wow, you're a miracle. You could have been paralyzed. At that moment you believed it was an angel, and you believed that everything would be fine? Was it like an embodiment?

Columba: It was like an energy; like something that hit, and I realized that I will be fine, I will be okay. From that moment, I think I became a new woman. I was born again.

After the surgery, it took me three months to recover. I started to learn to walk with a walker about a month after the surgery. I couldn't sit down for more than a minute. I was in pain, but I was ready to move on. I said, "Mom, I want to go back to college. I want to finish."

Sonia: What made you feel that you were born again?

Columba: Because God gave me a second chance. I always think that things happen for a reason. And I don't see it as a negative thing. After the accident, I thought, "Okay, let's keep going. You're going to move eighty-eight degrees." I became more of a positive person and I was always smiling.

Also, from that moment on, I had the feeling of wanting to help people. I wanted to help my community. I wanted to help Latino families.

Sonia: Did you feel like this second chance brought more purpose to your life, like you are here for a reason?

Columba: Yes. I went back to college. My best friend would pick me up from my house with my walker and my plastic vest because of my surgery. It was just incredible, yet so hard; things happen for a reason and God knows why. I think the accident made me the woman that I am today. I got married that same year, and then two years later I had my first child.

Sonia: It's like your life began during that time.

Columba: Yes! Having a baby was the happiest thing that had happened in my life. After that, I went into real estate and I enjoyed helping people. I loved giving them the key to their first homes. As soon as I would tell them that they're approved to get the house, I could see their faces. That's the thing that keeps me going—seeing their happy faces and helping them.

Soon after, I had my second child and then we moved to Texas because my husband wanted to open an ice cream business. For five years, he had been telling me, "Why don't we move, why don't we try something else?" On day one of the business, a lot of people came. It was called Ando-Kito-Kalitos. It was a blessing because so many people were there. God has blessed us in so many ways. We worked from seven a.m. to seven p.m. every day, and I think we did a good job on everything with the business.

We were there for two years, but I felt like, "You only live once, so you have to feel happy about what you do and where you live." And I wasn't happy because I didn't have any family over there, and neither did my husband. I said, "Why don't we go to California?" And he said, "No, we're doing good." But I wasn't really happy. I knew we were doing good, but it wasn't all about the money.

Sonia: You were missing your family?

Columba: Yes, I was missing the family, and I was missing my job in real estate. We came back and started all over again. I started doing real estate again and enjoying helping Latino families. A month later, I got pregnant, and the next year I got pregnant again, so now I have four kids. I was taking care of my kids, enjoying California, and enjoying my family. My husband started doing construction again.

And two months ago, I started doing life insurance again too. It was important to me to not only help people get their properties, but to get them something in retirement. It was more like a complete transaction. I love helping the Latino market with these services. They need to know more about this. Many don't have sufficient savings, so they have to work. I help them to start saving earlier so they don't have to worry about the money for travel or things like that. I'm excited about it. So that's another blessing in my life that I can do both insurance and real estate.

Sonia: You have perseverance because you came from Mexico, and you came here knowing zero English, but you were determined to go back to school, and you did well there. And then you had a traumatic experience in your life; you almost died. You learned to walk again, and now you're determined to help people through your work. Where does that drive come from?

Columba: Maybe it is because my mom was always struggling, working hard, getting up at four a.m., going to bed at 1, 2, 3 o'clock—all for us. That drives me to keep on going, keep on going, until I reach my goals. I believe in God and I know that if I have God with me, everything is going to be better. I have this destiny, this big "why," and that's my kids. I do this for my kids. And if they see that their mom works for them, then they're going to be the same way when they have families.

Sonia: I'm seeing the legacy of your mom, faith, hard work, and family. How do those impact why you do what you do?

Columba: My path and my accident have led me to a career that makes a big difference for people. People tell me stories about their lives and the unexpected things that happen. I help them to be prepared when bad things happen. I want to inspire people to believe in God, believe in themselves. And when things happen, to keep God beside them, because great things are going to happen in their lives.

Life is hard and sometimes it will knock us down hard, but only by a measure of faith can we take that grip and say, "Okay, I'm not alone in this, I'm not alone in this world." Everyone should embrace this—everyone.

Sonia: I love your story. It is powerful. Thank you, because we all need a greater measure of faith, we all need to know our destinies and our responsibilities to walk in our destinies because we were made for them. Thank you so much; this was incredible.

ABOUT COLUMBA PEREZ

Columba Perez, a strong, caring and passionate Independent Business Contractor who specializes in helping families plan and protect their financial future. She uses several products as a foundation then uses other planning techniques to better protect her clients' financial plan and future. Her efforts and meticulous planning have helped many families start on their road to Financial Freedom.

Previously Columba, as a professional Real Estate Agent for 14 years, has helped many families find their dream homes. She has always loved helping families find a wonderful place they could call home, making sure they understood the whole process from start to finish.

She always has put her clients' interests first and has always continued her education to better serve her clients. She has been married to her husband Jorge Perez for 19 years and has four wonderful children, Aketzali, Yetlanezi, Jorge and Pablo, and her family resides in the San Francisco Bay Area.

To contact Columba Perez
Phone: (925)628-3390
Columbapereznunez@gmail.com

CHAPTER 19

Always Have a Plan B

Susana Alcala Wood

Sonia: I am here with Susana Alcala Wood, and she is going to share her story of courage, strength, and success with us. Susana, why don't you start from the beginning and tell us about your life.

Susana: Thank you so much, Sonia. I don't get a chance to talk much about my childhood, so I appreciate the opportunity. Both of my parents are gone now, and any time I can talk about them, it's a blessing.

I was born and raised in East Los Angeles, California, right in the heart of the ghetto, although of course, I didn't know that as a kid. I didn't know that we were being raised in a really impoverished community, because for me, it was just home. My grandmother and great-grandmother lived in a two-bedroom house, and my mom and my sisters and I lived in a little one-bedroom house behind them. I am the middle child of three girls. My two sisters and I shared the bedroom, and my mom slept on the sofa in the living room. It wasn't until much later, as an adult, that I realized we could actually see the buildings of downtown L.A. from our neighborhood. That's how close we were to the city.

My father was born in Mexico, and he met my mother here in California. My mom and dad separated when we were little. My last memory of them being together was when I was six or seven before they got divorced, and we lived with my mom. For that reason, most of my childhood memories were about my mom, my sisters, my grandmother, my great-grandmother, and my aunt. I'll talk more about my dad later. For the most part, pretty much all I grew up around was a strong female household. If anything happened in the house, a woman did it. My mom worked as a Spanish-language interpreter in the courts, so she was gone a lot, and my sisters and I took care of ourselves after school. We were what they called "latchkey kids." But of course, my grandmother and great-grandmother were nearby. My mom worked hard, so we were always taking care of her however we could, and taking care of the house. My older sister was like a second mom to us, and pretty bossy.

Now as I look back, I think that the best part of growing up that way is that we went without things, but we didn't realize it. For example, half the time we didn't have a car, or the car we had didn't work. Luckily, our schools were fairly close so we could walk or take the bus. But it got hard for my mom because she had to get to work.

Many times we didn't have something as basic as electricity. My mom had to make a lot of choices as to what got paid, and sometimes it was the phone, sometimes it was the lights. Food was whatever cheap food she could find to feed us. My grandmother and great-grandmother helped out whenever they could. We didn't do things like take vacations. We were always mindful about money, but I didn't know any different. I just thought that's how everyone lived. I grew up with so much love around me that I just didn't realize how little we had.

Sonia: How did that lack of money affect you?

Susana: It has had a lasting impact on me from the standpoint that I'm grateful for everything that I have in my life. Nothing that I have was given to me. Everything I have, I worked for. Everything. It always felt like we were making the best of everything, so I absolutely grew up as a glass-half-full kind of person because of that. No matter how bad it got, it was an adventure. For example, when the lights were turned off because we couldn't pay the bill, what did that mean? We went camping in the house. We had a lantern, blankets on the ground, and a picnic. And I also grew up knowing that I wanted more and that the only way to get more was through education. When my parents split up, my sisters were about nine and five, and I was about seven. My mom raised us to rely on ourselves over relying on a man, and told us that the only way to do that was to get an education, because nobody could take that away from us. Like my dad, my mom tried to go to college and even tried to go to law school at night. I have vivid memories of her taking us to the park so that we could play while she studied. But with three young girls and working full time, she just wasn't able to continue. But she instilled in us the knowledge that we could do anything we wanted because we're women. I'm glad that I listened.

Sonia: Did your mom create this for you guys so you wouldn't feel the burden of the lack?

Susana: Yes and no. Yes, she was definitely a positive, optimistic person, but there were many times that we were trying to tell her "It's okay, Mom. It's okay, we can do this, this is fun." Because we knew that she felt bad and felt like she was failing us. So we were cheering her up many times, I know that for a fact. She would apologize, or feel bad that there was something she couldn't get us. I can't even tell you how many times I told her, "It's okay, Mom, I don't need that," or "I don't really want to go," or "It's okay, we'll find another way to do something." After a while, it became like the four of us taking care of each other and trying to just get through. I had the role of being positive, reasonable, and easygoing, because I was the middle child. My little sister was young and funny and loving (but kind of bratty!), and my older sister was more serious, with responsibility for helping my mom take care of us. We all played our roles to take care of each other and do what we needed to do, while saying, "It's gonna be okay."

But a big part is that my mom loved to have fun and enjoy herself. She could make a party out of anything, and everybody gravitated to her. It was a part of her personality, and I know I got a big chunk of that from her. My mom wanting to create that kind of a positive environment definitely is something that affected us. It is certainly a part of me. We learned, "How can we turn this into a positive? How can we make this fun?" Oh my gosh, there were times when there was absolutely no money in the house, so then we invented the game called "penny hunt," and we literally looked everywhere for change. It was a big game. We ran all over the place looking in the sofa cushions, pockets, closets, out in the car, everywhere. And then everybody would come back together and see how much we had found. It was really fun! But that money we found was to buy gas so she could get to work, or to pay something else that was due, but mostly it was for gas until she got paid again. But here we were playing this game that was fun, and we didn't even realize how much we were on the edge.

Sonia: Something so difficult and probably painful for your mom, yet you made it into a game. It's like your psychology shifted to the positive. Did you feel that shift as a child?

Susana: No, I don't really think I was conscious of it—it was just what we did to get by. Part of the reason why we didn't have a whole lot of money is that my mom made a choice to send us to Catholic school. She was raised in a Catholic school, so it was something she wanted to do for her kids even though everybody told her it was a waste of money because she was raising girls and we were just going to get married anyway. Because we lived in such a bad area of East Los Angeles where the schools were not good, she made the choice to send us to the local Catholic school. I'm not saying that we wouldn't have gotten a good education in the public schools, but that was her choice. That's why sometimes she worked at a second job at night. She had all sorts of odd jobs. At one point, she sold knives, encyclopedias, and she worked at a donut shop. We also had a paper route. Well, it was actually my little sister's, but we all worked it. I started babysitting when I was twelve to earn money, and got my first job at fifteen. All my money went to the family.

When I was in grammar school, I didn't really notice the difference in economic levels because everybody was from the same neighborhood. It wasn't until I got to high school that I noticed what we didn't have. I could see a lot of things that we were doing without, that I hadn't realized before. But I still said, "It's okay, Mom, I don't need to do that, buy that, go there." But there were times I needed money to pay for something related to school—like a field trip or a class event, and I had so much anguish over having to ask my mom for it because I knew she didn't have it. That's when I really became aware of the worry about money.

Sonia: Wow. Did you feel like it would burden her more when you had to ask?

Susana: Absolutely. And all this time, I need to mention my dad, because although we weren't living with him, he loved us, of course, and helped however he could. He did love us. But if we called my dad and asked him for financial help, he would come up with something. He was working a bunch of odd jobs and I recall him doing work as an electronic technician. He didn't have a lot of money, but the worst times were when we were really desperate and then my mom would have one of us call him and ask him for money. And to this day, Sonia, it is really hard for me to ask anybody for money. I just remember that I didn't want to do it. "Hi Papi, how are you doing? Papi, you think you can send some money because we need to pay this or pay that," and then hearing him on the other end trying to be our dad, not wanting to disappoint, but knowing that he didn't have the money. That was tough.

Sonia: What was his response?

Susana: He always came up with something, like, "On Friday, I could have this much." I remember we all took turns making that phone call and I remember when it was my turn, I'm like "Okay Papi." And then there were a couple of times I remember when my mom said, "Well, that's not what we needed," in other words, we needed more money than he could come up with and I was a little girl and so I didn't know what to say. And then he would give us what he could, and we'd just keep going.

Sonia: He didn't ignore the situation, he did what he could. I can see the weight of the asking, because you knew you were asking for a lot, no matter how much you were asking for.

Susana: Right, and since we didn't see him too much, it was tough to just call him and ask him for money. After a few years, my mom would tell us that we needed to call our dad more and spend more time with him, so we didn't just feel like we called him for money. And so little by little, we started to call him to spend time with him. We'd spend the weekend in his apartment, and that was good. To know him as somebody other than a person we called for money. In my teenage years and beyond, that's when that relationship with my dad started to become what it needed to be, which was more father-daughter. That alleviated a lot of distress because then I knew I could call him about visiting or invite him to something, and every time I talked to him it wasn't just because I needed to ask him for money.

I'm very grateful that over the years my mom and dad were able to get along. It certainly didn't start out that way, but over the years, my parents' relationship got stronger, and that was a blessing. As we grew older, and my older sister got married and had babies, everybody was able to be together for holidays, birthdays, and all of that. So it ended well, with everyone focused on having a good, positive family.

Sonia: It seems like everything came back full circle. It wasn't dysfunction as much as it was just pressure.

Susana: Yes. Like I said—it didn't start out that way. When I was ten or eleven, my mom got married again. She got married very fast to a man who wasn't a good man at all. And I think she rushed into it because she was a bit old-fashioned in her thinking then that she should have a man to take care of her. He was not a good man at all. And that marriage only lasted for two years, but he lived with us. Some pretty awful things happened, especially to my older sister, and stuff that I know I've blocked out. But when it was starting to fall apart, I had feelings of guilt that it was our fault. My mom was very emotional and had a lot of anxiety. I see that now, but as a little girl, I didn't know what that was called. So when things got bad for her, she tended to lash out, and so for that reason, we felt a lot of guilt for the marriage breaking up, even though obviously we had nothing to do with it, and she never should have married him in the first place. That was a difficult time. My dad also got married again, and he was preoccupied with her, so it was a period of time when my sisters and I were more on our own, but it was okay.

Sonia: How did it make you feel in that time of transition, and did both parents get remarried around the same time?

Susana: I think my dad married first and then my mom. My mom was beautiful. She was maybe in her late thirties, and she was dating a lot and she worked someplace where she met a lot of people, and so why she settled on this man, I don't know, but she did. He kind of swept her off her feet, as those kinds of men do. And so when he moved in with us in our tiny little house, my mom's bedroom was the living room. Her bed was a sofa bed that she had open, so that's what he moved into with us. My sisters and I were still in our bedroom. We had bunk beds. My younger sister and I slept on the bottom. My older sister slept on top. We were just in this small, one-bedroom, one-bath house, and he moved into that. So it's not like he brought anything to her. She mostly gave him everything that she had, and so I don't know how it happened.

As far as how it affected me, I think for all of us, in addition to feeling like we were partly to blame for the marriage breaking up, we felt guilty for stuff that happened. Self-esteem was a big one. I saw how my mom was so devastated, and I wanted to make her feel better. Like I said before, it was like my job to cheer her up. I wanted to make her feel better but I had absolutely no capacity to do that, but I tried anyway, including by putting up with stuff that we shouldn't have had to put up with. But once he left, it was good, and she found her way back. That convinced me more than anything that you don't need to rely on a man, and a man doesn't define you. You have to be strong anyway.

Sonia: How did things shift after he moved out?

Susana: We felt relief. We had a deep understanding that this was a good thing, even though my mom was so sad. I think she just felt like a failure, you know, marriage number two. But it pulled us back into the four of us again, and we connected and just did things together again. It's not like we went on trips to Hawaii or on a cruise, we just did things together like going to a park, and we did a lot of camping. I still have a lifelong love of camping to this day, and I raised my kids to love camping as well. Then we got bikes and we started to do bike trips, just enjoying being together, so it was a good thing. We never talked too much about him. It was like a bad dream that was over, and then we all kept going and thrived. My mom eventually dated this other man, a very nice man, for a long time. They didn't get married and that was probably good. And then she remarried, and I think she finally found the man who she was happy with. He is such a good man. She died when they were still married.

Sonia: So she married for the third time, and it was the "charm."

Susana: Yes, he was a lot younger than her, he was a "gringo," but he adored her. He treated her like a queen. My dad remarried too. He divorced his second wife and remarried, and they were married for thirty-three years. She's wonderful, and she's still a huge part of my life.

My mom died twenty-three years ago. I was pregnant with my first child when she died. All the weight of being a mom and raising children, and I just wish all the time I could talk with her and ask her questions.

Sonia: She was a form of strength.

Susana: Absolutely. She was full of strength and inspired me with the idea that you just keep going. You don't have an option to stop, so you just keep going. Nothing's impossible if you believe it can happen.

I remember her saying, "You can be anything you want to be, you just have to do it."

And of course, with her, education was the key. My older sister got married already so she didn't go to college, and I did. I didn't have any example to follow, I just grew up knowing that education was a key so there was no option. I didn't know how I was going to go to college, and I certainly didn't know how to pay. I didn't even know how to apply for it. I just knew I was going. It was like a puzzle.

Sonia: I love that, and I want to go into that journey. But first, going back to your mom, what would you say she gave you as a legacy now that you're a mom?

Susana: She gave me the strength to not give up. When I set my sights on something, I don't give up. Even little stuff. People can tell me something's not going to work, and if I believe that it will work, then it motivates me to "double down." Not to prove them wrong, but to prove to myself what can be done. I mean, sometimes it doesn't work out, but even then, I get so much further than if I had given up early. I believe in the power of what you can do, and it's hard for me to be around people who don't think like that. I just don't have any patience for people who aren't at least willing to try. And so that's probably the biggest gift she gave me. I am consistent in every aspect of my life in utilizing that, whether it's with people at work, with my own kids, and at home. I even have a magnet on my refrigerator with my favorite quote by Winston Churchill that says, "Never, ever, ever, ever give up."

Sonia: I love it. That grit is priceless that your mom gave you. How are you now an example of that grit to your family and your co-workers?

Susana: I think my co-workers hear me talking to myself as I talk myself into not giving up on something. Or I encourage them if they believe a certain course of action can work. Sometimes they look at me and they hear me saying, "You know you won't be happy with yourself if you don't at least try." So it's funny now that I think about it, by talking out loud is how it manifests for me. And certainly with raising my kids over the years and all the ups and downs when they were teenagers. I would say, "Okay, you can feel sorry for yourself, but what are you going to do next? You've got to have a plan. If Plan A doesn't work out, what's your Plan B? You've got to pivot. Sometimes you even need a Plan C."

Sonia: How are you using that powerful force in your life now?

Susana: Having to go through all of those struggles as children, and believing it would work out, became a part of me. There may be times of self-pity, and I will admit to that. There may be times when I just want to curl up in a ball on the couch and watch movies. But a part of me will always say that I never, ever give up.

Sonia: It's called being human.

Susana: There have been times when I have to tell myself to not give up and keep figuring out a way this is going to work out, because it's not acceptable to accept something that doesn't make sense or is a bad situation. I do bring the idea of never giving up to every aspect of my life.

Even something as simple as deciding to go to the movies and we don't have much time to get there and someone says, "Oh, forget it. We'll never make it." And I say, "Oh yeah? We can make it. Grab this, and let's run, and we can race in there real quick." And we get in and sit down just as the movie starts. I say, "See? It's all fine." It's hard for me to accept sometimes that it's not fine, or that I tried it and it didn't work. It's also probably a much better idea to leave for the movies earlier! I know my husband would appreciate that.

I love it when I hear my kids say the same thing. When they say, "Well, what about this? Well, that's okay." They've already moved past the disappointment and are figuring out how they can make it work. Yes, sometimes they call crying on the phone, and then we talk about the options, and I love that. I don't think we are ever victims. Struggles just mean we have to figure out another way that we can work this to our advantage, or to something that's supposed to be. There's always a way through. Pivot.

So, as I struggled through childhood and had all of this stuff that happened, I was watching. For me, my mom is a hero. I'm not saying that my dad isn't. My relationship with him evolved later as an adult, but my childhood was all about my mom. I'm watching that and just still feeling all the love and the joy and the wonderment of life, despite everything that was going on underneath.

Sonia: That's amazing. How have your children gravitated to this trait of having grit?

Susana: My kids are awesome. I tell them, "Wow, you guys are so much better than me." My husband Joseph and I are proud parents of two children. The oldest is twenty-three and is in Oregon and works as a caseworker for troubled youth, and finding a lot of passion and fulfillment in that. My youngest is a senior at Chico State, and as an artist, she wants to go into art education. What they both have in common is that they are activists and they want to change the world. They're very aware of social issues, political issues. They're not afraid to speak up. They are not afraid to even try to educate their friends. If there are people around them who say certain things that are homophobic or misogynistic, they are courageous, and they speak up. I wish I had that kind of grit at their age. Now after turning fifty, I realize I don't have to explain myself to anybody anymore. I earned it.

Sonia: What happened when you turned fifty?

Susana: I realized I could be a grownup now and didn't have to apologize for anything. I gave myself permission to speak out. I love that it manifested in my kids at an earlier age. They never knew their grandma. They never knew my mom. I've done my best to talk about her. They weren't raised around my husband's mom, because she died not long after we met. My kids don't know what it's like to grow up with grandparents. They were just raised with the idea of them. I love how much they tell me that they love me and admire me. I love hearing it. I don't need to hear it, but I love hearing it because that was my purpose—to raise two strong children and to model to them what's possible as a work ethic and life ethic. My husband and I both worked full-time, and we had to balance everything to raise them, and I think we did a great job.

Sonia: What a blessing, and to carry the legacy of your mom. Your mom's hard work ethic and doing the best that she could with what she had, and the lessons and the gifts that she gave you are priceless. Even if you tried to pull them out of you, I don't think you can, because it's what you know now. It has become a part of you.

Susana: Yes. It defines me. I just turned fifty-five and soon I'll be the age that she was when she died, and I think, "Wow, I can't even imagine stopping right now."

I feel like I've finally figured out who I am. I'm just getting started. There was so much that she still had to give, but then at the same time, it's okay. We're just taking it from here, and her spirit lives in me and my sisters and our kids. It's a beautiful thing because that is her legacy. That's how she manifests to us, and it's wonderful. My oldest looks a lot like her. Even when they were born, it was a little bit of a reincarnation.

Sonia: What a gift!

Susana: In fact, her middle name is "Mary Lou" after my mom's name.

Sonia: Wow, beautiful. So, let's talk about that driving force, the grit. I think we fast-forwarded into marriage, but now you're going into college. Let's talk about that transition for you. You didn't have much, but you wanted something better. What was that experience for you?

Susana: In high school, I knew that I was going to go to college, because that's what my mom said, "Education is the key." I didn't know what that looked like, and I didn't know how that was going to happen. I just knew I was going. Like one day I was just going to go out our front door and college would be there.

I had a high school guidance counselor who strongly encouraged me to go to community college, and I said, "No, I want a four-year university," because that's what I had read about and it's what I wanted, even though I didn't know how I would get there. I felt like I almost said, "Thank you very much, but no thank you," and then proceeded to figure it out on my own. I applied to one university, and now that I think about it, I'm like, "Oh Lord, how did that work out?"

Now, as you remember I told you that one of the ways we had fun growing up was by going camping a lot. We always went to a couple of campgrounds that were in Santa Barbara, which was only a couple of hours away. It was free, and it was on the beach. You just had to wait in line, and then you got a spot. We went there a lot. So, when I was trying to figure out where I was going to go to college, my mom said, "Well, I think there's a university in Santa Barbara," and I said, "Oh, okay," because I knew Santa Barbara. I applied to UC Santa Barbara and I found out that they had this educational opportunity program at the time which would help disadvantaged kids get into college. I applied, and I got into the university. After I got in, I realized, "Oh gosh, you actually have to pay money to go!" but then I just figured out how to apply for financial aid and I got loans and grants.

I remember right before I left for college, I really needed clothes. We didn't have money for that, but my grandmother had a Sears and Roebucks account. So she gave my mom her credit card and that's where we went shopping! I remember exactly what I bought there: two pairs of jeans, a couple of sweaters, and some bras and underwear, and then I think a pair of tennis shoes. That was my college wardrobe.

As soon as I got to college, my world blew up for me in that I saw all that was possible. Wow! It was a tremendous experience and I was so determined to graduate with my degree. I borrowed money the whole time I was there. That was when Ronald Reagan was president, and in 1985, he repealed a lot of the student loans. I remember that I was notified that I wasn't going to get any money or not enough money to finish my senior year. So then again, I thought, "Okay, I'm not dropping out of school." So instead I just got a full-time job and I just worked at night. I worked the graveyard shift in my senior year so that I could go to my classes during the day. That's grit but working all night long was the only option, so that's what I did. It is crazy to think about it now.

Sonia: The magic in the big Plan B.

Susana: Yes! I decided I was going to finish that thing, even if it meant I wasn't going to sleep well for a year. But I finished and graduated. I couldn't rely on my mom for money, because she still didn't have any, and by this time, my younger sister followed my example and went on to college too. She went to UC San Diego, on loans as well. To be honest, one time, my mom didn't have money to pay the rent and I got an emergency loan from UCSB and sent her money for the rent, and then I just paid it off later.

By the time I got to college, I had already been inspired to go into law because my mom was a Spanish language interpreter, and she would take us to court with her. We would just sit in the audience and watch the proceedings, and I was enamored by the judge and what was happening in the proceedings. I thought that I wanted to be a judge, and the only way I could be a judge was if I was a lawyer first. That's how I started to think about law school. I just figured it out from there.

Sonia: Tell me about law school.

Susana: I figured out that I wanted to go to law school just about the time I was getting ready to graduate from UCSB, but I really needed money. I graduated from college and then took a couple of years off to work. I found work in a law firm, and I just did everything they needed. I ordered sandwiches, I delivered mail, I answered the phones part-time. I was one of the go-to people, but mostly I wanted to just be in the legal field. I didn't care what I did, I just wanted to be around it. I wanted to be around lawyers. So, after my second year of working, I applied to law schools, and the only way I could really do it was if I went at night so that I could continue to work during the day and pay for law school. So, that's what I did. I applied to several American Bar Association-accredited law schools in Los Angeles that offered night programs. I started in 1987 and went year-round. I would work at my job until five, then make my way to school, and be in classes for four hours a night, four days a week. I did that for four years.

I wasn't married and I didn't have kids, so I could be selfish. My mom used to call and say, "Okay baby, I made you some food. You can take it to eat for a couple of days." It was pretty phenomenal. I loved law school, and I just squeezed classes and studying in the nooks and crannies of my day. I studied late at night until I fell asleep, I studied at lunchtime, and I studied on the weekends. I didn't do anything but study in my free time. I just got it done. I graduated from law school, and there's only one way to do that and it's to just do the work and get through it. There's no Plan B for graduating from law school!

Sonia: Commitment seems like a word that fits you well.

Susana: Yes, and you know what? I have a business coach, and she always tells me, "I know when you say you're going to do something, you do it." I tell her I know, and that's why I'm judicious about saying I'm going to do something!

Sonia: Plan A or B, done.

Susana: It's hard for me not to keep a commitment to myself.

Sonia: It's like you have the keys to success, because life happens. You were growing up with that hardship, with the resistance and saying no, and turning it into this Plan B. That's what gave you the position to never give up. If Plan A doesn't work, Plan B will work.

Susana: Sometimes a Plan C. Just be ready to pivot.

Sonia: So now you're graduating from law school. What did that do for you?

Susana: That was the best feeling because finally I was seeing an end to my formal education and I could get to the next steps that were in my head. I had seen a judge, right? I had to finish college, get to law school, finish law school, and then study and pass the bar exam. So immediately after law school, while I was still working, I had to study for the bar exam. I graduated in May and they gave the bar exam at the end of July, so I took two and a half months off of work so that I could study, because I knew one thing: I was going to pass the first time. No Plan B for that. No way.

And I did pass the first time. I knew that I could not afford to not be working as a lawyer, because I had all these student loans to pay off. I didn't work this hard to get this far and then not pass the bar the first time. So, I was one-hundred-percent committed to it. For two and a half months solid, I studied from eight in the morning to eleven at night. I had all this vacation time saved up, so I was able to continue to get paid most of the time when I was off for two and a half months. I was grateful for that.

I took the bar exam in July and then in November I got my results. It was the best feeling in the world. By this time, my mom, my dad, and everybody got along well. My stepmom was in the picture. Everybody was good. They were so incredibly happy. As you remember I mentioned, my mom had actually gone to law school for one year when we were little after my parents divorced, because she really wanted to be a lawyer, but she couldn't do it. Not with the three of us and working, it was too hard. So, she was living vicariously through me, and there was nobody prouder. It wasn't that long until I was actually a lawyer, but unfortunately, I only practiced for a little bit before she died. She never got to see me in the courtroom or anything. On the day I was sworn in, she asked the judge that she worked for to do the honors, and of course, he did. So, I was actually able to go to a special swearing-in in his courtroom and she catered lunch, and the whole family was there and we had a nice lunch, and it was just a beautiful memory.

I started working and it has taken a lot of perseverance to get to where I am now. I consider myself very lucky in my profession because I get to work for cities, and that has defined my career. I get to go and help these communities improve their neighborhoods, improve their streets, improve their circumstances, improve their parks, and just create better communities for everybody that lives and works there. And I get to improve the communities where I grew up. It's just a blessing to be able to take my experience and knowledge and do this for other people, after growing up in such a disadvantaged community.

I was working in the Los Angeles area. I broke up with an ex-boyfriend and decided I needed a change of scenery, so I answered a classified ad in the L.A. Times for an attorney in the city of Stockton, and at the time I applied, I didn't even know where Stockton was. I came for the interview, and they hired me, and I moved up here, just me and the cat. On my second day on the job in 1993, I met my wonderful husband, Joseph. We've been married almost twenty-five years and he is my best friend.

Sonia: Destiny.

Susana: Exactly. Everything that had happened in our lives to that point just prepared us to meet. It was very cool. We worked together, and not that long after, we started seeing each other. About a year later, we got married.

Now, I've worked for several cities throughout the state and now I get to work for the City of Sacramento, and I just love it. It's like I was always meant to be here, but it wasn't easy to get here, either. I applied three times for this job and was starting to think they didn't want me, but I couldn't give up without trying one final time to see if they were finally ready to hire me!

Sonia: Here you are with that determination again.

Susana: Yes. Don't ever let anybody tell you that you can't do something, because it's not true.

Sonia: If we believe we can, we will. If we believe we can't, we won't. It seems simple, but the inner reflects the outer.

Susana: And you know what? Sometimes you're scared and you're not sure, and when that happens for me, I think, "Okay, but what are my options here? I'm not sure how this is going to work out, but I just know that I'm going to be proud of my effort because I tried." It's not always easy to think that way. It takes practice.

Sonia: What type of law are you working in?

Susana: I'm a municipal law specialist, and that simply means that I work for cities. Currently, because I am the City Attorney for Sacramento, my client is the city of Sacramento. I'm appointed directly by the elected body, the Mayor and the City Council, and I work on behalf of the City. Anything that they need, any program in the city, any building that goes up, any lawsuit that we may get involved in, the city of Sacramento has its own lawyers, and that's me and the outstanding group of men and women who work in the Sacramento City Attorney's Office. Together, we take care of all the legal needs of the city. Cities like Sacramento are municipal corporations, and like other companies, they need their lawyers, and we are their in-house lawyers. We also do criminal enforcement work because the City adopts its own laws to protect the health and safety of people who live and work in the City. In my career, I've done lots of criminal prosecutions and enforcement work. I specialize in nuisance abatement, and that means things like taking legal actions against drug houses and gangs and slum housing. I have made a specialty career out of that, going after those kinds of nuisances that disrupt neighborhoods, and I have been privileged to use my skills and training as a lawyer to improve communities in a very real way that helps people's lives. It's been incredibly rewarding. I love it. I'm never bored because I am honestly always learning.

Sonia: You have the grit of having a Plan B, so that has given you creativity in your work as well.

Susana: Well, you know what? I think that's probably it. You have to be creative as a lawyer, because our clients deserve no less. I'm so proud to work for the city of Sacramento. It demands my absolute best. I know I'm with a great group of lawyers who are in our department. They never stop thinking about how to help our clients work through complex situations.

Sonia: It's your driving force that has become gold in your life. You strengthened that muscle as a child, and now you're using it today. I'm thoroughly enjoying your journey because I always look for the driving force. Each one of us has a divine purpose. Most of our purposes are birthed from pain of some sort, and when we connect with our pain, then we use our purpose in the area where we have compassion.

Susana: Yes, and don't ever think that you can't do something. It may be that it's going to be difficult. It's not easy, but you absolutely can do whatever you focus your mind upon. And if it doesn't work out exactly like you're thinking, then that's because it was supposed to work out a different way. You won't know until you try.

Sonia: I feel like you need to speak to youth in high schools and give them this driving force, this legacy.

Susana: I've had the opportunity to speak to high school groups before, by invitation, and I do know that walking in as a Latina and a lawyer with my background, it benefits a lot of kids, especially in the underserved communities and communities of color. I'm not the type of lawyer they see on TV. I want them to see, "Look, can you see yourself in me a little bit? Because if you can, then you can do this. Because I saw myself in others, and I thought that I could do that too."

Any chance I get, I tell youth, especially Latinas, "Don't worry about the money for college. You'll figure out the money as you go by borrowing money. It's how I did it," and I share with them freely whatever information I have that could help them. I freely tell everyone that I didn't even pay off college loans until I was married and had kids already and we just refinanced our house. A year ago I paid off my law school loans, believe it or not! It was crazy, but I did it. I got that piece of paper that said, "paid in full" and said, "Look at this!" I'm almost getting ready to start thinking about retiring, but I finally paid off those loans! But those loans got me here, so I'm grateful.

Sonia: What would you say to those women who want that grit and want to accomplish their dreams, but don't know where to begin and don't have that muscle yet, that driving force?

Susana: The grit's there. We were born with it, but there may be a lot of things piled on top of it. We forget that it's there, but it is our saving grace. It's our life force, and you just have to believe that it's there and do it anyway. Do it anyway. Even if you're not sure it's going to work out because it's a muscle, and the more you use it, the more it will come to you, it will be there for you, and the more you'll be able to rely on it.

As you experience it more, you realize, "I did that. I made that happen," and it will remind yourself that you had it all along. We all have it, and as women, we absolutely have it. Sometimes, especially women who have spent most of their adult lives raising a family, we are worried about everybody else but us. I still have to remind myself, especially in recent years, to "Remember who you were. Remember that girl who slept in the library in the middle of the day because you had to work at night so you could finish going to college. Do you remember that girl? She's still there. Go find her. 'Cause you got goals and dreams and you've got to make them happen. Go find her." You polish out that little rock of grit and just bring it back.

Go after that dream. Take that action and commit. Make a promise to yourself and commit to it.

Sonia: So incredible. Adults and youth definitely need to hear about perseverance. I love what you said earlier to "exercise that muscle" every day. Get out of your comfort zone and do what you need to do. Even if it's a tiny step forward. Whether it's that phone call or taking that first class.

Susana: Right. Stop thinking about it, just do it. I remember the first time I got an executive position where I was going to be the head of a department. I thought, "Oh no, what did I do? I feel like I've been invited to sit at the big people's table now." And this wonderful lady gave me a little book. It basically said, "You've always been at the big people table. You just didn't know it." It was profound. She said, "Own it." And I said, "Okay. Even though I don't know what I'm doing. Okay. All right."

In closing, I just want to remind women that we have to be our biggest cheerleaders. We have to be the ones who believe in ourselves the most. I have experienced a lot of people who didn't believe in what I could do, or they were stereotyping and trying to put me in a certain category. Somehow, I didn't listen. I managed to keep going, and that is all that has gotten me to where I'm at. I'm no different from anybody else. I certainly have a lot of flaws. We should never stop learning. We should never stop growing.

We're imperfect human beings and it's always about being a better person tomorrow than we were today, and not comparing ourselves with anybody because that's just going to kill us. Focus on who you are and who you want to be. Then always try to figure out a way, and no matter what's happening, make it positive. And always have a Plan B.

Sonia: That's incredible. Thank you for your incredible story, your journey of transformation, and sharing your driving force.

Susana: Thank you.

Sonia Hassey

ABOUT SUSANA ALCALA WOOD

Susana Alcala Wood was appointed as the City Attorney for the City of Sacramento on March 19, 2018, where she is the principal legal counsel to the Sacramento City Council, and oversees a large department of lawyers, paralegals and support staff. An attorney specializing in Municipal law, Susana has worked for multiple cities throughout California serving in various capacities, including as the Modesto City Attorney from 2006-2013 While at Modesto, Susana guided the City Council and Staff through their shift historic shift from general elections to by-district elections,

Susana also previously worked as a Deputy City Attorney for City of Stockton and for the City of El Monte from December 1991 to December 1992. In both offices, she was responsible to advise multiple departments including Police, Code Enforcement, and Fire. She has worked tirelessly alongside city staff and leaders to address and eliminating blight, deteriorated and dangerous housing, and all nuisance conditions including quality of life issues, drug, red-light, and gang activity that affect communities.

Susana has served on multiple professional affiliations including serving in various capacities in the League of California Cities, City Attorney's Department, her local Bar Associations and has also frequently provided various training and guest lecturing to organizations and public agencies throughout the state on the topics such as Local Government Law, Code Enforcement, and Charter amendments.

She was born and raised in the Boyle Heights neighborhood of East Los Angeles, where she lived with her mom and two sisters. She was the first in her family to go to college and she received her Bachelor of Arts in Philosophy-Ethics and Public Policy in 1987 from the University of California at Santa Barbara and received her Juris Doctorate from Whittier College, School of Law in May of 1991. She has been married to Joseph Wood, her best friend and adventure partner for almost 25 years and together they have raised two amazing humans – Sam and Madison who are going to change the world.

CHAPTER 20

Ripple Effect

Cheri Knight

Sonia: Hello, I have Cheri Knight with me, and she is going to share her story. Welcome, Cheri! Tell us about you and what you do.

Cheri: Hi Sonia! Thank you for having me! I'm a certified health coach, and I help people win, not just in health, but in all areas of their life! So for a little bit of backstory about me, I was born in Lodi, California. I have not traveled far since then. When I was about age four or five, we moved from Lodi to Orangevale because my dad got a job transfer, and around that time my parents divorced. It was a hard time for my mom. I can remember her lying on the couch crying because she was heartbroken. I know she'd be okay with me sharing this, but she later told me that was a pretty desperate time and that having us kids was the thing that kept her going. I remember kneeling by her and not being able to comfort her in her distress. And for good or bad, that moment in time really helped me develop into who I am today.

When my parents divorced ... it was a feeling of abandonment. Some people don't realize how devastating it can be, and it doesn't matter if you're three or five or in your twenties, divorce is a tragedy for any family. There are broken promises, and for me, I had resolved at a very young age that I never wanted to be that dependent upon a man, nor have my kids have to ever go through that, so I knew that when I got married one day, I told myself it was going to be for good. The broken promises and sense of insecurity that this brought me, however, caused me to be distrusting and have a lack of confidence. The unconditional love of my grandparents and my mother were what helped me through this, and formed who I am today; however, I've had a lot of growth and insecurities to overcome along the way. My resolve to not be dependent on anyone else was great in the sense that it has given me stick-to-itiveness, a grit-filled determination and drive in life, but it was not healthy in the sense that I was too fearful to give up that control of earning an income in order to be the stay-home mom and raise my kids that I should have been, and had always wanted to be. My FEARS kept me from truly living the path in life that I wanted to take.

When I was a teenager, I read a book called *A Woman of Substance* about a lady who started her own business and built an empire. It sparked something in me that I wanted to build something bigger than myself. Something that would continue beyond my life. Something I could create for my family, and so I've always been a dreamer.

Sonia: So this book specifically impacted you in a way that you knew there was a destiny out there for you?

Cheri: Yes, but I did get away from that thinking during my teenage years, yet God brought me out of that, and it was through Him that I really learned that there was a much greater plan out there for me. I struggled a lot as a teenager with depression and self-confidence. It was the only time in my life when I didn't have much in the way of self-confidence and I didn't really have much hope for the future. When I was sixteen, I had suicidal thoughts, and I couldn't imagine that I was ever going to become somebody or something of worth, nor that someone would love me. It was a pivotal thing for me to go through, that kind of desperation, and to find the strength to overcome it, and realize and recognize that there is hope. I was in a negative mindset and listening to negative talk in my head, and I had to overcome that.

I met my future husband, Chris, when I was sixteen, not too long after one of my darkest moments of almost taking my life. My brother worked with him and had brought him home. I was in a period of despair, but I felt assurance that God told me that I COULD go on with my life and that there would be something better. God gave me that hope, and then this man came into my life. I was only sixteen and he was nineteen, so we had a long courtship of dating for six years before getting married. When we were young and dating, he used to tell me, "Stick with me and life's gonna be great," and I believed him! He brought hope back to me. My husband is a big part of who I am. He built me up and gave me beautiful strength, and I thank God for bringing him to me just when He did.

We got married when I was twenty-two and I had my first child, Christopher, at twenty-four. I rededicated my life to Christ shortly after that time, and through my walk with the Lord, I grew more in being confident and secure in who I was as a child of God.

We had our second child, Stephen, three years after that. One of my biggest desires was to be a stay-home mom. Deep down, I just wanted to stay home and be with my kids. But there was a deeper-rooted part of me that said, "You've got to be independent. You can't rely on a single income of just Chris." Because I believe that deep down inside of me was still that fear or insecurity and wondering what if my husband left me … I wouldn't allow myself to be vulnerable to that; I was too fearful. If I could go back and relive my life, with the courageous faithful spirit I now have, I would have pursued my desire to be that stay-home mom, confident in the worthwhile life of raising my own kids, rather than someone else doing it while I was at work. I believe raising our kids is one of THE most important callings in any of our lives, and I do regret letting my own fears and insecurities dictate a different path for me in that regard. What we may not have had in quantity time, I tried to make up for in quality time, however, and I'm so proud of the two responsible, honorable, hardworking, and compassionate men they have become. They are now twenty-four and twenty-seven and yet they still love hanging out with my husband and me and have strong moral and family values, so I guess we managed to do something right!

Shortly after our second son was born, because of the long hours I worked and responsibilities of running my own business with employees, I was wearing a lot of hats, trying desperately to juggle everything. I started to feed the feelings of bitterness and resentment toward my husband, which ultimately had nothing to do with him, but everything to do with the result of my own poor choices bred out of my fears and insecurities. This was an extremely difficult time in our lives and in our marriage, to the point where I even questioned if I married the right person. In this day and age, it's so easy to throw in the towel on marriages, thinking that the grass will be greener on the other side … (he was NEVER unfaithful or physically or verbally abusive). Well folks, it really isn't greener on the other side usually, and I'm SO thankful that I didn't walk away from my marriage. It really is true that the grass is greener where you CHOOSE to water it.

Because of my frustrations and the stresses upon me of my numerous roles, from being wife, mother, running the household, chores, dinner on the table, grocery shopping, running a stressful, fast-paced business … I had no time for myself, nor time to really do anything well, because of how spread out I was between everything. It was making me crazy! A lot of people probably go through counseling at this point, and I encourage people to do whatever it takes to find common ground and work on their marriages and save the family. For me, I felt I had no one to turn to, no one exactly in my situation, and felt very alone and unhappy. I felt my husband was no support and that I did everything, even putting in more work hours at my business than he did. The reality, though, was that it was selfish thinking on my part and a lack of communication that got us to that point; and for me personally, my only resource was prayer, plain and simple. I had too much pride to be vulnerable and share with friends or with my mom what I was going through, and didn't feel they'd be able to offer me an objective opinion anyway.

I learned from this time in my life that you cannot depend upon any person to make you happy. You have to completely look to God to fulfill your needs and be happy in who you are … it's up to us and depends upon that relationship with our Creator! I prayed during this time for God to remind me of why I fell in love with my husband in the first place and I prayed for God to restore those feelings of love for him and to take away my bitterness, anger, and resentment. These feelings were really brought on myself due to choices I made out of fear that we wouldn't have enough money, fear of the unknown, and my lack of being able to communicate well with my husband. It was through a lot of prayer and personal growth that I had to go through during this time to realize that I was being selfish, had placed unspoken expectations upon my husband, and then was angry and resentful when those expectations were not fulfilled. I had to work on my communication skills and let him know what I needed from him, and I had to also work on my own heart and spiritual walk … it was only then that things turned around. I also learned that love is not an emotion … it is a choice. From my CHOOSING to honor God and my marriage, by sticking it out and going through the motions until the EMOTIONS returned, and also letting go of ALL expectations and focusing more on serving and looking at what his needs were … it was only then that Chris changed and became all I needed him to be. I believe God honored my choice and saved our marriage and worked in the hearts of both of us. Through the next couple of years (and this was a two-year-long process of growing and rebuilding and sticking it out), we grew closer than ever, more in love than ever, and truly ran our household and parenting responsibilities as a team as it was meant to be!

So my message to those out there who don't FEEL like you love your spouse anymore, is this: Please don't give up on your marriage … focus on the reasons WHY you fell in love with that person, communicate and work at your marriage, work on your own personal growth and development and spiritual growth … nothing great comes easy, and through working at being self-sacrificing and choosing to love that person, even if you don't feel it, I promise that in time it will be better than ever and God will honor your commitment!

Sonia: Tell me about your career path.

Cheri: The spark of the entrepreneurial spirit that the book I read as a teenager gave me really geared me toward wanting to create something bigger than myself. Or perhaps it was the spirit and work ethic of my grandfather in me. He spent a good part of his career as a grocery store owner. I started working after school for a legal photocopy company as a receptionist when I was sixteen. It was a very small company. I ended up becoming the office manager when the existing manager went out on maternity leave and decided to not return. I worked there for eight years, and then the company went out of business due to the mismanagement of finances by the owner. Because I had a good job during this time, I guess, college was never impressed upon me. I wish I had gone, but I didn't. So when I saw that this company, which I had worked for since I was sixteen, was going out of business, I thought, "Well, I might as well start my own company." So I did. I've always had that mentality that where there's a will, there's a way. I started it out of my home, and my office was in one of the bedrooms until about a year later when, after having a couple of employees, I rented office space. I had that business for fifteen years. I worked hard for the first five years. The second five years were great and I was making a great income and I had a great staff that enabled me the freedom of working maybe just twenty hours a week. I was able to go on field trips with the kids and help in their classrooms occasionally. Even at that time, I was inspired by that *A Woman of Substance* book.

But then the economy started tanking and I had to pay myself way less in order to pay my employees. For the next five years, I was working seventy-plus hour weeks again and missing out on a lot. My business owned me and dictated my schedule. It was a hard time in my life and in my marriage, as this was the time when I was pulled in so many directions and it was at this time that I started to harbor those feelings of resentment (that I previously mentioned) for my husband. We were just so on-the-go all the time. I told my husband, "I need to sell this. I'm not happy. I don't have a passion for it anymore. It's not my calling anymore."

My logical husband said, "How can you walk away from it? You have no college education. You can't quit on it, so you have to have a Plan B first." I prayed for God to make me a way to get out of it. Now I can see God's hands in things, allowing everything to kind of fall apart financially, until we realized that I was hardly making money for the hours I was working. My husband came to a point where he too said, "Let's sell it." It was liberating to walk away from it.

I was talking with my hairdresser about what I was going to do next, and she said, "You should do hair. You love people, you're great at relating with people." I knew I would love it because I had a heart for women and women's ministry. I wanted to empower other women and help them through struggles and to help them feel better about themselves, so I decided to get into doing hair. I could still be in control of my own schedule. I didn't have to have a boss or have employees. I wish I had done it from the get-go. I realized that I could help women to feel better, and it was my calling to serve others.

I built my clientele up in about three months working seven days a week. I had a lot of drive. It takes most people a couple of years to build up their hair clientele. I rented a space where I had my own room. I feel like it prepared me for what I do now as a health coach, a life coach.

But there was an interim time, after I sold my business, when I was home taking care of my grandma with Alzheimer's and then eventually also going to school in the evenings and getting established as a hairstylist. I was still running my household for my family and it was a very hard time.

Sonia: It took work and courage.

Cheri: Yes, and I was always trying to become a better person and to continually grow.

So before I started pursuing my career as a hairstylist, my grandma moved in with us and I became her full-time caregiver for over two and one-half years, and then I finally started going to school for cosmetology in the evenings during that time. My grandmother was one of the biggest role models in my life, next to my mom, because of her faith and her living loving example. She was my hero, and she lived a servant's life. She had a sense of peace and patience about her. She was loving and she never raised her voice. She moved in with us when my boys were twelve and fifteen, after our family meeting to talk about how grandma was going to move into our home because there were four of us to help. It was a hard time because it's one thing when you have a little baby getting you up at night, but it's another when you have an adult that is going back to that time of life, kind of like a toddler. And it was so hard because I didn't want to see someone who was such a big person in my life to have to change so much. I knew, however, that because of our love and respect for her, she would never get the kind of quality care and attention, if she went into a nursing home, that we would be able to give her. It was the least that I could do to take care of her in her end years of life after the self-sacrificing life that she had always lived out for others. For all of the challenges it presented, it was such an honor to provide loving care for her, and Chris and I and our boys loved having her with us.

She never lost her identity of being a child of God, but there were times that she would think I was her sister, or she would become combative if I wanted her to get into the shower or something. But it was also one of the best times of my life because I was able to be home with her, and to have dinner ready for my family, and have all my focus just be on family.

Sonia: It's such a place of honor when we get to care for our grandparents. Tell us more about your personal experience with your relationships with your grandparents.

Cheri: My grandfather was more like my father figure. My dad was around and we'd see him a couple of times a month, but he had another family. So I went to spend a week in the summers with my grandparents and saw them all through the year. We have so many memories, and they were always very loving. And every morning, I could never get up earlier than my grandmother. Every time I would get up, she was already in her chair in the living room, hands folded, head bowed in prayer, and I knew better than to interrupt her time with God.

That's still a big priority for me that she passed on to me ... quiet time in the morning. Faith was her everything and living a life of serving Christ and serving people around her. She would deliver little violets to the shut-ins, and baked cookies. She took me clothes shopping and helped to provide for us. And when I was thirteen, I think I saw a commercial with the ocean and I asked my grandpa, "What does it smell like there?" And my grandpa asked, "You've never been to the ocean?" And I said no. He said, "All right. We're going tomorrow." He took me on my first trip to the beach and I had salt water taffy, so now every time I go to the beach, I get salt water taffy.

Sonia: A beautiful memory.

Cheri: Yes, so getting back to when my grandmother had Alzheimer's ... Thank goodness my husband was on board with me when it was time to bring my grandma into our home. He loved and respected my grandparents too, and considered them to be his own grandparents. My grandpa passed away about ten years before my grandmother. My mom was living with her mother after grandpa passed, and she thought they were going to get to travel and do all these things together, but then my grandma started to have Alzheimer's symptoms and wasn't the same mom. It eventually became too difficult for my mom to manage everything and she was unable to ever leave my grandma unattended. My grandmother coming to live with us sent a good message to my boys of how we shouldn't abandon our elders and that there is still so much to learn from them. My son's friends called her Grammy G, and they all loved conversing with her. While she had her moments with the dementia, she never lost her sense of humor nor who Jesus was and her identity as a child of God. She still taught my sons and their friends life lessons, talked about Jesus, and they would play games with her, take her on golf cart rides around our property and had a lot of laughs with her.

Sonia: What a legacy your grandparents left.

Cheri: So yes, definitely, and my grandma's totally a big part of who I am, and I've always aspired to be like her. However, when I was taking care of her, I wasn't really focusing on myself, and neglected self-care. And I think that tends to happen a lot, especially with women.

Sonia: We can get depleted.

Cheri: Yes, and spend so much of our energy and time and effort taking care of others that we neglect our own self-care. But self-care is a top priority. After my grandmother passed, and I went on to my career as a hairstylist, I would be so tired that I'd have headaches, and my weight was going up. I wasn't making time to exercise. I was trying to build my business, and I was working six days a week after the initial three months of seven days per week to build my clientele. I loved being there, but it was taking away from my home life and I wasn't making the time for myself to work out. My health started to suffer.

I had been doing hair for a couple of years when I met my health coach at an event. I liked the idea of someone keeping me accountable. She was going to help me beyond the weight-loss phase. I wanted to learn how to properly fuel my body and improve my lifestyle. That's what I loved about her program … the lifestyle changes and education that would come along with it. As I got my weight under control, I felt better and had more energy. Now I realize that self-care is so important, whether you're a man or a woman. How can we fully serve others if we're not at our own optimal best? It takes dedication, intentionality, and commitment. Some people think it's selfish, but it's not. You can have the energy to play with your kids by going outside and running instead of just sitting there watching them, being on the sidelines, or not being able to go down the slide because you can't fit on it.

After dropping weight from our nutrition plan, I started to make exercise a priority and other people were witnessing my transformation and saying they wanted to do what I was doing. It had a ripple effect. Everybody's always looking to get healthier, but most just don't have the tools to make it a reality. I started doing health coaching to help my friend and her husband. Then as everyone in their Bible study was witnessing the success that they were having after having nothing else work in the past, they all started reaching out to me. I started offering this gift of health to everyone, and my coaching practice grew! The income I was earning as a health coach quickly overcame my hair income in a fraction of the time it took to earn the same amount doing hair. This gave me more time freedom as well, as I started to eliminate days at the hair salon and eventually retired from my hairstylist career. I was able to spend more time with my family, friends, and helping others on their health journey as I worked on my own health journey. I started incorporating my regular quiet time, Bible study, more regular sleep, and exercise. I was truly able to create my life centered around what is most important to me and have been able to help others do the same! This has truly been the vehicle for me to fully live out serving others, helping them in ALL areas, and not just one area as a hairstylist providing a temporary fix of feeling good about the way they looked on the outside. I am able to help them physically, emotionally, financially, and with stress reduction. And with them feeling better, their attitudes became better, which helped improve relationships. All of these areas are so interrelated to our overall sense of well-being, which defines how optimally we can live out our days!

As my health transformed, I felt liberated! Like I was in my twenties again, even though I'm over fifty! I did a sixty-five-mile hill ride on my bicycle, and I had never done that kind of thing, even in my twenties. It's been exciting to not be inhibited in the activities I can do, and to challenge myself. It's freeing to have so much energy. I gained an overall sense of well-being and a more positive outlook because I was feeling better. It totally overflowed into my marriage and my relationships. I discovered that hair was a temporary fix, but health could be a permanent fix if people followed the program, incorporated the healthy habits necessary and stayed connected to me as their coach. It has been life-transforming, and it's been a huge blessing to help others to find the same kind of freedom and breakthroughs in their own mindsets and physical health like I've been able to do. I realized that this is the legacy that I can build of helping others and my family and being an inspiration and light to those in my world, who then, in turn, are a light to those in their world, creating that ripple effect.

I realized that I can do anything I want, anything I set my mind to do. I've had three different couples tell me that by adopting these healthier habits and our nutrition plan, it has saved their marriage because of how it affected their attitudes about themselves and how they react to each other. It's so much more than just physical health. Our program is about a healthy body, healthy mind, and healthy finances. All of them are interrelated and affect our health. When you're feeling better, you have a more positive outlook, and you have the energy and confidence to react better to the people around you. We also work on personal development. You can't control all the circumstances in your life, but you can control what you put into your body and how you respond to circumstances, and it's how you respond that will dictate the outcomes of these circumstances that happen in life. Your health is your most important asset, and without it, you may not have the ability to earn an income or to enjoy life because of suffering or ways you're physically prohibited from participating in life.

This has become my passion and it's exciting to help people with their health journeys. It's my way to help people discover what they were born to do and what fulfills them and makes them happy, and to pursue it and keep dreaming. As adults, sometimes we give up on our dreams because we're dealing with the pressures and stresses of life, but we should NEVER stop pursuing our dreams and whatever it is that sets our souls on fire!

Sonia: Big things happen when you say yes to your destiny, your purpose, your dream. Just go after it and allow everything to flow.

Cheri: If it's truly your calling and it's meant to be, doors will open.

In my life, we've had our good times and our hard times. We've had some hard times in our marriage, especially in those earlier days I mentioned at the beginning, and also when my grandmother was living with us. But overall, it's been so good. I still have dreams of travel and seeing the world and being able to spend as much quality time to just BE with my husband. A few years ago, my husband started to have an issue with his leg not functioning, which has progressed to both legs, and we discovered that he has a motor neuron disease that's debilitating, and we are told it will continue to progress and there's nothing doctors can do to fix it. Even with his health challenges, he's been so positive about it. He's such a fighter and my true hero. He's always said that you can't dwell on things. We realize that we have to live each moment and be thankful and make the best of it. I don't know what lies ahead for our future, just as none of us do, nor do any of us know when life is going to throw us a gut-wrenching blow to the stomach like it's now done to us. No matter how much we can try to plan for the future, only God knows what's in store for us, so we have to learn to adapt, stay focused on the positive and focus on what we ARE able to do, and trust that God has a plan and a purpose, and it's up to us to live that out.

Watching someone you love struggle can be so difficult because it affects me, too, because I love him so much, and I just want him to be happy. I want to fix this and I want the doctors to "fix it." But we have to just roll with the punches. As it is becoming more difficult for him to move around and do his job every day, I can't even imagine what he goes through. He's always been my rock, the person who lifts me up. And now I need to be there for him. I think it's interesting how God paired us because since we met, positivity is one of my strengths. Today I'm hopefully helping him to be positive and thankful.

I've also realized that I need to be very intentional not just with my time spent with loved ones, but when I'm doing things with my business or helping other people. I need to be fully present, and I'm working on that right now. Both my husband and I are on a journey right now. God has his reasons for why he's allowing this to happen. God is helping us grow in our faith, and who knows what God has in store for us.

Sonia: You have a lot of courage. How does it affect you on a daily basis?

Cheri: I try to start my day off like I witnessed my grandma doing. It's become more of a priority to me now. I need that time to draw strength from God, and that's when I can pour out my frustrations or my fears. I don't want to voice my fears out loud, but I can voice them through prayer, and reading God's Word comforts me. God gives me hope and strength. No matter what happens to us in this world, I know where I'm going eventually, and I know it's going to be better.

Another outlet for me is to exercise. Working out always makes me feel better. I try to read books that will help me and try to work on areas of my life such as how to be a better communicator, a better listener, and ask more questions. Helping people is another outlet for me. When I'm doing my mentor calls or coaching people, I get lost in their stories and in their worlds, and it is a release to take my focus off myself during that time.

Sonia: I have interviewed so many successful women who have overcome, and have been transformed into someone great, and who are helping other people. There's no perfect life out there. We can look at someone who seems to have a beautiful life, but we don't know what they've gone through and what they're going through right now.

This is your journey, and you're successful, but you also have known the feeling of desperation and despair. It's an important component of our journeys because it reminds us of what is good. It reminds us to be in a place of gratitude. Deep suffering made us who we are today and built our faith. Faith is like a muscle, and we have to build it every day.

I love your courage. I love your story about foundation and your grandparents. Try to imagine that gap of time in your life after your family fell apart, if you didn't have your grandparents. It could have been ten times worse. God's hand was there along the path of your life. And now you are here on a new journey with your husband.

Cheri: Yes, and I feel like we just have to rely on God and know that it's in His hands. This gives me comfort. I don't know how people go through hard times without a relationship with God.

Sonia: We're not alone. He is our strength during tough times, and through Him, we know it's all going to be okay. You're absolutely right. He made us with so much grit and courage and strength that we don't realize it until it's time for it to come forth. God is molding us, so we can be even more impactful as women. Women have His power. There is a deeper meaning and purpose to everything we're doing. We may not call it a ministry, but in our hearts, we are serving in a ministry.

Cheri: Yes, and in developing relationships with people, I'm able to influence them in ways that I would not have otherwise. It's enabled me to open up and share my faith with them, or have them share their faith with me. I can speak Christ into people's lives and they can get their health back, and it makes them want more and they want to know their purpose and have more of a relationship with their Creator. That's been a huge blessing to me and those I serve.

Sonia: What would you say to women who are struggling, whether they are young women whose families are falling apart, or teenagers whose lives are hard, or women of any age who need hope?

Cheri: I would say that there's something better out there for you. Hang on; this is going to pass. Life is going to be great. Nothing lasts forever, and we go through different seasons. The tough seasons are building our characters. This time might be hard, but you're going to get through it. Lean into God. He's your rock. Just know that life's not always rosy, and sometimes we must do things we don't want to do in order to have a better life. You will get past this. You will be blessed for sticking it out.

Just be as compassionate and loving as you can, and try to put yourself in somebody else's shoes. Try to understand others, and don't make it all about you. Put your own ego aside. Find ways to feel grateful.

When you're frustrated or feeling hopeless or down, and you just want out, start counting your blessings and then think about how it will affect other people if you leave. How will it affect your kids, even if they're grown? It would be devastating. Help other people, and you will help yourself.

Sonia: Thank you, that was powerful. And what would you say to the women who say, "You look fantastic; you lost forty-two pounds. I want to do that but it's too hard to do the work."

Cheri: There's no magic pill! Having a coach is key because we all need a layer of accountability. It's in our DNA to have community with others. We need help focusing on the creative process and on creating healthier habits. If you start to create healthy habits, they will eventually replace unhealthy habits. Start with one small thing, because it takes time. Have a plan, and create accountability. I found it was easier than I thought it would be. The hard part is keeping it off because a lot of habits will want to come back, and that's where having a coach and a community behind you is so vital to long-term success.

Sonia: Your story will inspire today's women. What do you want them to walk away with?

Cheri: I want to encourage them to keep working at becoming a better person. Keep working on yourself and not blaming other people. If there are things in your life that you're not happy with, you have the control and power to change! There is greatness in your beautiful uniqueness that you alone possess. Be the person who's in charge of your destiny. You have that power, and life is all about choices. Work on staying positive and filling yourself with thankfulness.

Lean into God and have faith and hope that better things will happen. Dream big! People just think too small. Live in the moment, but plan for a future, and work toward finding your passion and following it. Don't let anybody else block you from your passion or tell you that it's silly. If something's in your heart, pursue it all-out with everything you have.

Sonia: I love it. Thank you, Cheri, for sharing your story. I feel very inspired. You've been on a beautiful journey and you know that life isn't perfect, but you focus on what we can become in our journeys, and that's key.

Cheri: Thank you, Sonia, it has been such an honor to share my heart with you, and if it helps even just one person, then it was worth being vulnerable and opening up my continual journey with others.

ABOUT CHERI KNIGHT

Cheri Knight has been an entrepreneur for the past 27 years. At the age of 24, she started and owned a legal photocopy service for 15 years, then was a 24/7 caregiver to her grandmother with Alzheimer's, went on to a career as a hairstylist where she built her clientele in a matter of 3 months, and now, for the past 8 years, is a Certified Coach. It wasn't until she met her health coach, lost weight, and regained her own health that she found her true passion and a vehicle to truly be able to make a meaningful impact on the lives of others, empowering them to create lives centered around what's most important to them by helping them to reclaim their health, confidence, and achieve a healthy mindset in personal growth and development, as well as financial and time freedom! Cheri currently lives in Wilton, a small community in Northern California, with her husband Chris of 30 years. She is the mother of two sons.

Certified by OPTAVIA in partnership with The MacDonald Center for Obesity Prevention and Education (C.O.P.E.) and the Villanova University College of Nursing.

916-752-6830
fitwithcheri@gmail.com
coachcheriknight.optavia.com

CHAPTER 21

Yes I Can!

Rosario Renderos

Sonia: I am here with Rosario Renderos. She has a wonderful story of courage and of knowing what it takes to continue to move forward despite people telling her no. Start from the beginning and just share your heart with us.

Rosario: The story I want to share starts in a small town called Tepetitan, San Vicente, El Salvador. As I talked to my mom about this project, she began telling me how she was trying to get pregnant for four years and finally the big day came when it was time to give birth, as she said, "It was a beautiful April day when labor began, I was scared and happy, and so was your dad." But something did not look okay. To their surprise, their firstborn and expected baby was not a healthy one. When I was born, I was not breathing, and I had to stay in the hospital. Even my name was picked by my grandmother in a sense of urgency that I might not survive. She was a very religious woman and believed that I should get baptized and named in case I died. When I was three months old, they found out that I had severe asthma. I remember growing up at the hospital more than at my house. There were times when my parents would see me only once a week on Sundays because that's what the hospital allowed.

I didn't see them much when I was little. I felt alone and with a strong sense of independence since I had to care for myself. One of the things that kept me at the hospital was that I couldn't handle hot weather, and ironically, El Salvador has very humid hot weather. At the hospital, they had special equipment to keep me in a cooler environment. I remember growing up in the hospital surrounded by children, and sometimes the children were crying for their parents because it might have been their first time in the hospital. But I was so used to it, that I went to the children and told them they were going to be okay. I remember when I was around seven or eight years old, I wanted to play like my sisters, but every time I wanted to run my mom would say no because I would get an asthma attack. I wanted to play in the dirt, and they said no. Even eating some stuff, I got a no because it seemed that everything in my environment would get me to long weeks at the hospital connected to an oxygen mask. Time passed, and I kept going to the hospital until I was around fourteen years old and my asthma got a little better. I had to miss a lot of school, but the times I went I enjoyed every second. I loved learning, and I believe it was a sense of appreciation of being alive and doing something that a normal kid would do.

As a kid, I was not able to play. I was not able to run. I couldn't even play in the rain. Still today, I don't like the rain. I think it's because I was always told that if I get wet with rainwater, I would get sick.

Even though I couldn't play or do too much fun stuff like any other kid, I knew that I was loved. I feel that all those NOs were because my family overprotected me. I felt that they loved me so much, and they suffered as much as I did every time they had to take me to the hospital. I was the oldest of seven siblings. But it was hard because they also told me that "You can't have this, you can't do this, you can't ... you can't ..." Everything that I heard was no. There was a point that I was so used to being around nurses and doctors that when I grew up, I told my parents that I wanted to be a nurse. I remember my father telling me, "You can't be a nurse because you are too sick." To a young woman, that was harsh to come from someone who you love. Therefore, in my school years, I did not apply to nursing school. Instead, I became a secretary and then I did a semester in law school before moving to the U.S.A. Also, I remember near where we lived there was a cabbage plantation near the cemetery, and my dad would play with me by telling me, "Oh the cabbage place is calling you." Meaning that I was on my way to die. I remember them taking me to the hospital at three a.m. or anytime I couldn't breathe. It was hard, but I think that developed the light in me to say, "Okay, you tell me I can't—I will prove you wrong."

Sonia: At those times, something happened inside of you that made you fight back and say, "I'm tired of the no." What changed you so that you could say, "I'm not gonna accept the nos"?

Rosario: I think it was seeing the other children at the hospital and hearing everyone say we couldn't do something. It empowered me to be able to help other children to stay calm. I have been battling this for so long and there were many times that I had to be connected to oxygen so I could breathe. I said, "I can do this on my own." I think I was born to do something different because I have always felt different from everybody in my family. I used to feel different because I was ostracized since they wouldn't let me do stuff. Even though I had to live at the hospital a lot, I still went to school and got good grades. My mom was proud, and I also felt proud. Now I feel different in a good way. Now my mom tells me, "You never gave me a hard time; you were always well-behaved. The hard times were just because you were too sick, and it was hard for me to see you fighting for your life. I always admired your courage. You would always fight. Still today you are amazing; you are my pride. Seeing the way you have flourished—it's incredible."

Sonia: What a beautiful affirmation, especially coming from your mom.

Rosario: When I was finally spending less time at the hospital and more time with my parents, our life changed in the most unimaginable way. When I was twelve or thirteen, my father had a big accident that didn't allow him to keep working. He had been the provider of the house, bringing food and everything. My mother had to emigrate to the U.S. and send us money so we could survive. My siblings and I lived with my grandmother for five or six years, and my aunt also took care of us. Here I was again without my parents because my father emigrated one year after my mom. However, having my grandmother in my teen years shaped the woman who I am right now. My grandmother not only took care of me and my siblings, but influenced us in a very positive way by telling us to always have faith, be kind, love, work hard but always stay humble and grounded. I remember her telling us, "Do not ask your parents for stuff, because they work really hard over there." She taught us to be grateful and to appreciate the hard work of our parents.

Years later, I was in a law school pursuing a degree as a lawyer, and my parents were here working, but no longer able to pay for my school. So I decided to emigrate to the U.S. Anyway, I was told that the U.S. was the land for the American Dream. So I came to this country without speaking the language and feeling lost. I arrived in San Francisco, California, where I still live up to this date.

Sonia: So you had to leave behind your siblings and your grandmother?

Rosario: Yes, and it was not easy because I was an immigrant and I didn't know if I would see her again. I remember the moment when I left, I can still picture her standing right in front of the black and white door. Her last hug … I remember NOT looking back, because I knew she was aging and the possibility for me to come back soon was uncertain. My fear became a reality: I never got to see her again before she died. Ten years later I went back and all I could see was a grave full of flowers with her picture, with those beautiful green eyes of hers. That's a pain that only an immigrant can relate to.

When I got to the U.S., I had to work two jobs. I was a cook at a fast-food restaurant, but I felt that I was mistreated because I didn't understand a word, and people were throwing stuff and making faces at me. I said to myself, "I have to learn the language." I used to work there for eight hours and then go to my second job as a school janitor for two hours. Then I would run to classes to learn English. Every day I went from five a.m. through ten p.m. But I was determined to learn the language because I didn't want anybody to take advantage of me or treat me differently because I didn't know what they were saying.

I remember in the first week I started working, I had to take a bus after dark, and I didn't know the bus routes or the roads. I got on a bus and ended up near the San Francisco International Airport. When I saw that the bus kept going and I didn't see any more houses, I got scared. I got off the bus and realized I was lost, and I didn't know what to do. I did not have a phone with me. I sat at the bus stop shelter and cried. I asked myself, "What am I doing here? Why did I come here? I do not feel I belong to this country." I remembered my country. Memories came into my head. I felt homesick; I missed my grandmother, my aunt, and siblings; and for a second, I thought I should go back. I sat down for a while and tried to figure out what to do. I decided the most logical thing was to cross the street and get on the bus right back to San Francisco. That's what I did, and somehow, I got to my house.

Sonia: You felt lost in a foreign country. But you stepped back a little bit and knew it was going to be okay. Did that determination come from your grandmother?

Rosario: Yes, when I left she told me that everything was going to be okay. Also as my fear of being lost grew my desire to fight for a better future, and this desire grew even bigger than my fear. It was like putting fire in my soul: The more I cried because of the sad moments I was going through, the stronger I felt. My grandmother would always tell me that wherever I go, have faith and stay strong. She encouraged us to be better, to work hard. I know she meant physically work hard, even though now I believe that you don't have to kill yourself physically; you are mentally capable of doing amazing things. She always told us to work hard, and I've always taken it to heart.

Sonia: Let's go back to you at age eighteen, in a new country and working two jobs. What happened next?

Rosario: Yes I was working two jobs and going to school, and the universe put the man who is now my husband (Walter) in my life. He's from El Salvador but he grew up and went to school in the U.S. He has played a big role in my development. He knew that I wanted to go to school, and he supported me. In fact, when he met me, he knew I was learning the language and he helped me a lot.

We have been married for fifteen years and have three wonderful, smart, kind, loving children. Which I thought I would never be able to give to him. When I was thirteen years old, a doctor told me that I would never have kids because my asthma medication did so much damage to my body that the chances of having children were slim. At thirteen years old, not only did I have the news of not having children, at an age that I would not even care or think about it, but also the treatments for my asthma started to take a toll on me. I developed a rare skin condition that forced me to hide my body because I was ashamed that people would see the rare spots in my body. Since I met Walter, I knew he wanted to have children. Telling a man who loves kids that the person that he wants to marry won't be able to have children was not easy. I still remember his answer: "I don't care. I love you." To our surprise and blessing, I got pregnant right away, and now our children are Kinna (fourteen), Yamil (eleven), and Ricardo (eight). They are now my drive and biggest motivation to raise my standards and have higher goals.

Sonia: What a blessing! You met your future husband, and he encouraged you.

Rosario: He still supports me today. He sees me as a very independent woman and knows that no one will stop me from reaching my goals.

Going back a little, I was married, going to school, working, pregnant, working, and going to school. I was in school through the birth of all three of my children. It felt like forever. After having all three, I decided to stay home to take care of them and go to school. Paying for a babysitter was too expensive. I not only learned the language, but I graduated with a degree in social and behavioral science with honors.

But while going through school and having kids, I became more overweight. Yes, overweight! I grew up overweight and it had to do with my asthma because I had to take steroids to open my lungs. The steroids helped me with my breathing condition, but one of the many side effects that I experienced was the uncontrollable appetite. However, after having my children, I got even heavier. I also got postpartum depression, and the medication and emotional imbalance led me to eat more. Feeling tired and heavy at some point, I felt like I couldn't handle it anymore. I tried many different diets, and nothing worked. I kept gaining weight. I think I wasn't mentally ready to lose weight. I believe losing weight is more emotional and mental than physical. I also remember going through financial hardships while married, in school, and with three children. Sometimes I barely had something to eat, but I was so determined to finish school that I kept going.

I was not eating healthy, and I didn't even have the means to eat healthy. I didn't take care of my body. In 2014, I wanted to have surgery because I had too much weight in my belly. I finally had the money for the surgery. But my husband didn't want me to do it. He is supportive of everything, but not surgery. He was afraid that I would die. I didn't have the surgery and I started looking at many different weight loss options. While searching online, I came across the Yes You Can! diet plan. I looked and looked at the plan several times, but I was hesitant until one day …

I said I would give it a try. Still not so convinced, I thought that I would be happy to lose at least =ten pounds in three months. But because of my dedication, self-love, determination, and discipline, I lost forty-two pounds in four months. I started and did not tell anyone because I always struggled with my weight and my family would tell me, "You have always been a gordita, and you're always going to be a gordita. Stop trying." Two months after I started, everyone started to notice my results. Fours month after December 31, 2014, to be exact—everybody was amazed with the new me!

At this point, I was working as a social service coordinator when I got a call from the CEO of Yes You Can! offering for me to be part of this journey. While I was in Miami, Florida, getting to know more about this project and how it was about to transform my life even bigger, I was getting promoted as the Social Service Supervisor. I loved my job in social services helping seniors with Medical, Medicare, and many other social services. However, for the very first time in my life, I was listening to something that I always dreamed about: inspiring people to find their better version of themselves, to end people's limitations and help them to start thriving for something bigger. I said, "Wow, yes, this is what I want to do." I would love to change people's lives. For six months, I did both jobs until I decided to only be part of Yes You Can! as an independent coach.

Since I've been working with Yes You Can! my life has become more meaningful, because every morning when I get up, I have the opportunity to transform somebody's life, to give them the opportunity that the CEO of Yes You Can! gave me. Not only to lose weight, but the opportunity to have a business. It has changed my life completely. Nowadays I have the freedom and flexibility to work from the comfort of my bed when it is cold, or from the beach during hot summer days. I have the freedom to travel anywhere, anytime, and to meet amazing people with inspiring stories that reaffirm that I am finally living with a purpose. When I was growing up so sick, I wouldn't have seen myself now surrounded by people telling me every day, "Rosario, thank you for this opportunity because now I have the money to send my children to school. I can bring food to my table. I can help my husband."

I like to know every person. What are their goals; what do they want; what are their visions? Where do they see themselves in three to five years? For me, it was the freedom, the opportunity to enjoy my children, to drop them off at school every morning, to go with them to their field trips, to have my husband going from more than one job to only one and being able to spend more time with our kids. That's what I value as being my own boss: the freedom and the opportunity every day to say, "I have an opportunity for you." It doesn't matter if it is someone professional with a well-paid job but without freedom, or someone who has never gone to school but has enough drive, passion, and bravery to stand up for their dream.

Sonia: You're right. Some people are way too busy with work that is unfulfilling, instead of doing what they really like and finding the balance, as you did.

Rosario: Fortunately, I was able to open my mind and heart when the opportunity was given to me. I remember when I told my mom I was going to quit my job and do this full time, and she did not believe it. She said, "Are you sure?" And I said, "That's what I want to do." I was determined. It was the best decision I have ever made. I am one of the fifty founders of the company and that makes me feel incredibly proud. It hasn't been easy to find my way in the U.S. I have cried so many times. I remember when I got lost. I remember when I didn't have food. I remember when I had financial hardships and I didn't have the money to do essential stuff. But now we can buy something that we really want, and we can also give somebody else an opportunity and say, "I understand you. I've been there." If you tell me you can't do it because you're overweight; you can do it because I did it. If you tell me you can't because you don't have the money; I didn't have money either and I did it. You can do anything you want, but first start believing in yourself and get past your fear.

I was so scared when you called me and asked me to be here because it's not easy to open up my challenges to the world. It's not easy to remember my childhood and my losses, and my family telling me no. So many times now when people say that I'm so independent, I say it's because I grew up by myself. I fell down; I got up. I cleaned my scratches and kept going by myself. But God had a purpose for me!

Sonia: We take it at a deeper level when it's people we love telling us "no you can't." Your language growing up was "no you can't," and now it's "yes you can." That's so powerful. You fought through your nos. You worked harder to get where you wanted to be.

Rosario: I am not what I want to be yet, but I am still working toward where I want to be.

Sonia: Success is in the journey; there's no destination. There's so much to be proud of even where you are right now.

Rosario: I am so proud because I have fought so many times. When I was pregnant with my third child, my asthma was bothering me so much that I could've passed. Changing my lifestyle definitely helped me a lot. I have been off inhalers since I did my transformation, since I lost weight, and since I adopted healthy eating habits. When I started my weight-loss journey, I walked around a lake, and suddenly I found myself running. I cried because I had been told that I couldn't run. I was running, and I felt powerful. I always tell people to do an exercise that you like to do to keep your body moving. Every time that I ran, I felt alive and I felt freedom.

Sonia: That's incredible. It's a personal transformation because you had voices on the outside and on the inside, telling you, "no, no, no, you're too sick." And all of a sudden, the more you believed in yourself, the more you took the risk.

Rosario: Recently, I was eating at a restaurant with someone very important in my life, and the person unexpectedly asked me, "Rosario, what is your drive? You're always fighting; you're always going after what you want." I said, "The nos that I have been given all my life." To me, nos were like vitamins because they made me want to do those things anyway.

I tell my children and others: Why would you limit yourself and your capabilities when you have a power within yourself? You have to believe it; it's not up to me to tell you. You have to find your drive and your "why." When I think about my "why," I have a flashback of seeing myself in the hospital and growing up not being able to do things, yet I don't want people to pity me because of how I grew up. I look back and see myself as a winner with high standards. I believed that I was born to do something different. To enlighten the world and be someone who can make a difference. I see that my life has a meaning, and I am living with purpose right now.

Sonia: What a beautiful place to be in. You've learned how to persevere, have grit, and live life with passion and love for what you do. And you tell everyone else that they have that opportunity, too.

Rosario: I can't say it enough: You have to believe in yourself and your abilities. Without believing in yourself, you won't get anywhere. You have to work for it. Everything has a price; are you willing to pay the price? I paid my price: learning English, waking up early to go to work, working two jobs, going to school, and earning my degree. I have both enjoyed and paid the price for every step to success.

Now I am focused on my business, and I also donate part of my time to a nonprofit organization called Mission Neighborhood Centers in San Francisco, California, as a member of the board of directors. The organization serves over three thousand low-income seniors, youth and families with young children at eleven sites throughout San Francisco. With a legacy dating back over one hundred years, its guiding principles remain the same: empowerment, cultural affirmation, and personal responsibility. It provides a continuum of educational programs and social services to the community populations most in need. I serve in this organization because it is a way of saying "thank you," because they helped me when I needed it. At the same time, it is an opportunity to give back to the community. I feel fulfilled because I am doing what I love and I'm helping people.

Sonia: It adds meaning and purpose to your life. You remember when you felt empty, lost and lonely, and now you're giving back.

Rosario: Yes, I want the immigrants we serve to know that they have a place right here and an opportunity to develop themselves. I tell them to work, become entrepreneurs, go to school or do something meaningful, but don't go home and watch soap operas. Now I feel that I belong here, I'm part of this society, I'm making money, paying taxes, and I'm giving back to the community. I have a purpose and I am fulfilling it.

Sonia: I see that in you. You are purpose-driven and fulfilled.

Rosario: My biggest dream right now is to create an empire, and what I mean by that is that I want to develop a big organization full of leaders. I believe that leaders create leaders, not followers. I love my team so much and I know they love me too. It's incredible to see them grow. For the very first time, I can tell that I am not alone and I building an empire that I cannot create by myself, but I can create it with a strong team of committed dreamers brave enough to fight for their dreams. I strongly believe that I have started to build it; I have a great team named "Team Juntos Somos Mas Fuertes," meaning Stronger Together. I believe that alone we can do so much, but as a team, we can do much more. Incredible things! Today, as I am finalizing this chapter, it was announced via Facebook Live that our team has been placed number one NOT locally but NATIONALLY. This is such a great moment for us. I have no words to describe how proud I feel to be the leader of the number-one team in the nation. I'm proud to be in the top ten highest earners within Yes You Can!

Sonia: What would you say to women who are afraid to move forward, whether or not they are immigrants? And women who may have heard a thousand nos and they can't get past them?

Rosario: First, believe in yourself. When you do, absolutely no one, not even yourself, will be able to stop you. Get up every morning with purpose, and do what makes you happy. Even if it scares you—do it. Go after it. Don't let anybody stop you. I tell people who have children that their children should be their motivation and their drive, not the stone in their shoes. They look up to you and will say, "If my mother did it, I can do it as well." After you overcome your obstacles, that's when you will cry out of happiness and say, "Oh my God, look what I went through." That's the most wonderful feeling.

There's something for you. Try to go back to when you were young and used to dream—whatever your dream/goal was. Why did you stop dreaming? Because you got comfortable, and you love the comfort zone. Believe me, I'm scared of making changes, but I'm even more scared of staying in the same place. So get out there and step out of your comfort zone, and fight for your dreams.

You can do it. You are more than those nos. Those nos are only building a stronger Rosario, a stronger Sonia, and a stronger you. They are preparing you for when things get harder. Everything we go through in life is with purpose or meaning, but we may not understand it at that moment. If someone tells you no, they are telling themselves no, closing a door of opportunity for them. But if you believe in yourself and what you are doing, no one can stop you. I believe in myself and I believe I can take my business to another level.

Go after your dreams and don't let anybody stop you—not even the person in the mirror every morning. Make that person in the mirror be your best motivation, and remember that "yes you can!" Your dreams and desires are yours, so go after them. You have big power, but you have to believe it. Yes, you can.

Sonia: I love it! That was wonderful.

Sonia Hassey

ABOUT ROSARIO RENDEROS

Rosario Renderos
Business and Weight Loss Coach
Inspirational Leader
Yes You Can! Independent Coach
Coach: ID 2458
www.yesyoucan.com/RosarioRenderos
Tel: 415.656.7166

Rosario is a very successful entrepreneur in the Health and Wellness industry creating opportunities for others. She is committed to empowering others to become strong and independent entrepreneurs while promoting healthy communities. Rosario has become an inspirational Leader, Leading an organization of over 800 hundred entrepreneurs across the United States helping them to reach their fullest potential. Her passion for developing leaders took her and her team to become the #1 Nationwide in leadership development within her company in 2018.

Rosario is one of the top ten successful Yes You Can! Independent Coaches holding one of the highest titles and several recognitions for her inspiring Leadership.

Rosario holds a degree in Social and Behavioral Science in which she graduated with honors, and in future times she would love to go back to school to pursue a degree in Psychology. Rosario also donates her time to the community and currently is the Board Secretary for the Mission Neighborhood Centers Board of Directors. Rosario is defined as an independent, strong, bold, confident, funny woman who enjoys life.

www.ingramcontent.com/pod-product-compliance
Lightning Source LLC
Chambersburg PA
CBHW020216170426
43201CB00007B/234